Chicken Soup for the Soul®

Answered Prayers

Chicken Soup for the Soul: Answered Prayers
101 Stories of Hope, Miracles, Faith, Divine Intervention, and the Power of Prayer
Jack Canfield, Mark Victor Hansen, LeAnn Thieman

Published by Chicken Soup for the Soul Publishing, LLC   www.chickensoup.com
Copyright © 2011 by Chicken Soup for the Soul Publishing, LLC. All Rights Reserved.

Scriptures taken from the Holy Bible, New International Version®, NIV®. © 1973, 1978, 1984, 2011 by Biblica, Inc.™ Used by permission of Zondervan. All rights reserved worldwide. www.zondervan.com and from the Holy Bible New King James Version. Copyright © 1982 by Thomas Nelson, Inc. Used by permission. All rights reserved.

The publisher gratefully acknowledges the many publishers and individuals who granted Chicken Soup for the Soul permission to reprint the cited material.

Front cover photo courtesy of iStockphoto.com/Zocha_K (© Zoran Kolundzija). Back cover photo courtesy of iStockphoto.com/mammuth (© peter zelei). Interior photo courtesy of Photos.com.

Cover and Interior Design & Layout by Pneuma Books, LLC
For more info on Pneuma Books, visit www.pneumabooks.com

Distributed to the booktrade by Simon & Schuster. SAN: 200-2442

Publisher's Cataloging-in-Publication Data
(Prepared by The Donohue Group)
Chicken soup for the soul : answered prayers : 101 stories of hope, miracles, faith, divine intervention, and the power of prayer / [compiled by] Jack Canfield, Mark Victor Hansen [and] LeAnn Thieman.

 p. ; cm.

 Summary: A collection of 101 personal stories in which the contributors recount incidents in which their prayers were answered, for health, financial, social, or other desires.
 ISBN: 978-1-935096-76-4

 1. Prayer--Christianity--Literary collections. 2. Prayer--Christianity--Anecdotes. 3. Miracles--Literary collections. 4. Miracles--Anecdotes. 5. Christian life--Literary collections. 6. Christian life--Anecdotes. I. Canfield, Jack, 1944- II. Hansen, Mark Victor. III. Thieman, LeAnn. IV. Title: Answered prayers

PN6071.P619 C45 2011
810.8/02/0382/4832   2011933080

PRINTED IN THE UNITED STATES OF AMERICA
on acid∞free paper
20 19 18 17 16 15 14 13   08 09 10

Chicken Soup for the Soul.

Answered Prayers

101 Stories of Hope, Miracles, Faith, Divine Intervention, and the Power of Prayer

Jack Canfield
Mark Victor Hansen
LeAnn Thieman

Chicken Soup for the Soul Publishing, LLC
Cos Cob, CT

Contents

❸
~Miracles~

❹
~The Healing Power of Prayer~

❺
~Let Go, Let God~

❻
~Ask and You Shall Receive~

❼
~Sign from Above~

❽
~Thanksgiving~

❾
~Trust in Him~

⑩

~Angels Among Us~

Introduction

Since the beginning of time and throughout all history, people have inspired and upheld one another by sharing their stories of faith, in times of trial and in times of joy. With that same conviction and mission we have gathered literally thousands of true stories from prayerful people around the world to continue this legacy. As you read how God answered their prayers you too will find peace and trust in Him.

These heart-warming, hope-filled stories prove the power of prayer. Some are as stupendous as the parting of the Red Sea and miraculous cures! Others share "Divine coincidences," the blessings of daily prayer or simple dialogs with God, proving His presence and guidance in our everyday lives. We only have to ask and count on Him, knowing there is no need too great or too small to be entrusted to God. As Corrie Ten Boom, a Christian Holocaust survivor said, "If a care is too small to be turned into a prayer, it is too small to be made into a burden."

These stories will lift your spirits and nourish your souls. Read them one at a time, alone or in a group. Savor the scripture verse or quotation. Embrace the message. Deepen your faith. Take God's hand as He guides you on your journey of hope.

~LeAnn Thieman

Answered Prayers

Divine Appointments

*"They also will answer, 'Lord, when did we see you hungry or thirsty or
a stranger or needing clothes or sick or in prison, and did not help you?'
He will reply, 'Truly I tell you, whatever you did not do for one of the
least of these, you did not do for me.'"*

~Matthew 25:45-45

Providential Timing

"For my thoughts are not your thoughts, nor are your ways my ways, says the Lord. For as the heavens are higher than the earth, so are my ways higher than your ways, and my thoughts than your thoughts."

~Isaiah 55:8-9

On a busy late Friday afternoon at my salon in Tulsa, Sandy the receptionist approached my station. "Emily Childers is on the phone. She needs help." I gave her the nod and she rolled her eyes. "You're a glutton for punishment."

We both knew that call meant an additional two and a half hours added to my workday. Most hairdressers have clients for whom they extend themselves, and Emily was one of mine.

Later, my assistant escorted Emily to the dressing room while I finished a client. She gave me a quick hug as she walked past, and I could see the need as her gray roots with faded honey-blond ends shouted for attention. Soon chattering voices, the ping of timers, whirring blow dryers all faded as the day's busyness waned and the remaining clients filtered out, leaving Emily and me alone.

I loved visiting with Emily. We always shared our faith and talked God-talk. About ten years my senior, her thoughts that late afternoon meandered down memory lane as she recounted the touching story of a dear friendship from past years.

Emily and Pat's lives had intertwined in a number of ways. Both were pregnant, Emily with her first child and Pat with her third. They attended First Baptist Church, sang in the choir, and belonged to the same women's Bible study.

After their Bible study ended one hot summer day in August, the two lingered to chat before heading home. Pat seemed to hold on to their parting moments as she gave Emily a farewell hug. Emily headed for home, but Pat had an errand to run.

"I was standing at the kitchen sink peeling potatoes when I heard the distant scream of an ambulance. An eerie feeling came over me," Emily said. "Later, our pastor phoned. The siren was for Pat.

"At the hospital, I found many friends and family gathered from the church. I learned Pat's car had stalled on the railroad tracks and an oncoming train broadsided her.

"The first person on the scene was a man who witnessed the accident and ran over to help. When he searched for identification, he found her Bible and church bulletin in the wreckage. He phoned our pastor immediately.

"We all sat in disbelief," Emily said. "Yet the most amazing story came from the ambulance attendant who recalled what took place during the transport to the hospital.

"He told us Pat faded in and out of consciousness, but he saw her lips moving as if she were trying to say something. Bending near, he heard her struggling to whisper a prayer, 'Please God, send a Christian to raise my children and be a good wife to my husband.'

"Pat lost her life that day, and I lost my best friend," Emily concluded.

A glance at the large round clock on the wall reminded me of the lateness of the hour. The cut hair on the floor, the used tint bowl and brushes in the sink would have to wait. I retrieved my keys and purse from the office, stuffed in the day's receipts, switched off the lights, and Emily and I left the salon. It had been a long day with a somber ending.

The previous night's clutter greeted me when I arrived at the salon the next morning. My thoughts were drawn to Emily's touching story as I began to clean up. The previous night's sad mood seemed to linger in the air like a mist.

Olivia's early arrival interrupted my cleaning efforts. As my first client of the day, her bedraggled appearance, crowned with straggling, dark brown hair, begged for a perm and cut. I paused to check her in, and continued with the clean-up. In making conversation, I related last night's moving story to her.

A shy, pleasant Christian woman, she had shared only glimpses of her own life story in past appointments. Her world revolved around her husband and two children. When I neared the end of Emily's story, I noticed a decided change in Olivia's demeanor. Her smile had disappeared. Tears, mingled with black mascara, trickled down her rosy cheeks. I handed her a box of Kleenex and apologized for anything I might have said to distress her.

She wiped her eyes and collected her emotions. "I've never heard the part about the prayer before. You see, I married her husband and raised her children."

~Jeanette Sharp

2

Miracle Soup

You may ask me for anything in my name, and I will do it.
~John 14:14

Our five-bedroom ranch house in the suburbs sold in the divorce proceedings. The boat, motor home and cross-country travels disappeared. My Chrysler LeBaron, the only new car I'd ever owned, was replaced with a rundown twenty-year-old clunker, symbolic of my own life—nondescript and nameless. The car soon fell apart, along with the dream I cherished. My bank account took a nosedive. Left with few options, I was forced into an efficiency apartment, which created a large gaping hole in my ego.

I frequently used the ten-minute walk to my barely-able-to-make-ends-meet job to convey my dissatisfaction to God. I wasn't sure He cared or even if He heard.

One evening at the opening night of a conference held close to my apartment, I bumped into Kathryn. She couldn't find a hotel room so I offered to let her stay at my place. She agreed to drive me back and forth to work during the day and we'd both attend the evening meetings.

The next morning I readied myself for work. As I approached the door, I felt a heavy presence, like a shepherd's staff on my chest, blocking my way. With every step it became weightier. "What is happening to me?"

I heard a still small voice say, "I have something else for you to do today. Go to the conference."

Counting the loss of a day's wages too costly, I resisted. "How can I not go to work?" My question dissolved into repentance. "Lord, I'm sorry for looking to my paycheck as my source of provision."

I phoned work, asking for the day off and received it. This time when I walked toward the door there was no restraint.

Kathryn and I quickly found seats in the second row. Before we sat down, Lois and Cindy from New York introduced themselves to us. Behind me sat Pat, from Indiana. Surprised that everyone around me was from other cities, I thought, "Invite them to lunch."

They all accepted the invitation immediately. When I realized the repercussions of their acceptance, I chuckled. "What will I feed these strangers?"

We ate chicken-broccoli soup left over from the weekend and chatted about family, work, church and life. After lunch, someone suggested we pray.

My own prayer shocked me when I said, "Lord, is there anything You need?"

Someone sang, "I will come and bow down at your feet, Lord Jesus."

"That's what I need," came His response, followed by another instruction. "Just ask."

We exhausted ourselves with asking, then agreed to rest before the evening service. Lois headed to the door, but turned rather abruptly to face me. "What do you need?" she said.

I searched for words but none surfaced.

"Tell me tonight." With that she was out the door.

I turned to the others in disbelief, repeating her question. They laughed. "It's obvious. You need a couch, a car, a better job."

They knew my needs better than I. I stepped outside to conceal the tears. Pacing back and forth in the parking lot, I asked God, "What do You want me to ask for?"

His response startled me. "Tell her you need a car."

I tried to gain composure while combating fear. "How can I tell someone I just met I need a car? I only gave her a bowl of leftover soup and you want me to ask for a car?"

I was still asking that question when Kathryn and I walked through the double doors of the 5,000-seat auditorium that evening. Lois saw us walk in and bolted down the aisle. "Do you know what you need?" she commanded insisting I reply.

I spit out the words. "I... I... need... a... car."

She grabbed my arm, walked me to her front row seat, and turned me to face the judge-like gaze of her three kids and their spouses. "Now, tell them what you need," she demanded.

I fidgeted, wondering if they would criticize me for answering honestly before sputtering, "I need a car."

They all howled with laughter!

I swallowed my tears and embarrassment.

"Let me explain," Lois said. "I didn't have to bring my car on this trip. In spite of the kids' opposition, I drove as well."

Another chimed in. "She told us last night, 'I'm suppose to give my car to the lady behind me.'"

While I was making soup in Kentucky, Lois was driving from New York. Neither of us knew the Lord was stirring our hearts to obey Him or that He would pour us into each other's lives.

Handing me the keys to a late model Ford Taurus, Lois beamed, "Next time, you drive to New York, and we'll have soup at my place."

~Deborah Howard

3

Beautiful Music for Tough Times

Brothers and sisters, pray for us.
~1 Thessalonians 5:25

Several women from our Sunday school class had the privilege of mentoring a group of young mothers who had recently lost their jobs. We met with them one evening a week, teaching them how to manage money, prepare for interviews and dress for success. We discussed proper nutrition and planned weekly menus for their families on a limited budget. The young women understood that the following weeks would be tough. Sacrifices would have to be made.

We went around the room, each sharing creative ways to cut expenses.

"My daughter takes clarinet lessons at school," one young mom offered. "We rent her instrument from a music store. Last night I had to tell her we could no longer afford her clarinet. Lessons will have to be put on hold, I'm afraid."

The tissue box resurfaced as Carol's eyes filled with tears. She quickly dried her cheeks. "I'm all right. I know that if God wants my daughter to make beautiful music, He'll find a way."

That evening I started praying for Carol and her daughter.

The next morning I made phone calls to find a warm coat for one of the children. The sweet lady on the other end readily offered one of her daughter's coats. I was about to hang up when she suddenly cried out, "Wait! I just remembered one more thing. Do you happen to know anyone who could use a clarinet? We have one tucked away in the closet and I feel God has someone in mind for it."

~Mary Z. Smith

I Wish

A prayer in its simplest definition is merely a wish turned Godward.
~Phillips Brooks

"What a perfect couple of days." I stretched out on the bed of the luxurious hotel room for an afternoon nap after another busy morning of sightseeing in New York City.

"Lord, thank you so much for this trip," I prayed. "We've visited so many sites I've always wanted to see. I never imagined we would be staying in such a beautiful suite." A thought niggled at the back of my mind, making me feel ungrateful. "Lord, I wish I could see a Broadway show, but I dare not ask. You have been so generous. Yet I've always dreamed of seeing one. It would be the final touch to a perfect trip—the caramel on The Big Apple."

I didn't want to ask my husband because tickets are so expensive and Mike probably would have bought them to make me happy. "Surely we'll make another trip up here in our lifetime," I told myself. "I'll get my wish someday."

With that, I fell into a deep sleep and woke a couple of hours later refreshed and ready to go again.

This trip was a shared birthday gift for my son-in-law and me. We drove up from Virginia in a rented van with my husband, two daughters and grandson. As a special treat my sister and her husband joined us from Tennessee.

We covered most of the city in a couple of days, sometimes

squeezing into a subway car and sometimes walking. At least some of the group walked. For physical reasons that prevented our walking great distances, my sister and I rode in wheelchairs pushed by our husbands. This was no small feat. We thought super-crowded sidewalks were the greatest challenge until we discovered what wheelchairs do in the subway—even with the brakes on. Think: roller coaster/bumper cars.

The afternoon of our nap was our last day there. My sister and brother-in-law had already headed back to Tennessee. One daughter, her husband, and son were going to a baseball game in the evening. My husband, other daughter, and I had no particular plans. We would rest, clean up, and go out to dinner.

We headed out to dinner and turned onto a side street to find our intended restaurant. We walked (or rolled) down Broadway looking at all of the theaters, admiring the marquees.

A clean-cut young man approached us. "Excuse me sir, would you like to have free tickets to a Broadway play tonight? They are $100 tickets."

"No, thanks," Mike said as we rolled on by. "I just bet they were free," he mumbled.

"Nobody would honestly give away $100 tickets," my daughter agreed.

"They're probably fake. I'd hate to take them and be turned away at the door," Mike added.

I thought of my prayer. "But what if they are real? What if we just gave up a Broadway show?"

Our daughter stopped walking. "Maybe he is for real."

"Okay." Mike wheeled me around. "Let's go back and talk to him."

We made our way back to the young man. "So, what's the deal with these tickets?" Mike asked.

"There is no deal. They are absolutely free and great seats." He handed three tickets to Mike. "Do you need more?"

"Yes! Thank you!" Mike exclaimed. "Sorry we brushed you off but it's hard to believe someone would just give these away."

"I know," the young man smiled. "We're up here with a group of children who have serious illnesses. The tickets were donated for them but they are absolutely exhausted. They've had a full day and want to go back to their hotel rooms." He shrugged. "I've been trying to give these tickets away for an hour. No one will take them; they all think I'm crazy."

We thanked him profusely and rushed to the restaurant. We had just enough time to eat before the performance of *Thoroughly Modern Millie*.

I couldn't believe I was sitting in a Broadway play, center section, row ten. It was the experience of a lifetime for me. After the play we walked back to the hotel amid city lights and the excitement of Broadway... amazed that God made the wish that I dared not ask for come true.

~Sandra McGarrity

Birth Behind Bars

Then I will give them one heart, and I will put a new spirit within them,
and take the stony heart out of their flesh...
~Ezekiel 11:19

I was getting ready for bed when the nightly news started. I was startled to hear the television reporter say a woman from a nearby county had been arrested for trying to sell her unborn baby for crack cocaine.

How could a mother even consider such a thing? My mind couldn't picture any circumstance that could lead a mother to sell her child. But my disgust quickly turned to fear. I turned the volume up. What county jail did they take her to? My heart sank as the camera showed this disheveled pregnant criminal being booked into the jail I would be visiting the next day.

Twenty years before, I'd felt a strong urge to reach out and help young pregnant women in trouble. I'd heard about the birth experience of a girl in county jail who went into labor. She was transported to a hospital but the location was kept secret since it could have been a security risk if street friends or even family discovered where she was. Once in the hospital, the inmate had one leg and arm shackled to the bed, and a guard, whom she had never met, watched as she gave birth. No encouragement, no support, no one to help make sense of what was happening. I wanted these young women to know they were loved and somebody cared about their babies and about them.

Working with our local sheriff, I proposed a program for pregnant inmates. The sheriff correctly complained that these pregnant women should not have made the choices that landed them in jail. But he also realized he had an innocent baby as an inmate, and that baby deserved a chance at a decent birth and maybe even a few hours of bonding with a mother who would be headed back to lockup while the child went home with a relative, or worse.

Years earlier I had taken the first step to prepare myself. I became a certified doula, a woman trained to coach and support a mother before, during, and after childbirth. Next I studied to become a Certified Childbirth Educator so I could help these scared girls prepare for motherhood. Along the way, I developed a team of women who shared my compassion for these women suffering in the shadows of our community.

From our very first day at the jail, the pregnant inmates came. Most were distraught that their babies would be born behind bars and they would only be able to hold them for a few hours or maybe a day. These girls sat in our jail classroom sobbing. They bore the marks of their lifestyles—tattooed and pierced in every place imaginable. But they also had a mother's heart and begged us to help them and their babies.

We implemented our program and a certified member of our team visited them in jail and began their childbirth education. When the time came for delivery, one of us met them at the hospital and stayed with them the entire time, even if that meant days. And as long as we were with them, it was our hope they wouldn't be shackled.

Two decades later we have attended more than 600 births. Some of the girls were homeless. Some, barely teenagers. Some were the victims of abuse. And almost all had been abandoned by the people they needed the most. But none of them, not a single one of the hundreds of drug-addicted mothers we had cared for, had ever attempted to trade their unborn child for a rock of crack cocaine. Until now.

I turned the television off and sat on the edge of my bed. How could I possibly love this woman who thought nothing about her baby's welfare? What would I say that could possibly make any difference? Did she really deserve help?

I bowed my head and said the only thing I could think of, "Lord I don't know what I will do if I see her. Please help me."

Early the next morning I packed my teaching materials and headed out to the jail. I tried to convince myself that I was scheduled to teach the child birth class and I probably wouldn't even see the girl who tried to sell her baby. But she stayed on my mind.

I called a few faithful women who interceded in prayer for us every time we went to the jail. My prayer request, however, had changed from the night before. I asked them to pray that the Lord would somehow give me a heart for this girl, for my heart was hard.

I stepped past the security desk, the heavy metal door slid open, and I walked through. Even after all these years I hadn't gotten used to the deafening clap of steel behind me as the door slammed and locked.

I made my way to the classroom. The guards did not stop me and tell me about a new prisoner. "Good," I thought. "She is locked up out of sight and I won't see her."

After class I packed up and headed toward the locked exit door.

A guard stopped me. "We locked up a girl last night that was ready to pop and they took her to the hospital. You better hurry."

I didn't have to ask. I knew it was her. Yesterday she tried to sell her child. Today that child would be born.

I headed to the hospital, driving and praying as fast as I could. "Lord, I need You, I'm counting on You. Please help me have compassion for this girl. Please love this girl somehow through me."

I pulled into the first available parking spot, grabbed my nametag and birthing bag and headed for labor and delivery.

Because inmates aren't allowed to take anything to the hospital, I packed a gown, lotion and baby clothes for a boy or a girl. The nurses recognized me. Even though they seemed appreciative of what I did for these troubled moms, their prejudice was often apparent. Today, I honestly admitted, my racing heart felt the same way.

I opened the hospital room door and the guard recognized me

and waved me in. That's when I saw her. She looked smaller than she appeared on TV. Her hair was matted and snarled on her head. The toil of constant drug abuse was evident on her face. She looked at me with a half smirk and her rotting teeth resembled those of other meth users I'd seen.

I said one last silent prayer and walked toward her. Suddenly it was though everything was in slow motion. In a flash across my mind the Lord simply said, "I can forgive her. Can you?"

It took less than three seconds for me to reach her bedside and in that short distance God worked in my heart. I extended my arms; the girl fell into them and sobbed. My first words to her were, "God forgives any of us who call out to Him. He loves you."

Her body wracked with sobs as she clung to me.

I stayed right by her side for the entire twenty-hour labor, holding her hand, stroking her hair and helping her breathe with contractions. Then I held her in my arms while she pushed and the armed guard watched. When her baby girl was born, she asked, her voice choking, "Can I rock her? Can I please rock her?"

"Of course you can."

Though her baby had been born safely, God's plan wasn't over. Because I stayed with her and loved her unconditionally for those few days, she trusted me and revealed that she wanted to surrender the baby for adoption. Instead of being sold to another addict, the infant was going to a loving family who had been praying for months for her.

Two days after my arrival, I finally left the hospital, unlocked my car door and slid into the seat. I felt exhausted, hungry, exhilarated and blessed. As I drove out of the parking lot I looked out the windshield at a clear blue sky and could only say, "Thank you, God."

As I drove home I cried harder than I had after any other birth.

~Janice Banther

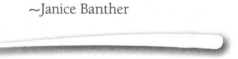

Old Faithful

Prayer is the soul's sincere desire, uttered or unexpressed.
~James Montgomery

"Hey! You!" I half-yelled at a man in the parking lot near Yellowstone's Old Faithful Lodge. Charmed by a bison rolling on the ground in the distance, he completely missed the one walking past his left shoulder.

When the man turned to look, my skin prickled. "Pay attention," my inner voice said. "Surprising things are afoot for you too."

Somehow I knew I was being put on notice.

We'd ridden roughly 370 miles a day on a Harley motorcycle, from Tucson to Yellowstone. The first few hours, because of a minor misunderstanding with a favorite publisher, I prayed for reassurance about the direction of my career as an editor and writing coach. Soon, I surrendered to the rhythm of the ride, the cleansing wind, and the creativity roaring within me in this beauty. How wondrous that Bruce and I could sit, blissfully connected, our helmets just inches apart for hours.

We ventured from the parking lot to the benches by Old Faithful, due to spout any minute. "Mind if we sit here?" Bruce asked a pony-tailed man.

"Go ahead, I don't bite."

Bruce loved meeting people on the road, which was a Godsend because I had no desire to talk, preferring to bask in the moment. I didn't want to be rude, so every once in a while, as Bruce and Mr. Ponytail chatted, I nodded in their direction, catching bits and pieces.

He and his wife were traveling with her mom and dad in their RV. He dedicated his life to helping gang members recover from substance abuse and violence. In fact, he ran a nonprofit called L.O.V.E. Let Our Violence End. He traveled around the country training police officers, judges, and health care professionals on how to interact with gang members. He was traveling now to de-stress and revive.

"Get his card," I heard in my head.

"What? No!" I protested, staring where I willed Old Faithful to rise. Normally I wanted to get people's cards. My favorite thing in the world was to write about inspiring people. What if I couldn't find a market for his story? Or I got too busy with other assignments? I didn't want to get his hopes up.

Mr. Ponytail kept talking, easy and soft. My senses wouldn't stop vibrating. His L.O.V.E. programs successfully helped gang members choose peace, again and again. I recalled how one of my best friends was a facilitator in Nonviolent and Compassionate Communication. We'd collaborated on a book about it.

When the geyser erupted, I barely saw it, so distracted was I by the voice in my head. "Get his card, get his card, get his card. This is why you're here."

I felt a quickening inside me. How melodramatic, I laughed at myself. The second the geyser died down, I heard myself gush, "I'm a writer. Can I have your card?"

Mr. Ponytail looked dumbstruck. He slapped the bench with one hand. Tears filled his eyes. His face reddened. "I'm sorry. I'm sorry," he said. "I've been praying for the last two weeks to meet a writer." He clenched the bridge of his nose between his fingers and shook his head.

My neck flushed.

"That's what she does!" said Bruce, astonished.

"Everybody's been telling me I should write a book," said Mr. Ponytail. "I just started taping my stories, but I've felt so lost. I'll fly wherever you are for a week to tell you my story," he said. "Whatever it takes."

Bruce described how I nurtured books into completion. I had no idea he'd been paying such attention.

I almost chuckled. As Bruce and I were thundering on a Harley from Tucson to Mr. Ponytail, God was orchestrating the answer to my prayer… and His.

~Jan Henrikson

Grandkids for Christmas

The deepest wishes of the heart find expression in secret prayer.
~George E. Rees

I was ten and my little sister was seven, the babies of a family of fourteen. Seven of my siblings had flown the coop, but my brother Wayne was the only one with kids. He and his wife had just been transferred across the country to California. Mama was looking at her first Christmas without little ones in the house. We all prayed she wouldn't be too sad, yet we suspected she was a bit depressed, though she didn't let it show.

On Christmas Eve we sat talking about my little nieces, wondering what they were doing. We imagined how empty the next day would be without them ripping open presents from Santa. When we couldn't stand it any longer, we called and passed the phone around, asked them if they'd been good girls and what they hoped Santa would leave under their tree. Mama busied herself in the kitchen, no doubt praying, as usual.

That's when our Christmas miracle began. We lived on a busy state highway in south Louisiana, on a section of road called Dead Man's Curve. The sound of screeching tires and smashing steel was not unusual to us. Many strangers found refuge on our living room couch while waiting for an ambulance, a tow truck or a family member to rescue them. Once a man died in my dad's arms on our front lawn, after being hit by a car as he walked along that treacherous road. My father, an ordained minister, baptized him there.

As we hung up from talking to our nieces, we heard the familiar sound of tires screeching. We held our breath, then heard an earsplitting crash. We bolted for the front door and rushed to the road. An eighteen-wheeler had plowed into a station wagon holding a young couple and their two little daughters. The truck was on its side in the ditch. The station wagon had crossed the road and a ditch, then landed inches from a row of trees. The truck driver and the young family crawled from the wreckage. Amazingly, no one appeared hurt, but the truck and car were going nowhere except the junkyard.

Someone stopped the traffic. Mom and Dad hustled everyone into the house, called the police and Mama started warming dinner. Next thing I knew the truck driver was gone. I guess someone picked him up. But the family was stranded. They were on their way to Mississippi to spend Christmas with elderly grandparents who were too old to drive and pick them up this late at night.

Within five seconds we all fell in love with the precious girls. The older girl was three just like my older niece, and the baby a few months younger than our little one. Mama rocked the baby to sleep and Daddy read Christmas stories to the girl until she dozed off in his lap. My sister and I offered to sleep on the den floor and give them our beds.

Mama scrounged around in her closet, found some toys, wrapped them and stashed them under the tree. Long after we drifted off to sleep ourselves, Mama's sewing machine whirred away making a painting smock, a dress and a pinafore for the older girl, a Christmas apron for the mother, and a bonnet for the baby. She wrapped up a handyman how-to book for the daddy and some of her popular homemade cheese straws.

When we woke up, Dad read the Christmas story from the Bible, then the three-year-old placed the figures in the manger, just like we did when we were that age. Everyone was amazed at the presents. The young couple was shocked to find something for them too.

About midday on Christmas, someone came from Mississippi to pick up the little family. We hugged goodbye and thanked each other for the wonderful Christmas we shared.

For many years after that, the family visited regularly every Christmas Eve. When their grandparents died and they no longer traveled to Mississippi, they stayed in touch, sent Christmas cards and even visited every few years. We marveled at how the girls, and later their little brother, grew.

There have been plenty Christmases since then. Now I spend them with my own four kids. There've been other miracles too. But I'll never forget the year God sent my mama grandkids for Christmas.

~Mimi Greenwood Knight

The Lost Coin

And when she has found it, she calls her friends and neighbors together,
saying, "Rejoice with me for I have found the piece which I lost!"
~Luke 15:9

"I've got something for you." I set down my cup of tea to take the thick manila envelope my co-worker held out to me. I tipped out a pile of papers, recognizing one as my son's official adoption certificate.

"Edie, where... where did you get this?" I gasped.

"At the children's home."

"What?"

She smiled at me, the same friendly smile I'd seen for three months as she and I answered phones for Trinity Broadcasting Network, praying for callers.

"Who are you? Are you... are you Ron's mother?" I almost whispered it.

"No," she said calmly. "I'm his sister."

I threw my arms around her. "This is unbelievable!"

We'd adopted Ron in 1958, when he was five. Our daughters loved him and enjoyed teaching their new brother about life on a Colorado ranch. Ron looked enough like me that one teacher accused him of lying when he said he was adopted.

But as he grew older, he asked the questions adopted children often have. "Why didn't my parents want me? Where are they now? Do I have sisters and brothers somewhere? Can I meet them?"

We'd tried to find his birth family, but the records had been sealed. There was no hope.

"They probably don't want to know me anyway," Ron finally said bitterly.

The morning after Edie's revelation, my husband and I met her for breakfast, carrying family photo albums. Joy in her eyes, Edie laid a handful of photos on the table and I put mine beside them.

Ron's little-boy pictures matched Edie's perfectly. His adult pictures resembled Edie's brothers. We read the reports from the orphan's home. There was no doubt. Edie really was Ron's sister.

My husband put his arms around me as I wept. Edie started to cry, too, and I took her hand. "How did you find us?"

"Our family was having trouble, and my parents placed Ron at the children's home when I was a teenager. The social worker persuaded them to relinquish all rights so Ron would have a real home, with a mother and father. My sister and brothers and I have been praying and searching for Ron for over ten years. We've asked and written and phoned and visited the orphan home, but the information was sealed."

"That's what Ron was told when he tried to find you," I told her. "So what did you do?"

"I called the children's home again," Edie said. "The woman who answered said they destroy all records after seven years, but she was willing to check the files anyway. When she called me back, she said she'd found the paperwork! I went there and she allowed me to copy everything. I couldn't believe it when I saw your name on Ron's adoption certificate."

"God connected us at work," I said, "so you could find me… find Ron."

We decided Ron's upcoming thirty-second birthday would be the time to introduce him to his long-lost family. This would be the best surprise birthday present ever.

Edie joined our family as we gathered that day. "Listen to this," Edie said when everyone had arrived. She started to read from Luke 15. "Suppose a woman has ten silver coins and loses one. Does she not light a lamp, sweep the house and search carefully until she finds it? And when she finds it, she calls her friends and neighbors together and says, 'Rejoice with me; I have found my lost coin!'"

Her unsteady voice continued, "I too lost something very valuable twenty-seven years ago. Today the Lord is restoring that which had been lost to me."

She put a fat brown envelope in Ron's hand. He shuffled through the sheaf of papers, stopping at the social worker's report of his stay at the orphanage. There wasn't a sound in the room.

"If this is a joke, it's not funny!" Ron looked around in desperation.

His dad and I smiled encouragingly.

"Are you trying to tell me that you are my sister?" he asked.

"Yes," Edie said, wrapping her arms around him. "Our father passed away several years ago. Our mother lives in Lakewood, just a few miles from here. You have three older brothers, Vern, Danny, and Richard, and another sister, JoAnn. The family's waiting at Danny's house."

"How far is that?" Ron stammered.

I spoke up. "It's just behind the nursing home where Grandpa has been the past several years. Every Sunday when we visited him, we were driving by your brother's house... and we didn't know it. If it's okay with you, they're coming over now."

When Ron's brother Danny arrived, he stopped and stared at our daughter Rosanne. "You... your son's on our son's baseball team!"

We were astounded to learn more Divine coincidences. When Ron drove a truck years before, he had frequently gone by his sister JoAnn's home in Albuquerque. And Edie lived within walking distance of Ron's house.

I started to put out refreshments for the birthday party. I cut the cake, scooped ice cream, and handed plates to all the strangers in my house, strangers who were now my family too.

When Ron's mother arrived, Ron ran outside to greet her and her husband. He brought them in saying, "Mom and Dad, this is Bernice and Rich, my mother and stepfather."

We'd all been praying silently, asking for the right words, and those prayers carried us through the momentary awkwardness. I offered them coffee and birthday cake and we sat down to share stories of Ron's growing-up years.

From the birthday party on, our family activities included both families and their extended families. When Ron had back surgery, we were all there.

"What a wonderful family you have," a nurse said.

Ron smiled. "You don't know the half of it."

~Lucille Rowan Robbins as told to Elsi Dodge

My Gift from God

The LORD will command His loving kindness in the daytime,
and in the night His song shall be with me—A prayer to the God of my life.
~Psalm 42:8

I sat at the stoplight, staring at the sign in front of a small church crowded between a diner and a park-and-ride on a four-lane highway. It was hardly noticeable when driving forty-five miles an hour in a rush to get somewhere. Yet this church had personality. They always posted one-line zingers to get people's attention. Today it read, "If you feel God is not by your side... guess who moved?"

I sat staring at the sign. It was true. I'd moved. What I didn't understand was, how did I move? When? I didn't purposefully walk away. I didn't say, "That's it. I'm done." Yet one day I woke up saying, "Where did He go?"

As my car proceeded through the green light, I decided it was time to have a talk with God. I used to talk to Him all the time. Typically, it was a daily conversation asking for guidance or help. I'd talk about the safety and health of my friends, family, and even strangers. But, that evening as I lay in my bed looking up through the dark, I decided to talk to God about me and only me.

"God, I don't feel You. Are You still there? I feel so disconnected. It's like You're not around anymore. What happened?"

I lay waiting for a magical answer. Silence.

I continued. "Okay, listen. I don't feel You. I need to know You're here. So if You could just do something. Do something so I know You are by my side. God, if You are here, give me a gift."

My immediate response to my own words was, "What kind of stupid thing is that to say? I'm asking God for a gift. A gift, of all things, not a sign, not help, not guidance, but a gift?"

I lay in bed thinking "Yeah, that's it. Feeling a little disconnected? Ask for stuff!"

I fell asleep feeling even farther away than before.

The next morning I rolled out of bed and headed for the shower. I had a child to get ready for school. I had clients waiting for me. I had yet another networking event that evening. My conversation with God was quickly lost in life.

A few weeks passed.

I stopped at my post office box on my way to the office, grabbed my mail and found a little yellow slip saying I had a package. I went to the counter to pick up my latest software purchase or client package. I looked at the sender's name. Carmen Cardwell. I didn't know the name. I checked the address. It was my box number and my name. Feeling a little awkward, I took the package to my car and sat examining it. "Who is Carmen Cardwell? What could this possibly be?" I slowly opened it, praying lightheartedly that it wouldn't explode.

Inside the box was a purse. A pink purse. Pink was my favorite color. I only had pink purses. All of them were pink. Now I had received a pink purse from someone I didn't even know. "Who is this person? How does she know me? And why would she send this?"

I noticed a small white envelope inside the box with my name handwritten on it. As I opened the card a small business card fell out: Carmen Cardwell, Life Coach.

It all came rushing back. I'd sat next to Carmen at a seminar the month before. We were both thinking about changing career paths and both excited to learn what our futures held. We'd exchanged information and agreed to keep in touch.

But why? Why would she be sending me a gift after our brief meeting at the seminar?

I opened the tiny card. It read, "Diana, I found this pink purse. I originally bought it for me. But God has placed it in my heart to give it to you."

I sat, holding my gift from God.

~Diana DeAndrea-Kohn

Ambulance Calling

Be anxious for nothing, but in everything by prayer and supplication,
with thanksgiving, let your requests be made known to God.
~Philippians 4:6

With our blinding lights and ear-piercing sirens my partner and I weave our ambulance in and out of traffic, complaining that the driver in front won't let us pass.

I re-read our call notes: male patient; conscious, breathing: wife states patient having neck pain for over a year: patient will be sitting in a chair in front yard.

My partner and I agree this sounds like yet another person trying to get a free ride to the hospital, most likely trying to get pain pills.

We pull down the street and I shut off the emergency lights as we see, sure enough, a male subject sitting in a lawn chair in his front yard. We advise our arrival to headquarters and step out of the truck and proceed to the patient. We are approached by his wife who states she is very worried about her husband who has been in unbearable pain for over a year now. She states that he has been to numerous doctors and through countless tests, but still no relief of pain, so tonight he decided to numb the pain with alcohol.

As my partner gathers more information, I begin to assess my patient, getting his blood pressure, medical history, and a strong foul odor of liquor on his breath. We both begin talking to the patient, but get no response. I think, "Is this guy just being stubborn or is he so heavily intoxicated that he can't answer us?"

When my partner goes inside with the patient's wife to get his medical records and medication, the man begins to speak to me like we've met before. He then asks me in the most horrific and crying-out-for-help voice, "Have you ever treated a gunshot wound?"

My heart skips a beat. Nervous and wondering how to answer, I tell him, "Yes, yes I have."

As many thoughts run through my head, I notice my partner coming from the house so I walk toward the ambulance to get the truck ready to transport the patient. My partner asks, "What did he tell you while I was inside?"

"He asked me if I have ever treated a gunshot wound."

I ask the patient, "Are you intending to harm yourself tonight?"

Before a second can pass the wife bursts into tears. She states that her husband has been very depressed and this is the true reason for calling us. She feared that if she did not make the call, her husband's life, or maybe even hers, could have ended tonight.

My partner and I begin to observe our patient very closely. Is this man hiding a gun? Does he truly intend to harm himself or even others?

The man then states he would like to go inside to use the bathroom. We both answer, "No, you are not going inside. We are leaving right now to go to the hospital and if you choose otherwise, the sheriff will be on the way."

The man agrees to come with us but states that he needs to get his wallet from his vehicle. As he is in his car, we see him pull a dark black object from the side of his seat. I flinch. Is it a gun? Do we run, call for help, or attack the man? To our relief, the man pulls out a CD case and removes a CD.

We then load him into our ambulance and begin our trip to the hospital ten miles away. En route, I reaffirm that this is a career that truly touches the lives of people and this is what I want to do with the rest of my life.

As I try to gather information from this stubborn man, I get childish answers or no answer at all. Annoyed, I ask him one final question, "Sir, what is your date of birth?"

"Passover. What is Passover? If you can answer this, I will tell you whatever you want to know."

Astonished by my quick response, I answer him, and to the amazement of both of us, I am correct. So as I begin to finally get information from the man, he surprisingly becomes compliant. He then asks, "Do you believe in God?"

Without hesitation, I answer, "Yes."

He then asks my name and says that he would like to pray for me. I tell him my name and he states, "I was talking with God while on my front lawn. I told Him that I was tired of living, tired of being in so much pain. I asked Him to please help me, send me a sign on how to get my life back on track, and you, you my good friend are that sign."

He then hands me the CD. "I wrote these songs telling people how it is not worth taking their own lives. You know anyone in need of help, give them this CD."

I tell the man that the only way to get help from the kind doctors at the hospital is to listen to what they say. I tell him that I will pray that he gets better.

The man then says, "You, my friend, truly are a sign from God. If not for you, I would have taken my life. While reaching for my wallet in my car, two options ran through my head... the gun on my center console that would take my life, or my music that I would give you to help others. Your kindness and willingness to help, to heal this hurt, made the decision for me that suicide was not the right option."

Before transporting the man into the ER, I thank him and wish him well. While driving away from the hospital, my partner and I talk about the call and I pop in the CD. The sound of the man's pain runs through his music, but his message stands strong. Give it all to God, life is worth living.

From that day on I appreciate every patient I come in contact with and try to get something out of every one of their words.

I'm humbled to be a vehicle for God's work.

~Trent Michael Larousse

Finding the Right House

Everything is in the hands of heaven, except the fear of heaven.
~The Talmud

"Got your cellphone? Glasses? Wallet? ID?" I asked.

"What are you doing, a pre-flight check?" my husband Avraham smiled. "Can we please get going? You've got to get to your interview before I go to see my patient at one o'clock."

"Right. Got your medical bag?"

"Check."

Even years after moving from North America, we still loved the half-hour drive to Jerusalem. The blue sky above the rocky mountains, the trees, and the ascent to the Holy City always filled us with gratitude for the privilege of living in Israel. My eyes drank in the greenery like an invigorating tonic.

As we sped along, Avraham commented, "Every day is an adventure here. I really do appreciate that everything is meant to be. Before coming to Israel, I knew that, but here I experience it every day."

We approached our favorite part of the journey, just past Mevasseret Tzion, where a panoramic view of Jerusalem suddenly appears above the roadway. Before we knew it, we were at the entrance to the city. We had made good time and arrived at my meeting with time to spare.

After my interview, I met Avraham at our favorite Angel's Bakery Café. Avraham ordered his daily dose of iced coffee and a bag of fresh, whole wheat bagels. Glancing at the clock, I suggested we get going to see his patient.

Avraham had received a request to make a house call at the home of an elderly woman in Jerusalem. Her daughter had called the day before to arrange the appointment. As there are very few podiatrists in Israel, Avraham would travel all over the country to see patients requiring specialized foot care. He searched his pockets for the slip of paper on which he had written the address. He checked his medical bag, his notebook, and even the bag of fresh bagels. The note was nowhere to be found.

"I don't believe it! I must have left the address and phone number at home."

I sighed to myself in frustration as I realized our "pre-flight check" had been incomplete.

"Do you remember any part of the address?" I asked.

"I remember that there was a 17 in it, because it was part of my birth date."

"Do you know the street name?"

"No. Just that it's in this neighborhood."

I had heard the family name mentioned briefly the day before and recalled that it sounded European. "Let's try looking at building number 17 on this street and see if the mailboxes list any familiar sounding names," I offered.

Avraham agreed. "I guess it's worth a try. We are already here."

We scanned the listings at number 17, but all of the names were Israeli. We tried two more nearby buildings without success.

"This is like looking for a needle in a haystack," I complained.

"Well, since we are already in the city, let's try one last building," Avraham suggested, as he whispered a prayer for God's help in finding the right house.

We wearily approached the entrance to an apartment house down another street and noticed all of the European occupant names. Taking this as a good sign, we entered the lobby and climbed the stairs. We encountered a young boy who informed us that indeed an elderly couple lived next door to their married daughter in the building.

We quickly went up to the first landing and knocked on a door covered with children's art. I recognized the woman as a teacher from an educational workshop I had taught.

"What a small world," I remarked. "We know one another from teaching, and now my husband is here to see your mother. Where does she live?"

"My parents live right next door," she replied, pointing the way down the hallway.

We proceeded to the neighboring apartment where an elderly gentleman answered the door. Avraham announced that he was the foot specialist whom their daughter had called. The delighted man warmly welcomed us. The couple had recently arrived from South Africa and were so pleased to find an English-speaking doctor who made house calls. The wife suffered from a variety of ailments which made it difficult for her to travel to a clinic. She sat in a reclining chair, her bare feet ready to be examined.

Avraham took a detailed medical history and conducted a thorough examination. After treating her and suggesting appropriate follow-up care, he packed his bag and we departed.

Moments later, as we buckled our seatbelts, we laughed about actually finding the house despite the incredible odds. "We certainly had some help from 'upstairs' on this one!" Avraham exclaimed.

As we were about to pull out of the parking lot, the daughter came rushing up to our car. She could hardly contain herself. "Thank you for coming to help my mother." Then she added, "But I have to ask. How did you know to come to see her? After you left, my father came over to thank me for calling you. I told him that I hadn't called. I thought *he* had called."

Avraham and I stared at each other. It was the wrong house! Or was it?

~Ruth Zimberg

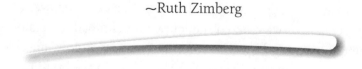

12

His Eye on the Sparrow

He prayed as he breathed, forming no words and making no specific requests,
only holding in his heart, like broken birds in cupped hands, all those people
who were in stress or grief.
~Ellis Peters

I stood in our yard on a beautiful late summer day, but I wasn't enjoying it. I hadn't been enjoying much of anything lately. Several months earlier my husband Grover had suffered a heart attack. The doctors warned us that even after recovery, patients sometimes suffered bouts of depression. Not my husband. He was doing great, back to work and exercising on his new treadmill. I was the one who'd been sinking into a despair from which I couldn't seem to recover.

As I headed back into the house our grandson Skylar, who lived only a few blocks away, appeared, a shoebox in hand. "Dad told me to bring this to you. He says you'll know what to do."

I peered into the box to see a tiny baby sparrow with only pin-feathers. It peered up at me with curious black-dot eyes. I wondered what I was supposed to do.

The little bird answered by opening its mouth wide in the universally understood command: Feed me. Skylar watched me expectantly. Clearly outnumbered, and without much conviction, I sighed. "I'll see what I can do."

That was enough to satisfy Skylar, who ran off to play. As soon as he was gone I turned away from the bird, convinced there was nothing I could do for it. An orphaned bird was the last thing I needed.

Retreating into the security of the house, I turned my mind determinedly away from the shoebox on the patio. Nature would take its course.

A short while later my friend Betty called. I told her about the little bird.

"What are you going to do with it?" she asked.

"There's nothing I can do. Besides, it's just a sparrow," I said, justifying my abandonment.

"You know, there's a great hymn, 'His Eye on the Sparrow.' Have you heard it?"

"Sure," I said somewhat grudgingly.

"And it says in the Bible, 'Are not five sparrows sold for two pennies? Yet not one of them is forgotten by God.'" (Luke 12:6)

"Okay, I get it," I snapped.

Betty chuckled, but after I hung up I knew I had to go look. Maybe I'd underestimated the bird and it'd already flown away.

No such luck. The little sparrow waited expectantly.

"Oh, Lord, tell me what to do now," I prayed as I carried the shoebox into the house. A quick Internet search gave me information on how to feed an orphaned bird, and before long I was mixing together a gruel made of canned dog food, the yolk of a hardboiled egg, a dab of turkey and vegetable baby food. Grover brought an old wire birdcage in from the garage and I placed the sparrow inside. It clung to the perch, looked up at me, and again opened that little beak wide.

Tentatively, I scooped up a pea-sized portion of the mixture on the end of a toothpick and offered it. The sparrow devoured the food and begged for more. Encouraged, I gave it several more helpings.

"Maybe this won't be so bad," I thought, and for the first time in weeks I felt a twinge of optimism. I put the cage with its tiny inhabitant in a spare bedroom.

That night as I lay in bed I thought about the sparrow. Preparing for the worst, I half-convinced myself I'd find it feet-up on the bottom of the cage in the morning.

But before I was even completely awake, I heard chirping from the next room. Lately I'd been turning over in my bed at the first hint of sunlight, pulling the covers over my head in an attempt to avoid the coming day. This was no longer an option. A small life depended on me.

"Coming!" I called, throwing back the covers.

For the next few days I focused on the little bird that needed my care. Without my even being fully aware of it, the fog of my depression began to fade.

The sparrow always greeted me as I entered the room and it hopped on my finger when I lifted the top from the cage. I whistled as I fed it, and it fluttered its wings and chirped in response. And always, it ate with gusto. Before long its feathers filled out and it pecked at the birdseed I placed inside the cage.

Finally Grover and I agreed it was time to set the bird free. Skylar came over to share in the moment. When we opened the cage the bird rocketed out, flew across the backyard and into a grove of trees where we lost sight of it. Without so much as a wave goodbye, the sparrow was gone.

That night I lay in bed and wondered if the little bird was safe, worried that it wouldn't know how to survive on its own.

Early the next morning I went outside, enjoying the sunshine more than I had in a long time. I heard a familiar insistent chirping. Even though I thought it was impossible, I looked around for the sparrow, and there it was, wings fluttering, on a low branch in our neighbor's tree several yards away. The sparrow flew out of the tree, swooped to me and landed on my outstretched hand! My heart lifted at the sight of this little creature. I felt a joy I hadn't known for months. A wild yet trusting gift with fluttering wings and a cheery chirp had lifted my depression.

I raised my hand and the bird flew back to the tree. I hurried into the house and quickly prepared a meal from the mixture I hadn't thrown out, with some bits of watermelon added as a treat. I returned to the yard and the bird again fluttered down to my hand. It ate its fill and then flew back into the high branches.

After that I continued to walk the neighborhood several times a day, whistling. Sometimes I'd walk as far as two blocks from the house before the sparrow flew down from some treetop. On one occasion I ventured into a neighbor's unfenced backyard. The little bird landed on my hand just as the neighbor came out her back door to witness this sight. "I've never seen anything like that," she marveled.

With each passing day I found the bird farther and farther from our house and it took longer to coax it from the trees. When it did come down to my hand it ate less, staying only for a bite or two before taking off again. "It's finding its way in the world," I figured, and knew the day would soon come when I wouldn't see it again.

That day came nearly two weeks after we'd released it. I walked around the neighborhood, whistling and listening for a responding chirp, for almost an hour before I gave up. When I finally headed home, I wasn't sad the sparrow was gone. It came to me and I healed it… and I was healed as well.

"Yet not one sparrow is forgotten by God," Betty had reminded me.

Nor are people, I understood at last.

~Jean Tennant

Chapter 2

Answered Prayers

God Will Provide

The prayer that begins with trustfulness and passes on into waiting will always end in thankfulness, triumph, and praise.

~Alexander Maclaren

The Christmas Bonus

And the apostles said to the Lord, "Increase our faith."
~Luke 17:5

My youngest sister called just before Christmas. "Guess what?" she began.

With Jacki I never knew what to guess. I worried about her... her safety in a tiny apartment in a bad part of town, her minimum wage job, her lack of health insurance, and her broken down car. Only four Christmases ago, she was earning hundreds of dollars working in bars, dancing, living a life far apart from mine. Miraculously, God had turned her life around. I was thankful for that, but her faith, still new, seemed fragile.

I braced myself. "What happened?"

"Remember how I told you we were going to get a Christmas bonus?"

I recalled how she had recently scoured the entire floor of the small convenience store where she worked, on her knees with a tiny scrub pad. It took her over a week, but she was so proud of the clean white floor. Even with her seven-dollar-an-hour salary, she was always doing over and above at her job. She even made little doggie treats for customers' pets. She always smiled and customers loved her. Now at Christmas, she really needed money for extra car expenses and just to pay bills.

"Well, I opened my bonus envelope to find three hundred dollars cash!"

"Wow!" I rejoiced with her. "I bet you hollered when you opened that envelope!"

"Yes! And I thanked God for always supplying my needs." She went on to say that she paid her bills and bought a few groceries. She giggled with joy, and I laughed with her.

The next day Jacki called again. This time her voice trembled. "My manager called very upset. She had opened her own bonus envelope to find a cash amount far below what she expected. 'I was supposed to get $300,' she said."

"On, no," I thought.

My sister continued. "I had a sick feeling. The manager and I have the same first name. What if there was a mistake? What if I got the wrong envelope? And now the money is gone! But I'm still going to call the store owner right away."

"Why don't you wait?" I urged her. "Give it some time. Think about it. The envelope did have your name on it."

"I can't. I prayed about it and I know what I need to do."

"But maybe it wasn't a mistake," I argued. "Maybe you were rewarded for all your extra work." I hated the thought of her talking to the owner, who was known to be a highly critical woman, downright mean at times.

"You deserve the money. I think you should keep it."

She didn't listen to me. Instead, she called the owner.

"You should have known you wouldn't get that much," the owner ranted. "We go by the rules here and low-ranking employees like you don't get extra. Only the managers get extra."

She told my sister that she must return the full amount immediately. There would be no bonus at all for her. What she couldn't pay back would be taken out of her paycheck.

Three hundred dollars… a fortune to Jacki, especially at Christmas. I was sick with anger. How could a person who owns several businesses punish someone who works so hard for almost nothing? I wanted to call the owner, write the newspaper, drive several hundred miles with all my friends to my sister's town and picket!

My sister said no. "I did the extra work for the Lord. And I know I did the right thing by telling," she said. "Besides, God always provides my needs."

Shaking, I hung up the phone. My first thought was to send her $300. I'd always wanted to jump in and fix things for her. I could afford it and I wanted desperately to make it right for her. It wasn't fair. She was still learning to trust God and now this happened.

In my heart, I heard God say, "Then let her trust Me. And you need to trust Me, too."

So I didn't send the money, but it was hard.

I got the call a week later. "Guess what?" Jacki chirped.

"What?" I asked tentatively.

"I bought a lottery ticket."

I groaned. I knew that every once in a while she enjoyed spending a dollar on a lottery ticket. I didn't think money should be used that way but I kept my mouth shut.

"I won something this time!" she exclaimed. "You need to thank God!"

My first thought was, "God would definitely *not* use a lottery ticket."

On the other hand, when my mind got quiet enough, He reminded me that He uses all kinds of things... a rib, a donkey who spoke, the jawbone of an ass, mud in a blind man's eyes, five tiny fish. He loved my sister and He'd reached into her world. Maybe it happened to be a lottery ticket.

"I won three hundred dollars!" she exclaimed.

Of course you did.

~Martha Moore

14

Dad's Dance

If you abide in me, and My words abide in you, you will ask what you desire,
and it shall be done for you.
~John 15:7

The call I'd prepared my heart for came from my sister. She was visiting my father in New Jersey and phoned me in Tennessee. "If you're planning on coming, you'd better come now."

I calmly took the recommendation and readied my three children and myself to leave in the morning. My husband remained home because one of us needed to be working for our family's survival. We also had a feeling there would be another New Jersey trip in our near future, one neither of us wanted me to take alone.

As I made the ten-hour drive, the most beautiful, yet surreal calm engulfed me. I concentrated on the road, aware that I was on my way to see my dad for the last time. To have that thought in my head and not be hyperventilating was such an odd place to find myself. Instead, I was focused on this amazing ten-hour gift of time I was suddenly presented with. I thought about all of the people in my life that had lost their own loved ones with no warning. With every breath I was thankful, not for my father's impending fall to cancer, but that God had given me the eyes to see the treasure within it all. I made peace with every moment I had not seen that way, and for times I maybe hadn't treated Dad as the gift he truly was.

I recalled the vacations we'd taken to the lake in New Hampshire when I was nine years old. Much to my chagrin, the sound of Frank

Sinatra flooded the car as we drove. It was absolute torture as far as I was concerned. After we unpacked and situated ourselves, my father taught me to dance for seven hours straight to music that had been the bane of my existence. My pajamas might as well have been a diamond-trimmed gown the way we twirled, dipped, and jumped on and off the furniture, rivaling Fred Astaire and Ginger Rogers. Nothing since has soothed me quite the same way as Ol' Blue Eyes.

I reminisced about the last time we'd danced together at a favorite cousin's wedding. In my Maid of Honor gorgeous, red, floor-length dress I twirled in Dad's arms around an actual dance floor to the music of Glenn Miller, not Frank. But I was dancing with my daddy so it little mattered. We used every inch of the ballroom floor because we were the only dancers… a good thing too because we were too good to be matched!

I drove along recalling the joy of that night, when we'd gotten our chance to dance in the venue that had always been in our imaginations until then. I replayed happy thoughts and memories of my father until I eventually reached his side.

My first sight of him was a deceptive one of health. He had discontinued his treatments and his hair and eyebrows had returned. He was thinner and smiling. I was so thankful he knew me right away. I didn't ask how he was feeling, guessing he was tired of that question, but instead we talked about the children and their fantastic daily chaos.

Over the days I stayed, he eventually slipped into a state where I became just as unrecognizable to him as he became to me. He spoke of things that made little sense, and my sisters and I did our best to guide him and each other through these times.

On my last day there, during one of his rare clear moments when I could actually see Dad behind those eyes, my six-month-old and I sat in his room with him. I put on Frank Sinatra and Dad began singing along! Then with Tucker on my hip and our hands entwined, Dad and I had one last dance… me with my feet, Dad with his heart… to "They Can't Take That Away From Me." I knew through my smiles and tears that I had just unwrapped one of the most amazing gifts I would ever receive.

I returned to Tennessee to work my job at a local restaurant. A week later I came home just before midnight. While everyone slept I sat in the chair under a wall of pictures my husband had put up in our absence. As I gazed at my father's photo I finally cried in brief cathartic sobs. Soon I climbed into bed and just as quickly as I closed my eyes they popped open again. I cried out to God, "Please take my daddy. Please God, take him and hug him like he's never been hugged before. God, please, please take my daddy." I said this over and over until I fell asleep.

An hour later the phone rang. My dance partner had gotten that hug exactly when I asked.

~Danielle Cattanach

No Matter What It Takes

God is faithful...
~1 Corinthians 1:9

When my mom called me to tell me the doctor didn't give Blu any chance to make it, I didn't panic. After all, my brother had been in and out of hospitals his whole life dealing with his hemophilia.

I drove to the hospital to be with my mom, praying the entire thirty-minute drive. When I got there and saw my sister, brother and my grandparents, who had also lost two sons to hemophilia, things became very real to me.

I walked into Blu's room to find him in more pain than I had ever seen him in. My panic moment came when the doctor told me Blu had a one percent chance of surviving till Christmas, just weeks away. The grief my family would soon face hit me. I couldn't even breathe. How could we ever survive this?

On my ride home I became angry with God. I wanted my brother to live, no matter what it took.

Then I got a call from my sister. "God spoke to me saying, 'I am God; don't ever doubt Me.'"

When she spoke those words, I began to feel God's peace and to trust His faithfulness.

That night I knelt beside my bed and prayed for Him to save my brother. I felt the Lord ask, "No matter what it takes?" That was the most difficult moment of my life, but after a while I said, "No matter what it takes." In that moment I put my big brother in God's hands. I had never trusted Him like that before and wondered where I got the strength to do it then. I got up from my knees, knowing that God would not take my brother until he belonged to Him.

On Friday night I went to work and had a couple of calls telling me Blu wasn't doing well. I began to panic and the Lord reminded me about the book of James telling us that a man who doubts His faith is like something being tossed about in the ocean. I needed a Bible, but I was at work and had left mine under Blu's hospital bed. In less than a minute a co-worker walked through the door with a Bible! I asked to borrow it and went to the break room. As I read, I felt the strongest urge to turn to James 5:15, "And the prayer of faith will save the sick, and the Lord will raise him up. And if he has committed sins, he will be forgiven." Even though they were written thousands of years ago, I knew God had intended them for me that day. I rejoiced and sent out a mass text to all my family: Find a bible ASAP, read James 5:15, God has spoken!

The next morning on the way to the hospital I prayed, asking for wisdom to determine if this was the right time to talk to Blu about the Lord. When I got to the room, my brother Jon was there and I knew the time wasn't right. We did talk and laugh together but when Jon left, Blu looked at me and said, "Terry, I am in the worst pain of my life."

"Can I pray for you Blu, for anything specific?"

"No."

"Do you want me to pray for your body and soul?"

"Yes," he said, and then took my wrist. "Thank you Terry, thank you so much."

I stayed all day Saturday, but went home that night for my son's twelfth birthday the next day. I woke to my sister calling to tell me they couldn't wake Blu.

I rushed to the hospital, begging God to give me a sign Blu would go to heaven. When I got to his room, he was not there, but in ICU. I ran to the nurse's desk and pleaded with them to let me see him before he slipped into a coma. Mom, Jon, and my sister Jen were there as I walked into Blu's room and found him conscious. I cradled his hand in mine and told him how much the Lord loved him. He couldn't talk but nodded his head as I prayed in his ear. By the time I said, "Amen," I knew my brother was going to heaven. God was faithful to my prayer. Within thirty minutes, Blu lost consciousness and was put on life support.

Over the next couple of days I watched my family go through so much pain. However, God continued to give me peace. At one point Blu opened his eyes and looked into mine with such intensity. I knew without either of us saying a word, that he felt the grace and love of God. At that moment the sight of him in ICU with all the tubes and lines, was no longer a picture of hurt and brokenness, but a portrait of grace, of how much God will do to save one lost sheep.

On December 23, Mom, Dad and his siblings surrounded Blu's bed, each taking turns telling him goodbye. I felt the presence of God so strongly I could hardly stand. A peace that passes all understanding consumed me; I couldn't even cry. Then a nurse, who would later tell us that God gave her an urge she couldn't ignore, walked into Blu's room and began to sing, "I feel Jesus in this place." When she sang the final chorus and turned to leave, my brother left this world... to Jesus.

Some people may question God, saying He didn't heal my brother, but I disagree. God was faithful to Blu and to me. He was willing to do anything to save my brother's soul, no matter what it took.

~Terry Sheri Kirkendoll-Esquinance

Unexpected Answers

Prayer is the mortar that holds our house together.
~Mother Teresa

Leathery wrinkled skin outlined the bones of my father's face. He sat slumped in the chair in my living room and stared out the window. I feared this man. He could make me cower with one stabbing angry glare.

As I stood in the shadows, a part of me wanted to walk away, give up, resign. Another part of me wanted to try one more time. I prayed, "God, I want a better relationship with my father and time is running out. It would be a miracle if he changed." Something deep inside opened up and I added, "God, if it be Your will, use me as an instrument to bring my dad back to You."

Quietly I walked over and sat down in the chair across from my father. He seemed unaware of my presence. I swallowed hard and reached across to rest my hand on his lizard-like one. He jumped, turned to me with a blank gaze, withdrew his hand and looked away.

I sat back in my chair and breathed deeply. My nursing skills were something he seemed to appreciate, so I started by saying, "Chronic obstructive pulmonary disease is a tough one. Most patients fight their own fear. When they feel the slightest constriction in their lungs, they panic and the panic throws them into a severe asthma attack."

He mumbled an incoherent curse word to the window.

I studied his gaunt face and rallied my courage. "Are you afraid?" I asked.

He snorted a scoff and the window kept his attention.

He was impossible. Nothing could melt that steely exterior. There was nothing to lose, so I went on: "Maybe I can help."

He looked at me critically out of the corner of his eye. "How can you help?"

"I have used a technique on myself and it works."

"You think you're some kind a miracle worker?" he spat.

His words hurt. He leaned slightly forward in the chair and there was a hint of a spark in his eyes. He wanted to hear more.

I cleared my throat. "You can turn your fear over to God through prayer."

The spark vanished and his head spun back to face the window.

My mouth felt like it was full of cotton balls as I continued. "When I needed help with fear, I invited God to sit down beside me and I told Him about my fears. Then I held out my hands and released my fear into God's hands. I asked Him to do for me what I could not do for myself, and He did. He took those fears away from me."

Dad shifted in his seat and folded his arms.

"A few weeks later when a similar situation occurred, the fear didn't come back. I put God to the test and tried my hardest to make the fear reappear. But I couldn't make it come back. It was gone."

He didn't move a muscle, except for his heaving chest.

"Dad, God can do the same for you."

My father grabbed the arms of the chair, sat straight up and stared into my eyes. His cheek twitched—and there was the expression that stabbed me! I cringed, cowardly, against his anger.

As an adult, every time I'd tried to talk to my father about God he'd always walked out on me. Would he walk out again? My own fear was mounting and I too wanted to run away. Instead, I applied my own technique of opening my hands and dropping my fear into God's hands. Regaining strength, I continued. "I know this works, but you have to do it for yourself. I can't do it for you."

"Well, it won't work for me! God doesn't answer my prayers!"

I spoke softly, "What do you mean by 'God doesn't answer my prayers'?"

"When we lived on the farm, we'd lost years of our crops to drought, insects an' weather. We were dirt poor. In '54, the crop was the best I'd seen. I was plowin' when dark clouds built in the west an' moved our way. I prayed we wouldn't get hail." He paused, as if he were reliving the event. "Me an' Willy were the only ones that got hailed out." His voice caught on the last words and he turned to the window again.

I waited.

"See," he shouted at the window. "God doesn't answer my prayers. God's against me."

My father had been living without God in his life since I was nine years old. It hit me that at the same time my father had given up on God, I'd found God and began my spiritual journey. My heart ached for my dad. I wanted to take him in my arms and hold him. I wanted to be that window that captured his attention.

"Dad," I continued, "I don't remember ever being hungry or without clothes. I don't remember being in need of anything. So, it seems to me, God took care of us."

He shrugged his shoulders.

I continued, "What do you think would have happened if God had answered your prayers as you had asked?"

"Huh," he huffed to the window. "We could have gotten out of debt."

"And then what?"

He shot me a quick glance, the one that said "You're stupid."

I shrugged it off. "What would have happened if you had stayed on that farm?"

"More years of drought and hail, I guess." His voice dropped to a whisper. "Then eventually back to being poor."

"See. I think God did answer your prayers, but He answered them in a way that you did not expect. He sent you in a new direction where you have prospered. You're not just a good cattleman, you're the best."

Dad's brow wrinkled and he scowled as he shoved back in his chair and resumed staring out the window.

After minutes of silence it was evident our conversation was over. I slid forward in my chair.

Dad grabbed my arm. "Pray with me," he said as he slid his hand down into mine.

~Betty Scheetz

Imperfection

For He spoke, and it was done; He commanded, and it stood fast.
~Psalm 33:9

I was the runt of the litter, the last of four children. At birth, my left ear was deformed. It had no shape or opening, just a thick mass.

As a small child I had several operations, but the only thing they could do was give that blob a bit of shape to resemble an ear. It would be impossible to hear from that side, even with medical science.

Growing up was a challenge. When you have a deformity, you instinctively hide things you feel ashamed of. I hid my ear. Fortunately, I was a girl and my hair covered it.

I had no thoughts about it as a young child, but as I matured, life dished out the old-school need for acceptance, love and approval. When you are flawed—and according to my definition, I was—those traits become high priority.

I sincerely believed I was supposed to erect change in myself, for God. Then I'd receive revelations of my deep inner struggles of the soul. But as those revelations came, they only created deeper disgust. I was powerless in my own efforts to really change. So the question came: Why should God love me? I was disgusting.

So I decided to go to a professional hairdresser and have a haircut and a perm. Through referrals, I finally picked the male stylist to perform this deed. He obviously saw my special need and I explained how I needed my hair to be cut.

"Oh, please be careful not to cut it too short, since the perm will make it shorter," I stressed.

He cut my hair and after the perm it went up like a venetian blind! I ran out of the salon in complete desperation.

Sobbing, I walked to my apartment. Thoughts swirled in my head that my life was over; I was going to hibernate for six months until my hair grew. I wished I had never been born.

In front of the mirror, struggling to stretch my hair down to cover my ears, with intense frustration, I threw the brush and yelled into the mirror, "You are so ugly. I hate you! I hate you, Sue!"

I put my head on the vanity and wept bitterly.

And then, I heard someone whisper my name. "Sue."

I recognized His voice.

"Sue, look in the mirror. Look in the mirror and say, 'I love you, Sue.'" This was scary to me. I heard this directive, yet was a smidge uncertain it was God speaking. I was afraid not to obey though, just in case it really was Him.

Reluctantly, I brought my head up and looked in the mirror, sheepishly saying, "I love you, Sue. I love you, Sue."

With all honesty, I sensed all of heaven joining the chorus of those words.

I found myself weeping again, not in desperation, but in discovering a glimpse of God's deep intimate love. He spoke His words to my heart, and filled them with power!

God had another lesson of His incredible intimate love for me. Years later, He answered my prayers and sent Gary into my life. During our courtship, I shared my life and its struggles with him, including my birth defect. It was one thing, however, for me to share openly with others, but another to truly let them see or touch the very root of my emotional pain.

As our love grew, we talked of marriage. God impressed upon my heart to show Gary my ear. After all, shouldn't he know what he was getting before he committed?

We went to church one Sunday morning and afterward had lunch together at my home. But the time did not seem right. Or perhaps I was too fearful. Nonetheless, that evening we planned to meet back at his house, before going to the evening service.

We sat on his sofa and began sharing again. I knew it was time for me to show Gary my ear. I simply asked him if I could close my eyes, then he could push back my hair to see my deformity.

I was nervous. In a moment I would either be received or rejected — true love would be made known.

I felt my hair gently pushed back, then I felt his lips kiss my ear with loving tenderness.

When I opened my eyes, Gary was on his knees. Little did I know he had been planning a marriage proposal for days. With tears in his eyes and an emotional voice, he extended me the most beautiful invitation to be his wife.

Then Gary gave me a lovely pair of ivory-carved earrings he'd bought years before in China when he asked God then to show him what to buy for his future mate.

I finally learned that God had always wanted me to push back my hair to reveal my imperfections, flaws and weaknesses. He only wanted to kiss them.

~Sue Stover Gaither

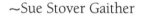

A New Heart for Pop

And He said, "I tell you the truth, unless you change and become like little children, you will never enter the kingdom of heaven."
~Matthew 18:3

Just before my daughter Brittany was born, my daddy suffered a devastating heart attack. Three years later, his health had declined to the point where he was put on the heart transplant list.

Our precocious daughter Brittany heard our many prayers and conversations about finding a "new heart" for her Pop. She knew that if they did not find one soon, it might be too late.

As Daddy grew weaker his health deteriorated. We became increasingly discouraged about his eligibility as a transplant candidate. Our fervent prayers increased.

One day, I heard Brittany's excited little voice calling as she ran up the stairs from our basement. "Mommy, Mommy! Guess what?"

"What is it Brittany?"

"You don't have to worry about Pop anymore!" she declared as she handed me a three-inch clear plastic heart-shaped box she'd discovered. "I found a new heart for Pop! Let's call and tell him."

Brittany's childlike faith bolstered the spirit of our entire family. We gave Pop his new plastic heart.

Within days another family, in the midst of their grief, gifted Pop with another "new heart."

With grateful hearts, our family sent the donor's family a framed, quilted patchwork heart, with a verse we wrote for them:

Our loved one treasures each new dawn
Because your loved one's heart beats on.

God's answers to prayers are always "right on time."

~Jamie White Wyatt

The Promise

"Before I formed you in the womb I knew you;
Before you were born I sanctified you."
~Jeremiah 1:5

When I was three years old my mother died of a heart attack giving birth to my sister, leaving my father to raise eight children. Relatives tried to help by taking some of us to live with them, but my father only relinquished the baby to my aunt Dorothy.

Life seemed pretty good growing up until things started to weigh on my father financially. At the age of five I was sent to stay with relatives I barely knew. My daddy promised it would only be for a year. It turned out to be much longer—in a house where I was sexually abused. My abuser didn't allow me to attend school for days. I was locked in closets and often sent to bed without food. My predator threatened that if I told anyone he would hurt me. I believed him. I promised not to tell.

A few years later, when I returned home, a bit of me was lost forever. My father remarried and for a brief time I thought I would finally be loved like a mother is supposed to love her child. But I was not her child. I did not feel loved. I thank God she took me to church. It was there I learned about Jesus and how much He loved me. I learned to pray and trust God. I felt His presence in my soul and, for the first time in my life, I felt true love.

At age twelve, another relative began sexually abusing me regularly and warned me not to tell. Again I promised.

In the fifth grade I saw some of my friends smoking pot behind a bush. They laughed and looked happy, something I hadn't felt in a long time. So I took a joint.

By the time I was fifteen I was smoking pot, chugging alcohol, and popping pills so I wouldn't have to feel.

One night, after a party, someone I knew asked me for a ride home. He raped me in the front seat of my car, grinning as he smashed my face into the dashboard. He was married. I knew his wife. He threatened that if I told I'd regret it. I promised not to tell.

I manage to graduate from high school and at eighteen I worked at a fancy nightclub. Wealthy men passed trays of cocaine. I snorted and felt like I was on top of the world. I needed to escape reality, to forget all the horrible things that had happened to me.

Finally I had enough. I asked a best friend who lived in California if I could stay with her and her husband to get myself straight. I prayed for a new beginning, a new start.

My girlfriend's husband worked as a security guard. Every day he came home, covered the windows with dark plastic trash bags, and smoked something in a glass pipe. I asked for one hit. "Please just one hit. I promise."

I was immediately hooked. I smoked crack cocaine for weeks. Finally I asked my father to send for me to go back home. But by then, crack cocaine had hit the streets of my hometown, Wichita, like a storm. I was sucked back in, a full-blown addict.

Over the next ten years, I had two sons. Their father, also an addict, left us with no money. To feed my kids and my raging addiction, I started dealing drugs out of my house.

One night, in a bar, I saw a guy I'd had a crush on in high school. David and I started dating and I found out he was an addict too, so he moved in and we sold cocaine as a team.

When we had a daughter together we promised each other we would quit, but we didn't.

Then one autumn day, I heard a furious banging at my front door. A SWAT team wearing masks and brandishing guns trampled the door and stormed my house. Our baby girl screamed in her highchair. My heart pounded as I lay in the entryway, handcuffed. In the police car the officer said, "You know you're looking at a lot of time." I had accepted $6,000 worth of cocaine from an undercover officer.

My whole life flashed before me. Scared and crying, I was booked and sent to jail. My life was over. I would never see my children again. I wanted to die. My court-appointed attorney said he would try to get me only ten years. The prosecutor was going for fifteen.

In my jail cell the call came for me to go down for breakfast. I pressed the intercom and said, "I'm not coming." Again for lunch and then for dinner, I declined.

In my cell I started to pray, finally able to reflect on my life. There were times I should have been dead, and here I was alive. I started to thank God for His grace and mercy.

I got off my bunk and sprawled on the cold concrete floor.

"Forgive me for my sins, God. And give me a forgiving heart so I can forgive all the people who hurt me." I lay there praying for hours. I prayed for my desire for drugs to leave me. I prayed for my children.

Then I prayed, "Lord if You allow me to get out of this situation, I promise I will change my life. I promise, if I'm released I'll dedicate my life to helping young girls not end up like me."

I had no idea that in another cell, David was praying a similar prayer.

Eight months later, dressed in fluorescent orange and hand-cuffed to a murderer, I was taken to court. At my sentencing, I didn't understand most of the legal language. The judge asked me for a statement before sentencing. I said, "If you give me another chance, I'll try my best to change."

He sentenced me to eighteen months' probation. "One condition is that you cannot have contact with David Gilkey."

"But I truly love him! We plan to get married."

The judge was shocked. "Two addicts cannot stay sober."

Then he added. "Okay, I'll remove the no contact order. However,

David was sentenced to three years' probation. If either of you breaks probation, you will have to each serve the other's sentence."

I left the courthouse homeless. I picked up my three kids who had been staying with a family member, and we moved into a family shelter. I started attending a Cocaine Anonymous 12-step program and went to meetings every day, sometimes twice a day. David went to treatment too. Together, we began attending church.

One day at the shelter I saw a flier for Dress for Success, an international non-profit that helps disadvantaged women find work. I felt like they were talking to me. At the meetings I met other women who had been in abusive relationships, addicted to drugs, or just lost their jobs. Dress for Success taught me about managing finances, getting a job, and even provided clothes for me to wear to interviews. They saw something in me I could not see in myself. The director encouraged me to apply to attend an international leadership summit in Washington, DC. There I met single moms who had become CEOs.

Inspired, I returned home. Keeping the promise I made in my jail cell prayer, and with David's urging, I created CLASS, Caring Ladies Assisting Students to Succeed. This weekly mentoring program has educated, motivated and encouraged hundreds of teen girls to graduate high school and choose healthy lifestyle behaviors.

Dress for Success asked me to share my story at their annual event. I was scared to share my past. I went to the restroom and sat in the stall and prayed. "Lord I can't do this, but I know through You I can do all things."

The next thing I knew I was on stage talking as if I were an evangelist. I spoke with confidence and without fear; I knew that God was speaking through me. The crowd gave me a standing ovation. A female attorney approached me after my speech and said she would be honored to expunge my felony.

With God's help, Dress for Success, my family and Tabernacle Bible Church, I changed my life.

I kept my promise and have been clean and sober for eleven years.

And I have come to realize that God will always love me and never leave me. That's the true promise.

~Lynn Gilkey

A Picture in a Prayer

God looks not at the oratory of your prayers, how elegant they may be; nor at the geometry of your prayers, how long they may be; nor at the arithmetic of your prayers, how many they may be; not at the logic of your prayers, how methodical they may be; but at the sincerity of them He looks at.
~Thomas Brooks

When our daughter announced her wedding would be in Hawaii where she lived, my husband and I started planning. Since we lived in California, it would be challenging to throw parties for the two weeks we'd be in Honolulu. We decided to lease a two-bedroom condo large enough for others to stay with us—the bridesmaids could dress there the day of the wedding, and we could host family dinners and a surprise shower for Kim.

During the months leading up to the wedding, I prayed over all the details. Every mother of the bride wants her daughter's special day to be beautiful and memorable. As I prayed, I visualized an open, airy condominium overlooking the ocean with a beautiful view of Waikiki beach and the famous Diamond Head crater. Whenever I prayed about it, the exact same picture popped up. I believed God was showing me the place He had for us.

As my husband and I made calls to locate a condo, we ran into a major roadblock. The week we requested fell over President's Day weekend. Everything in Honolulu seemed to be booked.

Meanwhile, I kept busy, shopping for my dress and designing and making invitations for a surprise shower with "location to be announced." Time was quickly running out. A week before the wedding, we still didn't have a condo lined up.

Two nights before I flew out to help with pre-wedding preparations, my husband got a call. A two-bedroom condo had opened up two blocks from Waikiki beach. Did we want it? We'd never rented something sight unseen, but this time there was no hesitation.

"Yes, yes!" Fred said.

He hung up the phone and I hugged him, relieved that our prayers had been answered. Joyfully, I anticipated a beautiful place for the festivities—the place I saw every time I prayed.

Soon I flew to Hawaii to help my daughter. I stayed with her until Fred arrived and we checked into our condo.

When we arrived at the high-rise, we were given the keys to our unit on the sixth floor. Fred opened the door and wheeled our luggage into the living room. I followed, my heart sinking lower and lower with each step. There was barely room to navigate around our luggage in the tiny room. This wasn't what I had pictured at all!

How could we have a party with twenty people in this cramped space?

The two bedrooms were hardly bigger than walk-in closets. No way would the bridesmaids be able to dress there; they'd trip all over each other. The small grubby bathroom had black mold in the corners. The view out the dark little living room window overlooked the roofs of neighboring buildings. No ocean. No Diamond Head. No Waikiki beach. Was this some kind of dirty trick?

I threw myself into a chair, held my head in my hands and started to sob. Fred tried to comfort me by saying something like, "We'll just make lemonade, dear."

"But this isn't the picture God gave me," I said between tears. I waved my arms around the tiny living space. "This isn't big enough for a shower, or even a family dinner. There's not even a table to sit at!"

Fred looked around and his silence told me he agreed. "Let's see if we can do something else," he said, picking up the phone.

I didn't hold out much hope. After all, everything was booked.

Why had God given me that grandiose picture if this was all we would end up with?

"Yes, yes, we'd like to take a look," I heard Fred say. He hung up and headed for the door. "Come on. They have a penthouse that's not rented because it's ready to undergo renovation."

"Oh, great. Another dump," I mumbled under my breath.

We got to the top floor and the clerk met us in the hall, explaining that all the other penthouses had been remodeled and were renting for exorbitant prices. This particular unit was the last to be worked on. Demolition would start next week. If we wanted it, he would let us have it for an additional, but nominal fee. He swung open the door and we stepped inside.

Huge glass windows showcased a 180 degree view of Waikiki, Diamond Head and miles of ocean. Sunshine poured through large windows in every room. Two large bedrooms bordered the living space, with two bathrooms complete with washer and dryer. The lovely living room had a wide screen TV and complete stereo system. A full kitchen had everything we needed. This spacious, light, cheery condo was exactly what I had visualized, but even bigger and better than I had prayed for.

Seeing images is another way God speaks to us, another form of listening to Him. When I flip through our daughter's wedding album and see the beautiful views from that penthouse, I am reminded of how God gives us more than we expect, through pictures in a prayer.

~Martha Pope Gorris

Evergreen Faith

Now my eyes will be open and my ears attentive
to prayer offered in this place.
~2 Chronicles 7:15

As I stood at the kitchen sink washing dishes that late October evening, I couldn't stop staring out the window. Thousands of sweet-smelling evergreen trees of various types and sizes dotted the country property we'd recently purchased. They looked beautiful to me, but because they hadn't been trimmed and shaped for years, the previous owner told us they were unmarketable. We'd hoped to sell the trees to offset the costs of repairs to our 150-year-old farmhouse.

"They ain't worth nuttin'," he had said. "They're too spindly on top."

Even my husband Chuck reluctantly suggested, "Maybe we should bulldoze them and start over."

I didn't believe they were worthless, and I especially didn't think so that night. With the soft light of dusk shadowing their majestic frames, the trees glowed.

I piled the dishes into the sink, unable to get my mind off the trees. As I kept glancing out the window, the view became more compelling, drawing me outside among the trees.

I thought I was being silly. Why would I take a walk while it was getting dark? Soon the skunks and bats would be out.

Then, out of nowhere, a voice inside me said, "Walk among those trees and pray over them."

The last golden rays of the setting sun were rapidly fading. It didn't make sense to go outside, so I decided to just pray from the kitchen.

But once again, more firmly, I heard in my mind, "Walk among the trees."

This time I obediently peeled off the yellow dishwashing gloves, tossed them on the counter, and without a word to anyone, slipped quietly out the front door.

The cool crisp air smelled of rich earth as I began my journey. A lone owl hooted in the distance. Dew was already forming on the ground as I climbed the steep hill that was home to several hundred Norway Spruces and White Pines. The closer I got to the grove, the headier the scent of pine. How I loved that smell. Happy, carefree childhood memories of Christmas enveloped me whenever I inhaled that wonderful, pungent aroma. Evergreens invite a sense of permanence and stability. Unlike other trees their needles don't completely shed, and they're hearty enough to withstand extreme weather conditions.

As I walked in and out of row upon row, an uncanny sense of oneness with the trees filled me. They were part of God's creation, alive and vibrant. Like me, they had worth and merit. And, like me, they weren't perfect, but still had a reason for being.

I stooped, noticing patches of tall grasses softly matted down where deer had nestled for the night. God used these pine trees to bring protection and pleasure to His creation. Birds softly chirped and their light feathers rustled as they settled in for the night in the thick pine boughs. I began softly singing, in awe of our Creator.

I continued walking, reflecting on how a few weeks earlier I had contacted several local tree nurseries in search of a buyer. Just a few were interested, but none had made us an offer. Having always lived in the suburbs I had no idea how expensive it would be living in the country. It seemed we were always putting money into something: tractor repairs or new attachments, gravel for our long lane, auto repairs for all the extra driving on rough country roads, pond upkeep, garden equipment, and of course the ongoing expenses of our old farmhouse.

As I turned and started toward home, I prayed, "Please God, help us partner with someone who wants and needs these trees."

The outside lights glowed when I finally reached the bottom of the hill.

"There you are," Chuck said, sounding relieved. "What are you doing out here? It's getting dark."

"Thinking... and praying over the pine trees," I said. "I know they are worth something and I think we should contact more nurseries to see if anyone is interested."

"Sure, honey. If it makes you feel better, I'll give Bill another call tomorrow," Chuck said, a slight teasing tone in his voice.

Our friend Bill owned a nursery and was very knowledgeable about pine trees, but when he'd come to look at them, he hadn't seemed interested.

At that moment, as we stood outside the front door, the phone rang. I dashed inside to answer it, almost with a sense of anticipation.

"Hello?"

"Hello, Connie? This is Bill. Is Chuck there?"

I ran out the front door and told my husband who it was.

"Yeah, right," he said, reaching for the phone in my outstretched hand. "You're kidding, aren't you?"

"No, honey... here!"

I walked back inside and refilled the sink with fresh hot water, barely resisting the temptation to stay outside and eavesdrop.

When Chuck finally came in, he slowly hung up the phone, shaking his head in disbelief.

"What did Bill want, honey?" I asked, although deep down I already knew.

"He wanted to know if we still had some trees for sale." Chuck paused and swallowed hard.

"He has an interested buyer."

~Connie Sturm Cameron

God Is Still Here

Pray to God at the beginning of your works,
that so thou mayest bring them to a good ending.
~Xenophon

The old church listed badly to the left, like an arthritic senior citizen leaning on a cane. The tornado that skipped across the Texas prairie had shattered the glass and forced the wide oak floorboards upwards off the foundation that had supported them for well over a century. Until the storm struck, the Eagle Springs Baptist Church had stood as tall and straight as the men and women who built it. The tornado lifted it off its stacked rock foundation, moved it over several feet, and set it down again, gently, as though Mother Nature realized she was making a mistake. Still, serious damage was done, and many members of the congregation, already holding services in their recently completed new church, didn't think the old building could be saved. Reluctantly, they scheduled it for demolition.

The church stood beside an old cemetery just across the back fence from our farm. A wave of sadness swept over me as I surveyed the damage. This church was the last remaining structure in the vanished town of Eagle Springs, a once flourishing pioneer village. The dusty streets had been lined with stores, doctors' offices, a cotton gin, a blacksmith shop, and a one-room schoolhouse. Like many other small towns, its fate was sealed by the path of the railroad. When the tracks were routed through other towns, Eagle Springs declined.

Recently retired after three decades of teaching history to middle

God Is Still Here : God Will Provide   77

school students, I discovered a small knot of rebellion forming in my chest at the thought of losing this link to our ancestors. In earlier times, my children and I had crawled under the fence to sit in the shade of the live oak trees and explore the remains of the ghost town and its primitive church. I remembered how astonished they were at the church's spartan furnishings and the uncomfortable wooden pews made by a pioneer parishioner.

They were amused to learn the church had two front doors. Women and children entered through the left door and sat on the left side of the church; men entered on the right. Legend has it that some of the men attended church with rifles balanced across their knees, in case services were interrupted by an enemy attack.

Older now and leaning a little myself, I wanted my grandchildren to see what churches were like before air conditioning and sound systems. I knew that no photograph could substitute for touching the ancient cypress boards, weathered to a soft silver, or inhaling the scent of dusty hymnbooks and frontier faith.

Before long I discovered I was not alone in my rebellion. My husband David, who grew up in the church, wanted to try to save it. Louise, my octogenarian neighbor, wiped away tears as she stood on the limestone steps where she and her husband had carved their initials as children. She looked into the battered interior. "God is still here," she said.

David and I agreed.

I wondered idly if there were others like Louise, David and me who weren't ready to give up on the old building yet. There was one way to find out. I sent an article about the history of the church to local newspapers. They printed it. Television crews came to shoot footage of the sagging relic. The public reaction took us by surprise. Although a few folks proclaimed that restoring the church would consume the fortune of a Texas oilman, many more joined with us, cheered us on, and prayed with us to save the church. Lots of small donations were made to assist with the project.

The congregation agreed to give us the old church on the condition that it was moved off their property. They were worried about liability. I thought this demand would be impossible to meet, until a landowner next to the cemetery volunteered to donate land for the relocated church.

A few people shook their heads at the damage and told us that the church would not survive the move. We called Mr. Booker, a contractor who moved buildings, and we met him at the church to hear the verdict. His weathered brown face and grizzled gray hair gave us courage—this man knew how to cope with aging. The truck he was driving seemed almost as old as the church. Mr. Booker walked thoughtfully around the building, peering through the windows and running his hands lovingly over the weathered cypress siding. Stooping, he picked up a few square nails. "This old church was built strong," he told us. "I can move it."

That was the beginning of the series of answered prayers that surrounded the moving and restoration of an old building too historically valuable to lose. Mr. Booker and his grandson pulled the slightly splayed walls back together and reattached the floor. A crowd gathered to watch as they jacked up the church and loaded it onto his ancient truck. Newspaper reporters and television crews stood among local supporters. When the truck's engine roared to life and the church began to move, you could almost see our prayers supporting its sagging walls. The antique timbers creaked and popped like old bones, but the repairs held. A cheer broke out as the truck repositioned the church in its new home in a grove of trees on the opposite side of the cemetery.

After this initial victory, the flow of answered prayers accelerated. A roofing company volunteered to fix the roof. An exterminator treated it for termites. Someone donated a piano, another an antique pump organ. Volunteers helped clear brush from around the church. More donations appeared in the church's new bank account.

Two years later, the Historic Eagle Springs Baptist Church reopened to celebrate the 150th anniversary of its founding. People came from as far away as Ohio, Alabama, and New Mexico to occupy their old pews again. The strains of hymns floated through the new windows and doors, filling the little grove with the sound of rejoicing. My grandchildren climbed under the fence and served cookies and punch. We all congratulated each other for our hard work, but we all knew who was behind this miracle. God was still here.

~Martha Deeringer

Answered Prayers

Miracles

*Remember the wonders he has done, his miracles,
and the judgments he pronounced…*

~*1 Chronicles 16:12*

Come Hell or High Water

Let my prayer come before You; Incline Your ear to my cry.
~Psalm 88:2

When I was growing up in South Louisiana in the 1970s, a hurricane brewing in the Gulf meant nothing more to my eleven brothers and sisters and me than the potential of days off school, a visit from our Gulf Coast cousins, sleeping bags on the floor, no baths or bedtimes, ice cream for breakfast ("Quick! Before it melts!") and hours spent by candlelight listening to the grown-ups reminisce.

We loved hurricanes the way northern kids love snow days, never understanding the very real danger because we were surrounded by grown-ups who were good at hiding whatever fear they may have felt. It never dawned on us that anything could actually harm us, not even a hurricane. Our parents wouldn't allow it.

All our lives we'd heard about "The Big One" possibly hitting New Orleans some day, but it never seemed like a reality. It was a ghost story the big people told us just as their parents had told them, right up there with California falling into the ocean. In our minds hurricanes destroyed coastal areas, and we were sitting an hour inland whispering in the dark as the winds whipped and our parents scurried about lighting candles and gathering water.

Now, thirty years later, it was my husband David and me protecting our four kids from the anxiety of South Louisiana hurricane season. On August 28, 2005, as we prepared for a visit from Hurricane

Katrina, I easily slipped into the mold my parents, aunts and uncles left me, going about storm preparations with an air of everyday calm. If I were scared, my kids wouldn't know it.

Katrina developed so fast that Friday seemed like any other day. By Sunday though, the weather reports looked ominous. I thought about the last two times we'd evacuated, only to have the storm change course and pass by. Evacuating four kids, two adults and three dogs from your country home was no small feat. Plus with everyone else evacuating, where would we go? I prayed and asked God to let me know if we needed to leave, but felt calm about staying.

I called our family on the Mississippi Gulf Coast and invited them to ride it out with us the way our Gulf Coast cousins had so many times—all those great memories—then I started battening down the hatches.

Our kids knew the drill as well as we did at their ages. Gather candles, flashlights, and battery-operated radios at a central location. Stash bikes, barbecue grills and other loose objects in the garage. I could feel that old excitement building. Call the neighbors to see who's leaving and who'll be riding it out with us. Buy plenty of ice. Just before the storm, fill all the bathtubs with water for potty flushings.

Twice my thirteen-year-old daughter Molly asked if maybe we should evacuate, but by then her own Gulf Coast cousins had arrived and the hurricane party was in full swing. To three-year-old Jonah it was one big slumber party. Nine-year-old Hewson showed definite signs of being a hurricane groupie like his mama. And fifteen-year-old Haley's only regret was loss of privacy since we'd declared her attic-turned-bedroom off-limits during the storm.

When it was announced that schools were closing, I felt like a third grader again, excited to know we'd be having ice cream for breakfast and brewing coffee on the barbecue. I remembered gathering downed limbs from the yard with my cousins as my dad and uncles cooked breakfast over the backyard grill in the 1970s, laughing and one-upping each other with stories. I was eight years old again and ready for the next hurricane party.

Katrina arrived at our house early Monday morning and lasted for nine terrifying hours. Through ceiling-to-floor windows we watched mammoth oak trees get sucked out of the ground like saplings.

"Please God," I prayed, "let me be as strong as I thought my parents were then."

The tin roof above our heads rippled and flapped. David's truck, tractor, our old pump house and the barn disappeared under mounds of trees. Our garage was flattened, our back deck smashed. A window exploded, sending missiles of broken glass flying two rooms away. The plate glass that covered two walls in our living room heaved in and out as if the whole room were breathing. "If it goes," I thought, "there's no place to hide from the exploding glass."

We'd bought this house because we loved the windows and trees. Now it seemed that the combination would be the death of us. Miraculously, all but one window stayed intact.

We watched hundreds of trees fall like a giant game of Pick Up Sticks. Eighty percent of the pine forest around our house disappeared, yet it was as if God had drawn a line around the home where we huddled and prayed, without a single tree allowed to hit us.

More than once during the storm, I noticed the kids searching my face to ascertain if they should be scared, yet I felt unexplainably calm. We hunkered in the hall, sang songs, told stories... and prayed some more.

When the wind finally stopped at dusk, we ventured outside. Our eight acres looked like a bomb had gone off. The devastation stretched for miles. "The Big One" had finally come. Lucky for us, we were on its weaker side.

Throughout the nine hours of the storm, two days trying to hack our way through the trees to civilization, days searching for family and friends, the good news, the bad news, the uncertainty of David's job, the loss of mine, and the month-long exile before we could return home, I came to a realization. As much as I was there to calm my kids' fears, in truth it worked the other way around. They were the ones who kept me grounded. When I told them things like, "All of this is just stuff. None of it matters. If we lose this house, we'll build another one," I was talking to myself. When I assured them the storm couldn't last much longer, that we'd be able to return home soon, that the important thing was knowing all our loved ones were alive, I mostly reassured myself.

This is one family that won't be riding out another hurricane. When we hear about a sizable storm heading our way, we're moving further inland. Still, this experience has become part of us, part of who we are. It's shown us what really matters in life. We've discovered things about ourselves and the people who love us we might never have known.

And through it all I've uncovered a secret about those big people who built a loving fortress around us for so many years. During the turbulent times in life, it's kids... by the grace of God... who keep their parents afloat—not the other way around.

~Mimi Greenwood Knight

Miracle in the Cane Field

"… I go and prepare a place for you."
~John 14:2

"Lord, we pray that you go before us as we meet with the plantation manager tomorrow morning for permission to buy the land for our new buildings," my congregation fervently prayed with me that Sunday morning.

Our church, located in the sugarcane fields on Oahu's North Shore, could not expand and build our preschool and community center without the purchase of land and approval of this powerful man. He had already privately expressed his opposition to selling any prime agricultural land such as that surrounding our church.

Bob, the son of Buddhist immigrants from Japan, was the dedicated chairman of the church building board. Bill, a stalwart church member, was the former plantation manager. Together we gathered for prayer in the church parking lot before the short ride to the sugar company offices. Cane ash from the recently burned fields blew into little piles in the parking lot. I raised my voice to be heard over the roar of bulldozers and cranes loading piles of scorched cane stalks onto huge tractor trailers next to the church.

Upon arrival, Bill led the way to the manager's office. We knocked, entered, and beheld a shocking sight. There, seated behind his massive wooden desk sat a physically robust, middle-aged man with a horribly swollen red nose. A blood-specked bandage covered his lip.

Bill and Bob pushed me toward the desk. Pretending not to notice his battered condition, I silently prayed for the right words.

I stammered, "Sir, we are here to ask your permission to buy two acres of land next to our church so we can build a community center and a preschool for the needy children in our community. We can't move forward without your blessing."

He stood, obviously in pain, and leaned with one hand on his desk.

"Gentlemen, we all know the dirty and dangerous work of harvesting cane. Accidents happen in the field and last night I nearly got killed. During the night we harvested the fields surrounding your church. One of the fires got out of hand and I was called from home to help supervise the fire control. I drove by one of the loaded cane haulers stuck in a muddy ditch. Seeing a fire jump the road, I climbed on top of the mired hauler to get a better view."

The plantation manager touched his bandaged lip as he continued. "It was windy and rainy and I slipped, fell, and smashed my face on the wheel well. I got knocked out and landed under a rear wheel."

His eyes misted as he said, "I woke up hearing the sound of the big D9 bulldozer starting to pull the hauler out of the ditch. No one saw me in the dark and smoke. I rolled out from under the wheels just as it lurched forward. One second later, I would have been crushed for sure. I figure the good Lord saved my life last night in that field. I thought, 'When that church asks for permission to buy that land, who am I to stand in the Lord's way?'"

My heart jumped and my soul rejoiced with a triumphant. "Yes!" as I comprehended his amazing story. Bob heaved a grateful sigh of relief. We thanked the manager profusely as we left his office.

Bill's eyes twinkled. "I guess we should be careful when we pray that the Lord go before us."

~David S. Milotta

Fishing for a Miracle

He said to them, "Let the little children come to me, and do not hinder them,
for the kingdom of God belongs to such as these."
~Mark 10:13-15

"Hey Mom, let's take the boat out today for a family fishing trip!" nine-year-old Steven suggested enthusiastically. It was a perfect day for fishing and before long Steven and his two teenage sisters scrambled into the boat. My husband, Jim, loaded the fishing gear and bait net while I stowed the picnic basket. Soon we were speeding across the sparkling water.

Steven, so passionate about fishing, was proud that he was learning how to throw Jim's large net.

As the boat slowed, Steven turned to his dad. "Will you let me throw the bait net today?" he asked with excitement in his eyes.

"Do you think you are ready?" Jim smiled. "You have practiced off a dock, but throwing the net from a boat will be different."

"I can do it, Dad. Trust me."

The family watched while Steven wrestled the large nylon net, bordered with weights. He took care to layer it over his arm. Then twisting his body like an Olympic shot put contender, he gave a mighty thrust and threw the net, nearly as big as he, away from the boat. It opened like a parachute, and landed in a circle on top of the water. We applauded. Steven beamed.

Suddenly, his delighted expression turned to horror as he watched the net disappear.

"Oh no!" Steven cried. "I was so excited I forgot to put the rope around my wrist! Now it's sinking to the bottom!"

We watched helplessly.

Steven interrupted our stunned silence with hope in his voice. "Wait! I can get it back! I'll just cast my fishing line out there and snag it on my hook."

Family members exchanged skeptical glances.

Jim steered the boat in wide lazy circles while we tried to remember the spot the net went down.

"It was over there," pointed Lori.

"No it wasn't, it was closer to right here," insisted Betsy.

"Look guys," Jim interrupted, "there is no way we are going to get that net back. Even if we knew the exact spot, the waves have moved the boat's position. By now the current has swept the net away or it's lying on the bottom. It's gone."

Steven's shoulders drooped. Then he turned to his dad. "Please let me cast my line and try to hook the net," he pleaded. "I know I can get it back."

"Even if you could snag it," Jim argued, "your hook would tear a hole in the weaving and ruin it. And besides, that small hook isn't big enough to snag the net and lift it into the boat."

Steven looked so dejected that Jim quickly offered a compromise. "Okay, son. You can try to snag the net, but your plan won't work. I'll give you three tries, and then we'll have to head home."

"Thanks, Dad. I know I can get the net in three tries." Steven prepared to cast his line.

He positioned his pole behind his shoulder then thrust it forward with a mighty cast. Staring into the water, he slowly reeled in his line. His hook came out of the water covered with green seaweed.

Steven's second cast caused the line to tangle in the reel and he fumbled to straighten it. Then he prepared for his third cast.

"This is your last chance," Betsy reminded from the back of the boat.

"Yeah, I know. But this time I'm going to pray." Steven bowed his head and mumbled, "Please God, let this last cast hook the net."

His trembling hand gripped his pole and he cast his fishing line several feet beyond the boat. He began to reel it in while the rest of the family prepared to get underway.

"Well, good try," Jim said as he patted Steven's shoulder. "Now it's time to pull up the anchor and head for home."

"Wait, Dad!" yelled Steven. "There's something on my hook! I can feel it!"

"It's probably a stupid catfish," Lori said.

"It's heavy!" Steven bit his lip and strained to reel in his line. Then he lifted his catch into the bow of the boat.

The rest of the family leaped to our feet and stared in disbelief.

The bait net dripped at the end of the line, the hook tightly secured around the plastic ring at the top.

"I have goose bumps," both sisters announced in unison as they rubbed their arms.

"I never thought this could happen in a million years!" Jim declared, shaking his head.

Tears filled my eyes as I witnessed my son's faith.

"You know," Steven exclaimed with a deep sigh, "the only way this hook could have snagged this ring was for God to put it there with His own hands. It's a miracle!"

~Miriam Hill

Black Flags

For your Father knows the things you have need of before you ask Him.
~Matthew 6:8

I'd spent most of my time in pools over the summer and was a fairly decent swimmer. When I was twelve years old, my mother took my two sisters, Samantha and Christine, and me on vacation to Mexico. Since my father had died a few years earlier, it was important to her that my family keep a tight bond. There was a big gap in ages between my two sisters and me, but they didn't seem to mind me tagging along as we explored the area. We did bond and we had a fabulous time together.

The irritating part of the trip was that the entire week in Mexico there were black flags in the sand telling us to swim at our own risk. My sisters, young and invincible, spent one day swimming and enjoying themselves despite the warning and were absolutely fine.

"Give it a try," Samantha encouraged me.

"Fine," I said reluctantly as I followed them into the scary water.

They were so right. The water was amazing. I easily jumped over or swam through large waves. We had a blast together.

The next day we went back to our spot. Everything looked the same. The waves were just as tall and nothing really had changed. Or so we thought.

"Mom, the water looks great. Will you join us?" I asked.

My sisters added their encouragement to win her over. Before long, all four of us headed into the water.

It didn't take long to realize just how wrong we had been about the conditions. Partway out, where the water had only been up to my neck the day before, I couldn't touch bottom! I started swimming alongside Samantha.

The waves grew six feet tall. "Dive in Angela!" Samantha yelled.

"I can't!" I screamed, afraid of the giant wave heading toward me.

"You'll be fine. You have to dive into it," she coaxed.

I jumped. I really had no choice. Under the water I felt pulled from every direction, like invisible strings held me down. I bounced off the ocean floor and looked up at a light above my head. I kicked and moved my hands as hard as I could but I didn't move. The breath in my body tightened as I started running out of air. The light was inches from my head but I couldn't reach it. I panicked. Twelve is a young age to think you're about to die.

It's weird how time slows at a time like that. I'm sure it was about a minute but it felt like so much more. I prayed, "Help me God! Save me!"

I was about done struggling and ready to give up when I felt something pull me up. I broke free of the chain that held me under.

"Are you okay?" Samantha asked as I bobbed out of the water.

"I think so," I coughed.

"We need to go!" Samantha said leading me back.

I swam for my life that day. As I neared the shore I saw my mother washed up on her side like a fish, scraped and beaten by the rocks. Christine was okay beside her.

I learned three valuable lessons in life that day. Always keep your family close because you never know when they may pull you through the storm. Avoid the Pacific Ocean when black flags are out.

And pray to God and He will save you.

~Ashley Townswick

The Miracle that Brought Miracles

This will bring health to your body and nourishment to your bones.
~Proverbs 3:8

W e were the couple living our dreams. My husband Bryan had a successful masonry contracting business and I worked with The Christian Broadcasting Network. We had a family, the home we always wanted, and life was great. We were so busy with our work that we took little time off to visit loved ones or really talk to each other like when we first married. But time has a way of eluding that thought as it races on.

But then I began to notice a dark feeling I could not shake. I'd be at my desk and suddenly a sad feeling would wash over me, as if waiting for something awful to happen that we could not stop. I mentioned it to Bryan and he simply said, "Pray about it."

And so I did. I didn't really think about it again until we sat in the doctor's office a few days later.

Bryan had been having back pain and the doctor ordered a routine MRI, predicting he'd probably need surgery. After reading the results the doctor said, "Well you won't need surgery." He paused with a grim look. "You have inoperable cancer in three places—on your sternum, backbone and pelvis."

We stood there together, hand in hand, staring at the MRI. We asked the questions one asks when given this diagnosis. The doctor shook his head. "There is nothing that can be done. It is a matter of months. I will send all the reports to your family doctor. I am so sorry."

Bryan and I walked out into the early winter's night feeling as dark and cold as the night itself. He was young. We had a child and a grandchild. We had a life. We had plans, hopes and more dreams.

The next morning when I awoke, my loving husband was sitting by our bed staring at me, tears rolling down his cheeks. "I do not want to leave you," he cried. We wept together that morning, canceling work and all appointments. We talked as we had not talked in years—not so much about the future, not about all the things we usually talked about—finances, dreams, and plans. We talked about our love, about the memories we shared, about our family.

Our family doctor called in a cancer specialist. We called all the churches we loved so dearly and put Bryan's name on prayer lists all over the country—and we prayed with a fervor we had never known.

A month passed. A myriad of tests were done and doctors seen.

One night my faith-filled daddy called. "I was praying and I sensed it was all going to be all right. And I believe it with all that I am."

Two weeks later we sat before the cancer specialist. He closed the folder on his desk and looked at us. "Well, we have run all the tests. There is good news. There is no cancer anywhere in Bryan's body."

I stammered, "What about the MRI? The other doctors?"

He smiled. "All I know is he does not have cancer. Perhaps the neurologist saw scars from an auto accident years ago. But there is no cancer. Your prognosis is—you are well."

It has been fifteen years since that day, and still whenever I look at Bryan I am reminded of how all our prayers were answered, and how our lives were changed forever. We focus more on each other and our family. We moved back home to a quiet town where neighbors know neighbors and hearts knows hearts. Our goals changed. We live one day at a time, and instead of planning so much, we simply enjoy the moments.

When I see Bryan playing with our grandchildren and great-grandchildren, I breathe a prayer of thanks that they know their Papa. Our house creaks at night and there are times when new dress desires do not match my pocketbook, but we are rich.

That one miracle birthed so many other miracles in our lives.

~Marsha Smith

My Miracle of Emmy

Is anyone among you suffering? Let him pray. Is anyone cheerful? Let him sing psalms.
~James 5:13

I was at home the night it started. After two years of trying to conceive our third child, we were finally successful. Now the sudden cramping and bleeding frightened me. I had a previously scheduled doctor's appointment the next day to confirm my pregnancy.

When I went in they drew blood to check my hormone levels. My levels were a bit low. I went back four days later for another blood draw to see if the levels were increasing, indicating a healthy pregnancy, or decreasing. I'd wait over the weekend for the results.

Prayer is something that had always come hard for me. I got distracted easily. Those next three days however, I prayed and prayed. I prayed that God would help me. I prayed that God would spare my child. I prayed that He would keep our little baby safe and not let it go. I prayed the blood levels would increase.

On Monday morning I was confronted with the news — my levels had dropped. I had lost the baby. My world turned upside down. The child we had been trying to have for two years was gone.

I'd always locked my emotions away. I didn't let people know how much I hurt, or how much they hurt me. This time was no different. I felt depressed for a week or two, and made my husband and our two kids miserable. I was hurting and didn't know how to grieve. The tears would start to form in the corners of my eyes, but I willed them back. I'd used that strategy for years.

One night my husband saw one lone tear escape and run down my cheek. "Amber, it's okay to let it out," he said tenderly. "If you need to cry, then cry."

That one tear would be the unleashing of many more to come for the next few hours. I lay on my bed, cradled in my husband's arms and began to cry. Those cries quickly became heart-wrenching sobs from the pit of my very soul. Unbearable pain pushed up into my heart. I found a small pink blanket with silk trim tucked away in my closet. I pulled it close to me; at that moment I knew the baby I had carried was another little girl growing within me. I cried my tears into that blanket until no more would fall. Later, I folded the blanket and placed it back in my closet as a reminder of the baby girl I had waiting for me in heaven.

A month later I began to feel fatigued and queasy. I took a home pregnancy test and was pleased to find it positive. I quickly called for a doctor's appointment, but they couldn't see me for a few weeks.

On the day of my appointment, the doctor reviewed the date of my miscarriage and determined I would be eight or ten weeks pregnant. He performed an ultrasound to confirm things, and surprisingly saw all the baby's parts. He did measurements and exclaimed, "This says you are fifteen weeks pregnant! That's not possible since your miscarriage."

He sent me straight down to see his ultrasound specialist. Her results were the same. I was carrying a fifteen-week-old baby inside me.

And she added, "It's a girl."

When I went back up to see my doctor, he shook his head. "We will never know how this happened."

But I know. Prayer changes things. My body may have gone through the miscarriage process but God heard the prayers of a desperate mother and granted her petition. He held my baby tight and protected her in my womb. He allowed me to have my miracle known as Emmy.

~Amber Paul Keeton

The Miracle
of My Father's Words

*Prayer has the power to generate insight; it often endows us with an
understanding not attainable by speculation. Some of our deepest insights,
decisions and attitudes are born in moments of prayer.*
~Abraham Joshua Heschel

Before my father's funeral service began, I stood in front of
the rabbi. He pinned a small piece of black cloth to the left
side of my blouse near my heart. While reciting a Hebrew
blessing, he made a tear in the cloth. This symbolized that my life
was torn by the loss of my dad.

It is now eighteen years since his death. I keep that very same
torn cloth in my father's shiny brass humidor. One recent morning,
while holding the cloth near my heart, a miracle happened.

Days prior to my father's service, the rabbi called. "I'd like to
know more about your father's life for my sermon." I told him a lot.
Yet the words that he ultimately spoke didn't describe my dad's life
even remotely. He said, "Samuel was a happy, fulfilled man who was
blessed with a loving marriage and a rewarding life."

He could have told the truth, though it wouldn't have been
appropriate to be candid about my father's quiet despair. But he could
have said, "With unwavering faith, Samuel followed the command-
ments of Orthodox Judaism. He honored his father and his mother.

He courageously sacrificed for his wife and his children." The rabbi could have gone on a lot about this. But he didn't.

Dad always did what he believed was right. The right thing, though, was for others' sakes. His parents sent him to the University of Maryland so he'd live with them in Baltimore. He wanted to be a lawyer. He graduated from law school and passed the bar. But his diploma was never displayed.

Instead of my father practicing law, his father decided he should take over the family's wholesale shoe business. Dad obeyed. He ran the company until he retired. And he hated every day of it.

His marriage was loveless. He had no hobbies or interests. He didn't even read the newspaper. He was a withdrawn, unhappy man around everyone except me.

If a heart could be metaphorically measured by its contents, 100 percent of my father's heart would have been filled with his love for me. I was his great joy. He adored me and I adored him.

When I was ecstatic about going to college, though it was very far from home, he was overjoyed for me. He never pointed out nor compared his slavery to my freedom.

By mere example, my father taught me how not to live.

"Oh Dad," I said to the heavens one morning. "I wish you had made your own choices and lived the life you wanted."

Then the miraculous moment occurred. It was just as if I heard his voice. "My shaineh maideleh (pretty little girl), I want you to know something in your heart of hearts: I did live the life I wanted."

I felt an unfamiliar sense of spiritual clarity I had never felt before.

Then I heard my father say, "Living a devout life gave me a connection to God. It gave me purpose."

"But you weren't happy."

"I chose a life of sacred devotion. That is what I held dear. And that is what I most needed to do."

This realization about my father's life brought me a sense of peace that was as astonishing as humbling. Who was I to judge what was best for my father?

And so, this year I began following the annual practice of Yahrzeit, which is lighting a candle and saying a prayer on the anniversary of a loved one's death. Next to the torn black cloth in the humidor, I took the small prayer book that was given to each of us at my father's graveside service.

As I read from the book, I held the cloth to my heart. "Oh day of sacred, solemn and sorrowful memories. The spirit of my father seems to hover over me. His memory penetrates my heart and my soul. Yea, as long as I live, I shall keep sacred this Yahrzeit as a tribute to my father whom I loved with a love everlasting."

And just as the miracle so clearly provided me with the direction I should take, I lit the candle to honor my father and the life he chose to live.

~Saralee Perel

30

Gifts from the Sea

The only way to pray is to pray, and the way to pray well is to pray much.
~John Chapman

My family members are people of the sea. Four decades ago, my parents moved us from the bustling streets of the Bronx to the pristine sandy beaches of Long Beach, Long Island. And we're all still here, my siblings and I, now raising our own families with sand in our shoes, salt on our skin, and the ocean in our souls.

My mom is the beloved principal of our town's Catholic school, a beautiful brick building directly across the street from the beach. A few years ago she chose the school's theme for the year: "Gifts from the Sea." I found that choice odd. What gifts? Seashells? Fish?

That fall I was waiting for my own gift to arrive. Our son Gavin was due in November and although I wanted to be excited, I was a nervous wreck. Gavin had been my fourth pregnancy in ten months, and although my doctor had resolved the minor issue that had prevented those previous pregnancies from developing, I knew I would not breathe easily until I held my baby in my arms. Gavin Thomas arrived two weeks early, two pounds lighter than my daughter had been at birth. I felt instantly protective of my little "miracle baby" as I called him. He seemed tiny and wrinkly and extra vulnerable. But nonetheless, I finally let out that sigh of relief. My baby was here, healthy, sweet and perfect.

When Gavin was four months old, I was changing his diaper

one morning and as I moved his leg he let out a scream. My stomach dropped. It was not a normal infant sound. I was terrified, but I decided not to panic and to be extra vigilant about that leg. A week later my husband Andy told me that Gavin screamed when he was changing him into his pajamas. I knew then that we needed to get him to the doctor.

Dr. Matt, our pediatrician, examined Gavin and said the tibia of his left leg felt abnormal so he sent us for an X-ray. The orthopedist examined the X-ray and then told us the unfathomable. "You need to have Gavin seen by a pediatric oncologist as soon as possible." Dr. Matt, who lost a sibling to cancer, just as my husband had several years earlier, promised an appointment at Sloan-Kettering in Manhattan the next day. Gavin would be seen by the best doctors in the world. We left Dr. Matt's office shell-shocked. A pediatric oncologist? Gavin was only four months old! This couldn't be happening.

At Sloan-Kettering, Gavin had several X-rays and we met with several doctors who diagnosed multiple tumors in the tibia, which had shattered his little leg. One oncologist wanted to do a full body scan because the tumors looked aggressive and probably malignant and most likely the cancer had spread throughout his tiny body. Then we met with an orthopedic oncologist who suggested a biopsy first.

During the two weeks of waiting for the results of the biopsy, the most difficult and distressing weeks of my entire life, the prayers started.

My mom had hundreds of children and teachers from her school praying for Gavin every day. Our family of teachers received endless calls, e-mails, and cards from former students and co-workers who were praying for Gavin. As an English as a Second Language teacher at the Adult Learning Center, I had people from all walks of life and all corners of the globe praying for my little baby. A student from Ecuador told me her mother back home asked her priest to pray for Gavin. One of my Muslim students said her family in Iraq was praying for him too. Two fellow teachers told me their rabbis were keeping Gavin in their prayers. He was the special intention at Masses said in parishes throughout New York State, where we had family and friends. People sent miraculous medals, blessed rosary beads, and prayer cards, all of which we placed in Gavin's hospital crib as he recovered from his biopsy. And of course we sent prayers via Andy's father in heaven, whose name was Gavin's middle name, and his sister who had lost her battle with breast cancer seven years before.

In addition to teaching, I also work as a co-host on a Catholic television program called *Good News with Father Jim*. Father reached out to all who were watching and asked them to keep Gavin in their prayers. I started receiving phone calls and cards from concerned and caring viewers who had prayed for my pregnancy just months before. We had constantly discussed my growing belly on the air. When Gavin was finally born, a film crew was dispatched to my living room to capture footage of our new baby boy. After that episode aired, cards and gifts for Gavin flowed into the station. And now those same dedicated viewers were among the literally thousands who were praying for him. This helped me through the darkest period of my life.

One morning I collapsed on the floor in the shower, sobbing at the thought of my sweet little baby having an aggressive cancer attacking his body. I let myself imagine him losing his battle. I envisioned his funeral. I thought about who I would become—a broken, depressed, and angry woman. I grieved for my three-year-old daughter who would lose the mother she knew, for my husband, siblings, and parents who would never have the real me back again. I prayed with the scalding water pounding against my back, the only words I could find, "Please, please, please, God. *Please.*"

After two agonizing weeks of waiting, we went back to Sloan-Kettering for the biopsy results. We were literally on the edges of the chairs in the waiting room, where it felt as if time stood still. I tried to read the doctor's face when he entered the examination room, trying to measure the tone of his voice when he greeted us. He got right to the point.

"The tumors are completely benign." The rest of what came out of his mouth was a blur. Thankfully my mother took notes. Gavin had aneurysmal bone cysts, something common in ten-year-olds but never seen in anyone younger than four. Gavin would need surgery to fix his shattered tibia and would hopefully be as good as new in a few short months.

How would they fix his broken leg? With cadaver bone fragments, which is a common treatment in a case like this. But they were also going to use cutting edge technology and fill his leg with coral reef, a live element that would grow through and with his broken tibia.

"Coral reef?" my mom asked incredulously. "Like as in coral reef from the ocean?"

"Yes, exactly," responded the doctor.

"A gift from the sea!" Mom exclaimed and then started to weep.

Our Gavin was going to be just fine. Those thousands of prayers from Long Beach to South America to Iraq and back were answered.

~Karen Danca-Smith

31

A Miracle for Mom

"For I will restore health to you and heal you of your wounds," says the
LORD…
~Jeremiah 30:17

When I was a little girl and lost something, my mother always said, "Pray to St. Anthony." When I got older and had problems in school, Mom would say, "Pray to St. Jude." We didn't pray *to* the saints, but *through* them, believing in their intercession with God to help with our needs. Over the years, there was always a saint I could count on for help.

When my husband and I took a cruise with our friends, Barbara and I, like most moms, spent some time talking about our families. I shared a personal problem one of my children was having and how I'd been awake nights trying to figure out how to resolve it. I had even considered canceling the trip.

Barbara immediately said, "Pray to St. Monica. She's the saint for parents who need help; she's the patroness of mothers."

I'd never heard of St. Monica, so Barbara eagerly told me that she was St. Augustine's mother back in the fourth century. Apparently her son Augustine was a real handful in his youth. He abandoned his Christian faith and gave his mother a lot of grief. St. Monica devoted herself to prayer and fasting for Augustine's conversion, and after a time, he turned himself around.

I thought to myself, "I've had lots of help from St. Anthony and St. Jude, so why not St. Monica?"

My husband and I left the cruise ship with our friends and boarded a tour bus to visit La Popa Monastery, located high on a hill in Cartagena, Columbia.

Built in the early 1600s, the monastery's grounds were green and lush and the view of the city spectacular. We all entered a tiny chapel and marveled at the huge gold leaf altar and gold statues standing in front of it. I knelt down to say my first prayer to St. Monica. I looked up at the sun shinning on these, the first gold statues I'd ever seen. Their faces radiated beauty. I glanced to the carving at the bottom of one: St. Augustine. And on the other: St. Monica.

Stunned, as if by a bolt of lightning, I knew in that instant that all I had to do was ask St. Monica for help and I would receive it.

When I got home, I found the longstanding problem resolved.

~Rosemarie Miele

Please God Make It Snow

*"Assuredly, I say to you, whoever does not receive the kingdom of God as a
little child will by no means enter it."*
~Mark 10:15

One November, my Sunday school class of five- to eleven-
year-olds was learning about the power of prayer. I
explained that God *always* answers prayers. His answer
may be "Yes," "No," or "Just wait." As a part of our lesson, we discussed what to pray for as a class so we'd all see God's answer at the
same time.

Some children suggested parties, others a vacation spot, still
others, toys.

Then one child piped up, "Lets pray for snow; I have never seen
snow!"

None of the other children had either, and suddenly everyone
was chattering excitedly as if it would snow any minute!

So together we held hands and prayed, "Please God, make it
snow here."

The weeks went by and every Sunday the children talked about
the snow God would send to our small East Texas town.

At that same time, my husband and I were leading a Bible study
at a youth prison in town. We told the juveniles the story of my
Sunday school class's prayer, hoping their faith would be rekindled.

Two boys challenged, "It never snows in this part of Texas! You
lied to those kids!"

"You'll hurt their faith; they should have prayed for something else."

I answered, "With God all things are possible."

But as the months went by, the children stopped talking about snow. Even my faith was being tested.

April arrived and Easter approached with balmy weather and temperatures in the 70s. On Good Friday I prepared my Sunday school lesson with a sad heart. It was 75 degrees and sunny. No one had mentioned snow for weeks.

Then the next day, the temperature dropped dramatically. I gazed out my window to see snowflakes falling... then more... and more... until two inches blanketed the earth.

My phone started ringing.

"Look outside, look!"

"Our prayer was answered 'yes!'"

"We're going outside to play in snow for the very first time!"

The next morning, on Easter Sunday in church, one of the girls from my class stood before the congregation, smiling brightly. "Last November I wrote in my diary, 'Today our Sunday school class asked God to make it snow here in East Texas,' and yesterday He answered our prayer! It snowed two inches!"

Everyone applauded.

At our Bible study class at the youth prison, the two young men smiled meekly.

"We saw the snow," one said.

"Sorry we ever doubted you... doubted God," said the other. "He answers our prayers too."

~Angela Closner

Reprinted by permission of Off the Mark
and Mark Parisi © 1992.

Specific Prayers

In that day you will no longer ask me anything. Very truly I tell you,
my Father will give you whatever you ask in my name.
~John 16:23

I heard the rumbling loud noises of my station wagon as I drove into my employer's parking lot. Several employees turned their heads. I am not a mechanic, but I knew it did not sound good. The noises had started several days before but there was nothing I could do about it. I was broke.

That morning my boss called me into his office and asked me to close the door. This only happened once a year, during my annual appraisal. I'd already had that. I tried to recall if I had done something wrong. Nothing came to mind.

"I've been noticing your car's loud noises lately," my boss said. "My wife and I know you are going through a divorce. Every few years we donate one of our vehicles to a charity organization. This year we wondered if your church would allow us to donate one of our cars so you would receive it."

Shocked, I stammered, "I don't know, but I'll be happy to check with the church office."

"We have a newer model Mercury station wagon we would like to donate. It is in excellent condition with a burgundy leather interior. It will be a great car for you. You'll enjoy it."

I walked back to my desk in a stupor.

Just one week earlier I had been teaching a Christian women's support group for single mothers. Each week I told them to be specific in their prayers. Whatever need they had, they were to tell God specifically. Prayers they had prayed for years were finally answered. Miracles happened weekly. That night I added my personal prayer request. "I desperately need a car and there is no money for it. I'm really stepping out on faith and asking specifically. I need a station wagon and I would love for it to be white."

All the ladies had laughed and giggled at the request. No one had ever heard a prayer like this before. I knew it was going to be a real test of faith.

The next week, after work, my boss and I walked to the parking lot. He pointed. "This is your new car."

Wouldn't you know it? It was a beautiful white station wagon.

~Dot Beams

Answered Prayers

The Healing Power
of Prayer

*Heal me, O LORD, and I shall be healed; Save me,
and I will be saved, for You are my praise.*

~Jeremiah 17:14

That's Who I Asked

I love those who love me, and those who seek me diligently will find me.
~Proverbs 8:17

I've heard it said that religion is for those who don't want to go to hell, but spirituality is for those who have already been there and don't want to go back. I guess that makes me a spiritual man.

I found myself, that first day of February, in hell without hope. There I was, a forty-eight-year-old man, divorced and childless, going through the most painful detox I had ever experienced, following two days of ceaseless drinking which were abruptly interrupted. I was at a convention in Las Vegas, working a sales booth for my employer, who had discovered my drinking the day before. He forbade me from drinking the rest of the week under penalty of termination. Paralyzing cramps racked my body, and sweat dripped from my face as I tried to pretend nothing was wrong and make small talk and sales.

That night, alone in my room at the MGM Grand, their trademark green floodlights casting a nauseating pallor over my room, a war raged in my body and in my soul. Violent cramps tore at every muscle without relief. I thought I wouldn't survive the night, and in some ways, that was fine with me. At least death would end my physical suffering and finally stop the daily cycle of drinking, hangover, remorse, resolve, and relapse that defined my adult life.

I was the son and grandson of alcoholics. From the time I was five years old I watched my father drink himself to death following his automobile accident that killed my oldest brother. I first got drunk when I was fifteen, majored in it in college, and pursued it beyond the gates of insanity as an adult.

Ironically, life had always come easy for me. I did well in school, earned a scholarship to college where I maintained good grades, played in several professional musical combos, advanced rapidly in the business world, and for many years, enjoyed an enviable social life, traveling to all parts of the country following my whims and pleasures.

But what was at first "having a good time" eventually became an everyday occurrence that took everything—jobs, homes, relationships, health, joy—and ultimately would have taken my life, just as it did my father's. Two months before that fateful business trip to Las Vegas, I was released after spending my second three-month stay in jail, this time following my conviction for a third DUI.

I went home to a tiny trailer in a rundown trailer park, surrounded by fellow alcoholics. I drank at least a quart of cheap vodka every night, straight from the bottle. I had nothing to show for my life, no possessions to speak of, no bank account, no credit card, not even a driver's license. All of the "stuff" I had owned in my life—the fancy cars, the big televisions, the nice furniture, the expensive clothes, the musical instruments—were all long gone. In fact, I had stopped playing music entirely seventeen years before. All the talents with which I had been bestowed, the gifts, all for naught, squandered in a vain attempt to find love and happiness in a bottle.

Three days after returning from Las Vegas, deeply shaken by my horrendous experience there, sober since, and avowed to try something—anything—to change, I found my way to Alcoholics Anonymous. The meeting, a few blocks from my work, was in a one-story warehouse down by the tracks. I walked into the large room with its stained carpet and sixty chairs of all different types. An old desk sat at the end of the room; banners and slogans covered the walls. There, men and women told stories like mine, but laughed about their past exploits instead of hiding them in shame. They were happy and smiling, and clearly sober. I wanted what they had, and immediately became willing to do whatever it took to get it.

After the meeting, I approached the chairman. "Where can I buy one of those Big Books?"

A man standing next to him handed me his, and smiled. "The first one is free."

Together they gave me four suggestions to "get" what they had: read the Big Book, attend ninety meetings in ninety days, find a sponsor, and start working on the 12 Steps program.

I followed those suggestions, and it turns out, what they had was God, a power greater than themselves that could end their insanity. The conduit to that higher power was prayer.

In fact, daily prayer and meditation were primary elements of the AA program. But I didn't know how to pray. Sure, I had said my share of Lord's Prayers and dinner graces, but I had no experience in how my personal prayers should be rendered. This wasn't because I didn't believe in God. I did. I saw evidence of Him in the lives of others and had witnessed the palpable presence of the Holy Spirit at my grandmother's funeral. I had come to believe that the God of the Bible was indeed the Creator. I just didn't think He was relevant to or interested in me, so I hadn't petitioned Him with prayer, other than in the darkest moments of the loneliest nights, when impassioned pleas were painfully uttered to an empty silence.

At the AA meeting, I heard an old immigrant, gray-bearded and stout, bellow to the newcomers in his Slavic accent, "You must humble yourself before God!"

So when I got home, I got on my knees with my face on the floor—no small feat for a 6' 6" man—and awkwardly began with the Serenity Prayer. "God, grant me the serenity to accept the things I cannot change, courage to change the things I can, and wisdom to know the difference." Then I added, "Free me from the bondage of self, let it be Thy Will, not my will, always." Then piecing together things I had heard, I offered God glory and thanksgiving for the blessings in my life, for my mother, for a mate who loved me, for the roof over my head, for my employment. I begged him for the guidance and strength to do the right thing. "In Jesus' name I pray, Amen."

Then I stiffly rose to my feet.

Within the first week of attending AA meetings and praying every day, God did for me what I had never been able to do for myself. He miraculously removed all my cravings and obsession for alcohol, 100 percent! In its place, He planted a seed of understanding, and a grateful desire to nurture that seed, to live the life He intended for me.

Now, over four years later, my life is better than I could ever imagine. I have a loving wife, a secure home, a rewarding job, a wonderful church family, and I play guitar in several musical combos, including our Praise Team at church.

That isn't to say that my life has been idyllic. Three months after God got me sober, my seventy-seven-year-old mother suffered a major stroke, and my then-girlfriend (now wife) and I had to move in with her to provide her care. Seventeen months later, she passed away. The events that followed—the memorial service, the settling of her estate with my brother, the cleaning and selling of her home, the transporting and burying of her ashes 1,000 miles away—were all things I could never have done when I was drinking or without God in my life.

And if someone asks me, "How do you know it was God who got you sober and did all of those things for you?" I simply explain, "That's who I asked."

~Dan G.

Reprinted by permission of Dan Reynolds /
Cartoonresource.com © 2010.

One Year

Is anyone among you sick? Let him call the elders of the church,
and let them pray over him, anointing him with oil in the name of the Lord.
~James 5:14

One year. What can I do in a year? Should I make a list? Should I just play it by ear? Words spun in my brain as I left the doctor's office. I did not want anyone to know. Then it would become real. But of course I had to call my daughter.

"Hi Lisa, not good news. The PET scan shows cancer in a neck lymph node."

"What did the doctor say?" Her voice quivered.

"That I have only about a year."

A death sentence is a death sentence. Or is it?

After my automobile accident in 1967, how long did I lie in the hospital hallway after the doctor said, "She will not live"? They had walked away leaving me to die. Hours passed. My dad caught the doctor's attention. "I think you should do something for her." A blood transfusion was started. Then a lung specialist was called in for my collapsed lungs. He placed tubes into my chest and I was transferred to the ICU.

The doctors continued to tell my family each time they visited, "We really don't know why she's still alive." Several weeks later I was well enough for a surgeon to remove the crushed vertebrae causing pressure on my spine. The surgery left me paralyzed from the waist down. But I would live. God answered my prayers, though as usual, in His own way.

Would God answer my prayers again forty-two years later? Could I escape another death sentence?

My good friend Kerry and I faithfully had our mammograms every year. We made it a fun day, doing lunch at a special restaurant. Then one year my insurance would not pay for my mammogram at my usual clinic. I insisted Kerry have hers, then I'd have mine at an insurance-approved clinic. Finally, after six months, I went for the mammogram. I was disturbed to hear that a spot needed to be rechecked on my left breast.

"Dear God, let the biopsy be negative."

But it was positive. I had cancer. The doctor recommended surgery. My first reaction was, "I'd rather die than have surgery." Then I realized that was the choice God was giving me.

I decided I could do breast cancer once — not twice. I did not want to do seven weeks of daily radiation; the decision was made to remove both breasts. I would be back in commission in a matter of a couple weeks that late December.

The surgery went like a charm, but to my horror one cancer cell had metastasized, hopped into the blood system and traveled to parts unknown.

I now had Stage III cancer. Life changed just that fast. Christmas was a dim fog. I needed six months of chemotherapy, followed by seven weeks of radiation. This was a far cry from over and done within a couple of weeks.

My family and friends took me to all my appointments and brought yummy food. I lost all my hair, was very tired, and threw up a lot. When I was in the hospital having the lymph nodes removed, my daughter announced she was pregnant. This was exciting; now we both had a "throw up buddy."

My newest grandson was born the day after I finished chemo. As I held the little bundle in my arms for the first time I understood. God was giving me a new life.

I made it through radiation, then had hormone treatments and monthly doctor appointments, blood tests, and PET scans.

Now this scan showed the cancer had moved into my neck lymph node. Stage IV cancer. One year to live.

"Dear God," I prayed, "please remove the cancer."

I prayed the same prayer for a year and a half.

At church one Sunday the pastor offered to pray for people using the type of oil that Jesus used. I rolled my wheelchair to the front of the church as the music played. "Please pray for my cancer to go away."

Pastor touched my forehead with oil, took hold of my hand, and began to pray, "Dear Heavenly Father..."

A gentle breeze wrapped around me; I knew this was my Heavenly Father. I knew then everything would be fine, Stage IV cancer or not.

Two months later, I paused before entering the doctor's office alone to hear results of the latest PET scan and blood tests. The nurse guided me to a small room and handed me the test results. I scanned them knowing anything abnormal would be in bold, as usual. Just then the doctor walked in.

"How are you?" he asked.

"Fine," I smiled, repeating the same routine we followed at every appointment. "Or am I? You tell me."

"The PET scan shows no cancer."

Stunned I managed to say, "Does that mean I am cancer-free? I can say I am cancer-free?"

"Yes, Beth, it does," he beamed.

"Cancer-free!" I nearly shouted.

God had once again commuted my death sentence.

~Beth Davies

36

The Swing

Evening, morning and noon I will pray and cry aloud
and He shall hear my voice.
~Psalm 55:17

The wooden porch swing hanging in my living room surprises visitors. In my unexpected, garden-like sanctuary, vine-covered chains descend from the ceiling, wrapping the swing in an embrace. Lazy clusters of purple lilacs fall from above the bay window. Wandering ivy explores a birdbath and trellis. Tumbling fountain waters serenade the soul. This place was my refuge, my safe haven... until the night the tall police officer and the professionally dressed lady arrived at my door. I knew what they were going to tell me, although I prayed I was wrong. Our sixteen-year-old son C.J. was late coming home. My voicemail messages to him were unanswered. When the woman asked my husband Don and me to sit down, we went straight to the swing. Seconds later she spoke those words. "C.J. died tonight."

Many insensible weeks passed as March turned into April and April into May. It was impossible to reclaim my garden room. Hellish memories echoed from there now. More than once during those weeks, I stood in the kitchen doorway that framed a view of my swing and the horrific scene replayed for what seemed the billionth time: the swing... my husband... the lady kneeling in front of me... my face buried in my husband's chest... his arms around me tight... my eyes clenched shut… my hands over my ears… shouts of "No! No! NO!" followed by my own unearthly sobs. Now I hated that swing.

One early May morning I was home alone and once again seized by grief. God, my Father, listened as I lashed out and hurled angry words of confusion at Him. I cried and yelled, ultimately ending up in the middle of the garden room. Completely spent, I plopped down on my swing. That swing. The swing I wanted to be at peace with again.

I asked God, "Why? Why?"

I knew there would never be an answer to satisfy me. Still, my very soul cried out, "I need to know he's okay, God. Please, please, show me that he's okay." The words poured from my mouth, but even more so from my spirit.

At some point, out of sheer exhaustion, I stopped and waited for an answer. I gently swayed back and forth, to and fro to the creaking rhythm of the chain.

Oblivious to time, I sat for quite a while, until I finally accepted the fact that God wasn't going to drop a postcard from the sky. I got up, cleaned myself up, and drove to my ex-husband's, C.J.'s dad, house to deliver some photographs. Steve was remarried to a wonderful woman named Kathy, and they had a boy, "little" Steven, who was almost four years old.

As I approached their house, Kathy drove toward me. We stopped and rolled our windows down to talk. I passed the manila envelope of photographs to her.

"Oh, Karen, I have to tell you something," she said. "Little Steven wanted me to call you yesterday. He had a dream. C.J. told him to tell you that he's okay."

My mouth dropped open.

"Steven was really persistent. C.J. told him it was really important that he tell you that." My jaw was still hanging slack. Little Steven was much too young to make up such a story. I told Kathy about my morning, begging God to let me know C.J. was okay. This time, her jaw fell open.

From that day forward the swing became a part of my healing, not hurting, and in time, it grew to be a peaceful place for me once more, even joyful at times.

I've come to accept that as long as I'm here on this earth, I won't have all the answers I yearn for surrounding the death of my son. But I do know that God heard my cry from the swing that day and mercifully answered my prayer.

~Karen L. Freeman

37

A Miracle of Song

But you, when you pray, go into your room, and when you have shut your
door, pray to your Father who is in the secret place; and your Father who
sees in secret will reward you openly.
~Matthew 6:6

N ormally on Saturday mornings I slept in, but, excited about singing a special Mass on Monday, that morning I threw the covers aside and sprang out of bed. I was eager to rehearse and organize my music. As I headed to the bathroom, I cleared my throat, a regular habit for me. As a singer, a clear voice was essential. For me, it was more than that—my clear voice was a miracle.

It had been a while since the church organist had walked up to me and asked, "Would you consider singing for Mass?"

It would have been easier if he'd asked me to take a flying leap to the moon. I had never sung solo in my life. In fact, except for at church, I sang only in private. I figured I was one of those people who think they sound good in the shower but are really bad singers.

Yet, in the past months, numerous people had turned around after Mass, telling me I should be singing up front. It was a strange and very frightening prospect to me, since I was the type of person who couldn't say her name at a baby shower without breaking into a sweat. I was scared to death and worried I'd fail. Yet I knew God was up to something, so I began to pray for courage and read scriptures to strengthen me.

Finally, with my knees knocking and stomach churning, I had sung solo in front of a full congregation. I felt God's peace come over me. Only God could have given me the voice and the courage to serve Him this way. I wanted to praise His name forever with my voice and my life.

To my dismay, however, I began experiencing long bouts of hoarseness. I'd wake up hoarse with no other symptoms. Sometimes my voice was completely gone. As frustrating as this was, I was determined to keep singing. I babied my voice, drank water and used any other medicinal concoctions I could find.

And I prayed; oh, how I prayed.

More than once I was hoarse the week before I was scheduled to sing at a wedding, and yet somehow, by God's grace, my voice cleared just in time. Still, I couldn't deny the problem was getting worse and more frequent.

Now, with the Mass just two days away, I was apprehensive.

As I stepped into the shower and cleared my throat repeatedly, I had to face the painful reality—my voice was gone.

"No... not again... please, Lord." I leaned my head back and let the hot water pour over my neck. I knew deep down, though, that the problem was too serious to be fixed by a hot shower. Soon, my tears flowed with the water.

Afterward, I drank hot tea and told myself to have faith, that it would get better; but contrary to my positive thinking, my voice got worse throughout the day. By late afternoon I was trying to decide whether to call in a substitute singer. But I had helped select the music, rehearsed it over and over to give God my very best. I just didn't want to give up.

Crying, I fell to my knees. "Oh God... why? Why me? I have tried so hard to serve You. Why would You help me sing and then take my voice away?"

Sobbing, I felt a bit of shame with each selfish prayer, but I couldn't stop. I was well aware that God knew my thoughts and intentions and I knew He understood and forgave my sorrow. Sure enough, within moments, I began to feel more peaceful.

"God, show me your Word that will give me an answer, or at least help me accept what I can't understand."

I let my Bible fall open randomly, and my tears formed a "lens" that magnified Psalm 40:1-3 and read, "I waited patiently for the LORD; And He inclined to me, and heard my cry. He also brought me up out of a horrible pit, out of the miry clay, and set my feet upon a rock, and established my steps. He has put a new song in my mouth—"

I cried even harder, because I knew that those words were written for me. Not only was God assuring me He heard my cry, He acknowledged my efforts to continually praise Him by giving Him all the credit for any courage and talent I possessed. Only God completely understood why I sang with such passion.

Feeling God's powerful presence, I felt led to sit down at the piano. God's blessing flowed through my mind and fingers as I composed the melody and words to a song I entitled, "Why Me?" Psalm 40 spoke of putting a new song into my mouth, and indeed, He did. With renewed confidence, I knew my voice would be back in time for Mass.

The next day, I sang nine songs, including four prelude solos. It was a miracle I will never forget as long as I live.

In the months following, doctors diagnosed that acid reflux from my stomach had created ulcers on my vocal fold. When I was wheeled into the operating room for surgery to correct it, I didn't say, "Why me?" I surrendered my life into His hands and He did not let me down.

I sing for Him.

~Elizabeth Schmeidler

The Power of Prayer

Faith makes things possible, not easy.
~Author Unknown

My heart stopped at the sight of the Eagle Med helicopter flying over the football stadium at Bishop Carroll High School. Dad muttered, "It's not good when that thing flies." It was halftime and my sixteen-year-old brother Aaron had yet to come find us at the game. My little sister Olivia, Dad, and I had all gone to watch my brother, Ben, play his first football game.

Little did we know, Aaron had gotten off work at approximately 6:30 and headed home in a hurry to change clothes and leave for the game. Mom had been getting ready for church when he arrived and he asked if she would like him to wait for her until Mass was over. She declined his offer. As Aaron headed out the door, Mom hollered, "Aaron? Don't forget to buckle up!"

"I won't, Mom. I never do," Aaron replied. He jumped in his car and hurried down the driveway, stopping at the end to click the seatbelt in.

Back at the game we were still looking for him. I could tell by the look on Dad's face that he was starting to get a little worried. "Maybe he had to work late and he's just now leaving," I suggested.

"Yeah maybe," Dad responded. With his reply, I knew Dad was trying to hide his real feelings.

Everything changed when Dad answered his phone at 9:45 to hear a frantic voice on the other line. I couldn't hear what was being said, but I could tell something was going on by the way Dad walked over to the fence so we couldn't overhear. Obliviously, Olivia turned to me and piped up, "Boy! Dad's gonna be mad at Aaron for not coming and finding us during the whole game! He's gonna be in big trouble!"

Dad walked back over to us and said, "Jussy, I need you to be a big eleven-year-old, take Olivia's hand and walk her to the van. I'm going to go find Ben and then we'll be there." I did what I was told and ten minutes later I could see Dad and Ben running through the parking lot towards our van. They scurried in silently, but quickly, and Dad drove off.

We arrived at my dad's office, and to my surprise, my mom and older sister Amanda were waiting for us. Dad told Olivia and me that Amanda would be taking us home so we needed to get in her car. Puzzled, I got out and made my way over to Mom. She was crying.

"Mom what's wrong?" I asked.

She said softly, "Aaron's been in a car wreck, honey. Just quickly get in the car. Hurry up! All you can do now is pray extra hard!"

At that moment, everything broke down around me. The next thing I knew, my sisters and I were riding back to our house in silence. Poor Olivia was only nine and didn't have any idea what was going on. She kept asking questions like, "Why did Mommy and Daddy leave in such a hurry? Is Aaron in trouble? Why can't I go see him?"

We arrived at our house and patiently waited by the phone. Grandma and Grandpa came over and said that they were going to the hospital. Before they left, Grandma helped Amanda put us to bed, but of course I couldn't sleep. My mind was racing sixty miles an hour. "What if he's not going to make it? How bad is it really?" I kept thinking.

The next day, we found out what had happened. The wreck occurred only four miles from our house. Aaron had taken a dirt road to the game because nobody was riding with him and he wanted to make it to the game as quickly as possible. He had been going too fast and hit a dip in the road, taking out a mailbox and rolling the car four times. The car landed upright in the middle of a field on a country road. When the paramedics found him, he had a seatbelt on but was lying down on the front seat with his legs out the window, as though he was trying to get out. He was in shock and as one of the paramedics tried to sit him up, he yelled, "Mom!!!"

According to the paramedics, it appeared that as the car was rolling, the window broke and Aaron hit his head on the ground each time, causing closed head injuries. As it turns out, the Eagle Med helicopter that we had seen at the game was on its way to rescue my brother.

The next morning, Mom called around 11:30 and explained that he was in the Intensive Care Unit on a respirator and in a coma. She and Dad finally agreed, later that day, to let us come up to the hospital for a while.

When we arrived at the entrance to the ICU, we were told we had to put on gloves and masks in order to go in. As I walked into his room, I glanced towards his bed and saw a lifeless creature lying there hooked up to many different machines. This creature looked nothing like my brother! His head was swollen and was the color of my purple shirt. His eyes were covered with a wet cloth and his fingers looked like little sausages. I wanted to scream out in fear and help him, but instead of a scream, only tears came down. I looked up at Dad and tears filled his eyes too.

"He looks a lot better than he did last night," Dad whispered to me.

"Better?" I croaked. "He doesn't even look anything like the brother I've known all my life! What happened to my Anno?"

Olivia and I spent the next two weeks traveling from house to house while Mom and Dad spent every waking hour at the hospital. I could only think about how angry I was that this had to happen to our family.

Why had God chosen us? Eventually with time, I realized that Mom was right. The only things that we could do were hope and pray. "God will watch over us. He has a plan," she would tell me.

Within two weeks our prayers had been answered. Aaron had come out of the coma and improved enough to be taken off the respirator. The doctor informed my parents that he would be in rehab one week for every day he had been in the coma. After being in a coma for eleven days, my brother threw the doctors for a loop and was out of rehab within one week of admittance! The doctor told my mom he had no explanation for why he was doing so well.

Mom looked up at the doctor and said, "I know exactly what it is. It's called the power of prayer." You see, the seniors and juniors at Bishop Carroll had handed out blue ribbons to all the kids in school to remind them to pray for Aaron. Before each class, they would say a prayer for him. Many people from our parish were also praying for him along with family members and friends who lived out of state. Aaron had his own prayer chain.

It's been a little over five years since Aaron's car wreck and he's fully back to normal. He now spends his time fighting for our country in the Air National Guard. He's always on the go, helping people. Right now he's stationed in Afghanistan, working in munitions. I thank God each and every day for saving my brother's life. I look back now and can't believe how much pain and anguish my family went through. The doctors said Aaron shouldn't even be where he is today, but it's like my mom always said: "With the power of prayer, and God watching over us, anything is possible!"

~Justina Rausch

39

Care Plan

For the eyes of the Lord are on the righteous,
and his ears are open to their prayers....
~1 Peter 3:12

While other parents celebrated the exciting moments of a child taking first steps, stringing words together and building towers of blocks, we watched... and waited. But those moments didn't come for our precious granddaughter Millie. Special tests and evaluations changed the landscape of our lives forever when our daughter Laurie, in words thick with painful emotion, explained, "Millie's been diagnosed as severely autistic."

Our family learned more about autism than we ever wanted to know. We watched in shocked bewilderment as the condition swelled to epidemic proportions, now affecting one out of every 100 children. I watched autism grow bigger than any of us and completely overtake my daughter's life, marriage, and family.

We prayed diligently, trusting God to set Millie free from this mysterious disease. We thanked Him for giving His children the spirit of power and love and humbly asked Him to fulfill His Word and bless Millie with a sound mind.

For years we prayed and for years there was no change. In fact, life became worse. What first appeared to be a hide-and-go-seek game soon became a serious issue as Millie began to run away.

Gates, locks, deadbolts and alarms were installed, but with the agility of a pre-school gymnast and the nearly inhuman strength of someone much older and larger, Millie overcame all security systems. One chilly spring morning the inevitable occurred.

Barefoot and clad only in her underwear, Millie slipped from the house and wandered two miles onto a major highway. God intervened that day and answered our continual prayers for Millie's protection. Miraculously no one was hurt during the tire screeching, car spinning ballet. Quick thinking motorists used their cars to corral Millie. Highway patrolmen transported her to the emergency offices of family services and after hours of interrogations and phone calls, Millie was reunited with her mother.

Laurie kept Millie's escapes to a minimum by sleeping with doors and windows blocked by heavy furniture. The family primarily lived indoors in a house resembling a high-security prison that nightly violated fire codes and general safety rules. Violent temper tantrums reduced Millie's room to a space with no closet doors and furnished in the battered remains of a once-beautiful canopy bed and dresser.

When school finally began, additional prayers were offered for the peace of Christ to surround and fill Millie, enabling her to focus and learn. Friends and family joined us in prayer for her school, teachers and other parents.

Our prayers were answered when a speech therapist began working with Millie using picture and word communications. As Millie was able to more easily express her needs, the violent temper tantrums lessened.

A specialist in behavior modification helped Millie develop behaviors appropriate to retail establishments, grocery stores, restaurants and swimming pools. We were thrilled to hear of her first trip to the movies.

As encouraging as these advances were, birthdays came and went with Millie remaining nearly nonverbal, eating only a few foods, roaming the house at night and still having violent tantrums with head banging.

Equally distressing was her inability to comprehend or be sympathetic toward pain and distress of other living things. She nearly drowned kittens, forced them into a zippered bag, and then used it as a seat cushion. Pets inflicted blows that left Millie bleeding, but laughing.

Eventually Laurie's best efforts at providing round-the-clock supervision, structure and routine ended with a terrifying crisis. One afternoon, while baking cookies, Laurie caught a flash of movement in the hallway and looked up to see Millie dragging her preschool brother across the floor by a cord tied around his neck. His face had already turned dark blue. Laurie screamed for help and managed to free her son from the noose. Millie simply covered her ears and left the room.

My heart broke when my daughter called and, between racking sobs, in nearly indistinguishable words said, "Mommy, I don't know what to do! We can't go on like this."

We held an emergency family meeting where the heart wrenching decision was reached to explore avenues of full-time care for Millie apart from the family.

As in most states, live-in facilities for the care of severely autistic children are few and far between.

Another birthday passed and Millie was approaching puberty. Medications were changed and the side effects were devastating: weight gain, sullen moodiness, physical awkwardness, and an increase of major meltdowns so powerful that Laurie was no longer able to physically restrain her daughter.

Hope was nearly gone when, during a meeting with Millie's family services team, a member mentioned a group home opening for three autistic girls. Unsure that space was still available, Laurie immediately rushed to the site. The house, location and staff were perfect. But the timing seemed impossible. There was only one opening and just six weeks to complete a mountain of paperwork, medical exams and evaluations. Applications were arriving daily and the window of opportunity was closing rapidly. What had seemed like such an obvious answer to prayer now seemed a crushing disappointment.

I poured my heart out to a dear friend. When she asked if I had been praying, I nearly lost it. "Praying? My knees are sore from praying! I've prayed so long and so often I don't even know *what* to pray anymore!"

My friend patiently listened, and then lovingly said, "This is the perfect situation for God to do something big." She reminded me that it is when we come to the utter end of our human resources that He delights in demonstrating His ability to work miracles.

We ended our conversation in prayer. "God help me to put my trust in You and Your care plan."

Incredibly, at that moment, I let go of the situation and placed Millie in the hands of her loving Creator.

The series of events that followed could only have been orchestrated by God's handiwork. Weeks earlier I had written a letter to Senator Strom Thurmond asking for his assistance in securing placement for Millie. Now, with only five days left to qualify, a member of his staff phoned promising to see what could be done; no guarantees.

Two days later Laurie called. "Mom, Millie was accepted!"

I fell to my knees and raised my hands high as rivers of joy and thanksgiving rolled across my cheeks.

Millie is now seventeen years old, well adjusted to group home life and through her public school's special education program, has made great strides. She speaks in complete sentences, writes her name, works simple math problems and reads at a second grade level. Her drawings won blue ribbons, and at a fundraising event one created a vigorous flurry of bidding.

New challenges and her future as a severely autistic adult continue to keep us praying, but now we've learned to trust in God's plans.

~Penny L. Hunt

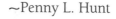

40

Gnarled Hands and Lives

Then Jesus said, "Father, forgive them, for they do not know what they do."
~Luke 23:34

"What's to become of me?" my ninety-three-year-old patient frowned as I massaged lotion into her gnarled fingers.

"What's the matter, Bonita?" I sensed she was referring to the end of life. I nodded toward the bookshelves. "You have a picture of Jesus there. He'll show you the way."

"That's just it." Bonita seemed to struggle for words. "I'm afraid to go. I'm afraid Hank will be there."

"Hank?" I knew her husband, children, grandchildren and neighbors. Never in the seven months I'd been her caregiver had anyone mentioned a Hank. I squeezed a puddle of lotion into my palm and picked up her hand.

She heaved a sigh and turned her head away as a tear trickled down her cheek. "My first husband."

"Oh, I didn't know." I massaged her gnarled knuckles.

"No one knew. I was sixteen, a waitress in Tecumseh, Michigan, where my only brother was stationed. To get in the army, Joey had lied about his age. Momma and Papa died when we were ten and eleven. A few years after Joey enlisted, he was sent to war and killed."

Her tone told me she needed to reveal more. I pulled up a chair, cradled her frail hands and waited.

"I took the train from El Paso to Chicago, then a bus to Michigan and rented a room in the hotel above the café where I worked. Hank lived there too. He was twenty-six, a shoe salesman, nice looking and friendly. He took me to the picture show and boating in the park. I loved him so much I let him have his way with me. I didn't know anything about anything."

Tears rolled down her cheeks. I gazed at her withered body in a hospital bed, in a sitting position with pillows supporting her head, elbows and knees. She kept pressing her lips as if trying to stop words from tumbling out.

I reached for her water glass and steadied the straw so she could sip. Then she continued. "I got pregnant. Hank married me. But he didn't want anything to do with me after that. 'You're no fun,' he'd complain. The closer my time came, the more Hank stayed away. Our hotel room was his stopover for clean clothes. I'd watch him going into the bar across the street, coming out at closing time, drunk. One night he walked out arm in arm with some redhead; they got into his car and drove off. I cried my eyes out and cursed him. I hated him."

I stroked her forehead, surprised, yet glad for her sake, that she'd shared her burden with me.

Caregiving is intimate work—bathing, dressing and feeding another person. As we breathed in silence and I concentrated on the bony bulges of her fingers, I became aware of the small painful knobs on my own hands. I recalled someone suggesting that arthritis might come from hidden resentment. Was Bonita's body so distorted from years of hating Hank that now she needed a hydraulic lift to move from her bed to her recliner?

Her story reminded me, in part, of my life. After she drifted off in peaceful sleep, my head dropped; tears fell. With all the resentment and betrayal from my past, I was surprised my own bones weren't more misshapen.

Bonita stirred and opened her eyes. "You're crying."

I didn't want to burden her with my story, so I said, "I'm praying for forgiveness." I sighed and Bonita did too. In truth I was praying for my dad and my own forgiveness as well. I went into the bathroom, washed my face, and came back with a warm washcloth. She wiped her face, and then sighed. "I'm feeling better," she said. "I'm glad we talked."

"I guess we're having a moment of truth." I set the cloth on her bedside table. "I don't know why Hank betrayed you, but I believe we get back what we've done. And I know that's a difficult idea to swallow."

She nodded. "As we sow, we reap. But we make such a mess of things. I can't imagine a God giving us only one try at life. I didn't go to church much; I was busy working and raising a family."

She closed her eyes, so I got up and turned off her bedside light.

"Wait," she urged, "there's more."

I leaned close. "Hank died that night in a car wreck. The woman with him was badly injured. Police took me to the hospital to identify his body. When I saw him I whispered, 'You got what you deserved.' When the baby was born, a dark-haired boy like Hank, it was so bittersweet, I gave him up for adoption." Her face contorted with pain.

We had seldom talked about religion, but when she was having a bad day, I'd hear her pray.

"Bonita, Jesus said, 'Forgive them; for they know not what they do.' (Luke 23:34) Today, some spiritual teachers say, 'Forgive us, for we're all so unaware and so darn stupid.'"

Bonita chuckled and squeezed my hand.

"Sometimes I feel resentment toward people who've done me wrong," I confessed, "but I hope and pray, some day, to say 'thank you' for teaching me an important lesson. I'm not there yet, but I know my own gnarled past has taught me to affirm others. And I've found comfort in the prayer of Saint Francis. 'It is in pardoning that we are pardoned...'"

"'... and it is in dying we are born to Eternal Life,'" Bonita said, her face softening. I, too, felt a peace.

In tending Bonita and others near death, I've felt like a faucet where a compassionate presence streams through me to them. During my fifteen years as a caregiver, I prayed for the right words when patients revealed a hidden wound that helped them let go. And in their process, they nudged me toward a deeper compassion for my own gnarled past.

I kissed Bonita's cheek. When I left she looked happier, relieved and relaxed.

"Goodbye," she whispered, her eyes gleaming brightly.

Three nights later she died in her sleep.

~Shinan Naom Barclay

41

My New Best Friend

Watch and pray, lest you enter into temptation.
The spirit indeed is willing, but the flesh is weak.
~Matthew 26:41

My husband Bob and I took turns puffing on our last cigarette until all I held was a charred filter. In a nearby planter, I partially buried it with other cigarettes. They reminded me of miniature headstones. While I gazed sadly at the tiny cemetery, I said farewell to my best "friend" of twenty-two years.

We, my cigarette and I, met the summer before my senior year in high school. Terribly shy, I was delighted to be included in a summer picnic with a few of my classmates. After lunch at the city park, the other girls lit up. "Wow," I thought, "this is grown-up stuff." I pictured sophisticated ladies holding cigarettes between polished nails while dashing gentlemen flicked silver lighters.

When a friend offered me drags on her cigarette, I readily accepted. Soon she corrected my crude attempts saying, "Inhale and exhale, like this."

"This is easy," I told myself. "All I have to do to be accepted is smoke." By dusk, I was hooked.

In the decades that followed, I smoked at least 154,000 of those gleaming white tubes of tobacco. I could always depend on my "friend" to give me a boost, calm my fears or blow away my anger. My doctor disagreed. He said my friend gave me bronchitis, asthma and poor circulation. When he said my buddy and I would have to part, tears filled my eyes, and I choked out, "Really?" He just nodded.

Following his orders, I tried to quit. I refused to buy any more cigarettes. If I didn't have them around to tempt me, I reasoned, I wouldn't smoke.

When smoking friends visited and left my home though, I grabbed the ashtrays, searching for viable butts I could finish. I had flashbacks of Seattle's Skid Road's homeless retrieving discarded smokes from the dirty sidewalk and I chided myself.

I gained weight, eating instead of smoking. Soon I broke down and bought cigarettes. I was skewered on the old adage, "Quitting smoking is easy, I quit many times," but I couldn't resist my cigarette "friend's" siren call.

A luncheon with a former smoker reinforced my guilt and frustration when she inquired about my attempts to quit smoking.

"You know I quit," she said. "I don't even think about it. When I decide to do something, I do it. No problem… easy as pie."

I stared at her, secretly imagining throwing that pie right at her.

At another lunch, this time with a friend who still smoked, I heard, "I know I should quit. But this isn't the time. You know the divorce and all."

I thought that getting a divorce would be a perfect excuse to keep smoking.

I tried every stop smoking technique I knew. Once I quit for three weeks, but always found a good excuse to start again. My husband was determined to stop too. I thought if we both quit at the same time, it might be easier. When I heard a local church was sponsoring a smoking cessation program, we signed up.

Bob and I snuffed out our "last" cigarette and entered the church auditorium. After the program director's brief introduction, the room darkened and scenes from an actual lung cancer operation flashed on the screen. The grim images erased all desire I had for cigarettes that night.

Terrifying facts may work for a while, but we learned it takes more than fear to erase an addiction. Successive nights of instruction bolstered our weak intentions. We learned more about tobacco's harmful effects and healthy alternatives to smoking. Fellow smokers supported our efforts.

When our leader suggested asking for God's assistance, I realized that was one technique I had not tried.

I begged God for His help. Without His intervention, I knew I would smoke again.

In the morning, when I craved a cigarette with my coffee, I prayed. When a friend offered me a cigarette, I prayed... and refused. After dinner, when a smoke would have tasted the best, I prayed—always the same prayer. "Lord, I'm helpless. Please help me. I can't quit." And I truly believed I couldn't.

Early one morning, I woke, prepared coffee and drank an entire cup before I realized... I hadn't craved a cigarette! Astonished, I held my empty cup and looked out the window. To the dawning sky, I whispered, "You did it, Lord. You really did! Thank you!"

It had been three weeks, just when I usually started smoking again. My craving for cigarettes had really died. Before, my nicotine addiction had screamed for relief. Now, there was silence. I could live without cigarettes.

Later I helped a group of anxious smokers and told them how many times I'd failed to quit. I recounted my winning technique... I asked for God's help and He answered my prayer.

Thirty years later I live high in the Colorado Mountains where I hike, kayak and ski with my husband and grandchildren. I'm free—no longer a slave to cigarettes, thanks to my Best Friend.

~Carol A. Strazer

42

Hannah's Story

You can do more than praying after you have prayed.
You can never do more than praying before you have prayed.
~Corrie Ten Boom

We were young, naïve, happy and so excited. The first ultrasound confirmed we'd be painting the baby's room pink.

The time went by quickly and at my final ultrasound my husband Larry joined me with our two-year-old son. Larry patiently kept him occupied while they watched the screen.

Lying there, my head filled with many thoughts. "Would she have much hair? Would she look like me? Would I be able to handle two small ones? Would I be a good mom to her?"

Like a bubble, my thoughts burst when I looked at the nurse's face. Something wasn't right.

"What's going on?" I asked.

She said nothing, just did a lot of typing. Worried, I repeatedly asked her questions. No response. Finally she broke her silence and told me she was going to get a radiologist to come and talk to us. I tried to ask more questions, but she left the room without another word.

While we waited, my mind raced. Was our baby dead? Was she deformed? I fought the urge to cry as we waited.

The radiologist came and gave very vague answers, telling us we should go to a larger city, an hour from us, and have a more advanced ultrasound done.

"What do you think is wrong?" I asked. She said she couldn't guess, that we needed more testing.

We left the hospital so confused and worried. I cried at the weight of it all.

After the next ultrasound we spoke with a specialist. Our baby had a cyst on the bottom of her spine, but more likely, she had spina bifida. We'd need to schedule a C-section then immediate surgery for our precious baby. That doctor then sent us to a neurosurgeon who, we were told, was world renowned.

He was quite knowledgeable about spina bifida but lacked bedside manner. He told us all the possible effects and outlined what the surgery would entail. His next statement nearly sent me to my knees. "It's common for these children to have numerous other health problems—blindness, deafness, mental handicaps, and holes in the heart. If your baby has any of those, I recommend that you just let her die, as opposed to putting her through all the surgeries and poor standard of living."

Numbly, we thanked the doctor for his time and walked out of the office in shock. Hand in hand, no words were said. We had none.

We went to our church with the news. Everyone rallied around us, cried with us, and lifted us up in prayer. Our faith was strengthened. And oh how we needed faith.

A week later, I entered the operating room. My teeth chattered from nerves and the temperature of the room. The anesthesiologist came in and his kind words put me a bit more at ease. I received the epidural and my legs began to warm, from the toes up. Then they brought Larry in. I knew he was nervous, but he was steady for me. Soon the doctor came surrounded by a crew of nurses, some from labor and delivery and some from neonatal intensive care.

Before long I heard the sound I had been longing to hear, the squeal of my precious baby girl. I wept. Nurses worked quickly to check her and within minutes, whisked her away to surgery. As they pushed the incubator, they stopped to let me see her, my beautiful red and squalling baby girl. Her face was so round. Her feet were so small. I laughed and cried at the same time. Then, just that fast, she was gone, out of my sight and away from my arms.

I thought I'd be scared, that I'd cry uncontrollably until I was able to see her again. Instead, an indescribable peace came over me. Filled with faith, I knew she was going to be okay. Hand in hand, Larry and I waited for our baby to come back to us after her surgery, knowing in our hearts that she was okay. God had it all under control.

After a couple of hours, the doctor came to tell us how well the surgery went and how he had done all he could to help our daughter. He said that her heart was fine; she was quite healthy. He went on to say that although he did what he could, he was not God, and that time alone would tell the outcome. He predicted that she would never sit up by herself, crawl, or walk.

Larry went to see her and brought pictures back. The nurses had placed a ribbon in her hair. I longed to hold her.

When my doctor gave the okay, I went right away to the NICU, sat in a wooden rocker by her incubator, and I held her like I'd never let go. She was beautiful. She was precious. I sang to her. I loved her with my whole heart. Filled with faith, I prayed over her.

After a week, we took her home and began physical therapy, doctors' appointments, and lots of waiting and watching.

At her six-month neurosurgeon appointment, I told the doctor that she was sitting up on her own. He urged me not to get my hopes up, as she would probably never crawl.

At her eighteen-month appointment I told him she was crawling. He urged me to not get my hopes up, as she would probably never walk.

At her two-year appointment I told him she was walking. He urged me to not get my hopes up, because she would probably never run. But this appointment was different. He looked like he had gotten his hopes up. He told us she did not need to see him any more. He asked that we send a letter every once in a while so he could keep up with her progress.

It has been thirteen years since we first heard that wonderful squealing cry. Our little girl has been through so much since then, but she's a bright, energetic child who gets good grades at school and enjoys reading and writing. She does run, in her own way. She has some physical limitations, but she has never let them hold her back.

She is our gift, our beautiful Hannah Faith.

~Carrie M. Leach

43

Mom's Miracle

And the prayer of faith will save the sick, and the Lord will raise him up.
~James 5:15

When the phone rang at 3:00 a.m. in my college room, I wiped the sleep from my eyes and tried to comprehend what my younger brother was telling me.

"Something is wrong with Mom! They took her to the hospital in an ambulance. She can't walk or talk. Dad went with her...."

I quickly dressed and rushed to the hospital, scared and confused. I met my panic-stricken father in the waiting room as they checked my mom into the emergency room. I started to cry, and my dad put his arms around me. "She's going to be okay."

I found Mom hooked up to numerous machines as the testing began. She lay still while the nursing staff shouted orders and rushed around her.

Several hours later, we still had no answers and Mom was admitted for further testing. Over the next few days, she deteriorated quickly, slipping into unconsciousness. The doctors determined that at the age of forty-two, she had suffered a massive stroke.

Surrounded by my four younger siblings, my dad, grandparents, aunts and uncles, the neurosurgeon gave us Mom's prognosis. "She has a less than one percent chance of survival," he stated in a monotone voice, "and if she does survive this surgery, she could be a vegetable. In most circumstances, I'd say it's too late, but I'm willing to try to remove the damaged tissue in her brain because she is so young."

He then asked if my dad even wanted him to go through with the surgery.

"Yes," Dad said, "try to save her."

In the pre-op holding area we huddled together, crying, telling Mom that we loved her as she teetered somewhere between heaven and earth. Nurses looked at us with big eyes, filled with pity, as they assisted my mom in mechanical ventilations. I sensed they were keeping her body alive for us so that we could have this time with her.

During the eight-hour surgery, countless friends and family stopped by to visit and pray with us. We waited for any news, sick with anticipation. Finally the surgeon stood in front of us. Mom made it through the surgery, but the next several days would determine if she would ever live a normal life.

That night I went home to my apartment, exhausted emotionally and physically. As I prayed, I wanted to beg God to save her, to bargain anything just to keep her with us. But instead, I turned it over to Him. I told God that no matter what happened with my mom, I would accept it and I wouldn't be angry with Him.

I slept fitfully that night and dreamed vividly. My mother was on trial. God was the judge and I sat in a church pew, watching her plead with Him for more time. As His gavel came down, He awarded her more time on earth.

I awoke with a sense of surreal peace. I quickly showered, dressed, and rushed to the hospital. I tiptoed into my mom's room in the ICU and was shocked to see she was no longer on a respirator! She turned to me and said in a raspy voice, "Hi hon."

"Mom!" I rushed to her side, filled with a relief and thankfulness I'd never felt before. My mom, alive and speaking, had defied all odds.

Three years later, fully recovered, she sat in my delivery room and held my baby boy in her arms. She looked at me with tears in her eyes and said, "I'm so thankful to be alive."

~Melissa Dykman

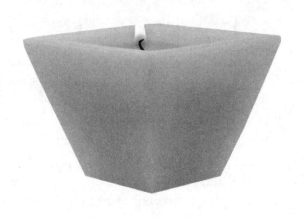

Answered Prayers

Let Go, Let God

*Prayer means placing ourselves at God's disposal so that,
for a moment or two, He may accomplish what He has always wanted
to do in us and what we never give Him a chance to.*

~Louis Evely

44

Giving Up

Pray without ceasing...
~1 Thessalonians 5:17

I lost it, not lost like a set of keys or cell phone. Lost it as in blew my stack, screaming, hollering, hand waving, spit flying, lost it. The stress of the past several months had pulled me so far down I had been reduced to something from a horror movie. As I sat on the bed that night and I tried to contemplate all we had gained and lost in this short amount of time, holding onto my faith was becoming an overwhelming effort.

The avalanche started as a small snowball when my husband came home and told me he had lost his job. He was an electrician, a skilled laborer and I was confident he'd get another job shortly. Then the snowball got bigger quickly.

Two days later we came home to a notice on the door of our singlewide trailer. The mobile home park was being sold and our family, along with 1,000 others in the park, had to vacate. Most of us had homes too old to move or could not meet new strict mobile home moving codes. In a short emotional battle with the city and the new park owners, we had to leave our trailer and sell it as scrap metal to the mobile home company, according to a Pink Slip Eviction clause in the state law.

I was devastated. It had taken me four months when I was a single mom to save the down payment on that trailer, sleeping on a friend's floor while throwing three newspaper routes. It was not my dream home—it was not anyone's dream home—but it was a place for us to live and now, a year later, it was gone.

My husband, child and I moved to a rental home. Then the snowball grew even bigger. My husband had something seriously wrong with him. He fell asleep standing up, while watching TV and even driving a car. I was scared, waist deep in distribution routes, and he could not help me keep up with all our delivery schedules.

We had no health insurance and no money, and we couldn't afford for him to see a doctor. So I shouldn't have been surprised when I got a phone call that he had been in an accident. He'd T-boned a brand new Crown Victoria. The accident, combined with the two tickets he had gotten the previous months, resulted in our auto insurance being cancelled.

Several days later I received a phone call from the landlord of our rental home. It seemed the neighbors did not like the hours we kept and had complained several times, so we were getting the boot and had ten days to move out. The phone call was like the roaring sound of snow falling down a mountain in an avalanche.

Sitting on the floor in the house, crying, I wondered where we would go and how we would manage. No job for my husband. No medical insurance. No healthcare for him. No car insurance. No savings. It was like a bad movie being replayed over and over again, only this was my life and I couldn't shut off the projector.

One more time we packed everything up, put it in a storage unit and went to stay with friends temporarily. But my friend had a family of six and had taken in a homeless teen, along with the three of us, and there was not enough room at the inn. My husband and I finally swallowed our pride and asked his mother if we could stay with her until we found a place of our own. She graciously said yes, so we relocated once again two miles across town.

For months I had prayed to God, tithed, named and claimed everything positive I could think of. I read scriptures of promise and prosperity, and still here we were living in my mother-in-law's home. I was snow blind. That's when I lost it.

I felt horribly guilty for my loss of control. Sitting on my bed, my mind filled with the words of a sermon about the Lord being our Provider and how we are not supposed to carry burdens alone.

Rivers of tears ran down my face. "I can't do this anymore," I cried. "There's too much to handle. I'm buried, suffocating and can hardly function. I hereby give up. I turn every problem and every issue over to You Lord."

I wiped my face and blew my nose, then went to my husband and told him, "God will have to handle it. God is the provider, not me. I am done. I give up."

Then I crawled into bed and slept peacefully.

Early the next morning my best friend called. "What are you wearing?" she asked.

I was in no mood. "I am in bed."

"Get dressed. I will be over in ten minutes," she said, and hung up.

I got dressed haphazardly and waited for her to arrive. We drove down the boulevard, turned into a driveway next to a rundown motel, through a gate, and onto a piece of waterfront property. She stopped in front of a cottage that sat not twenty feet from the river and fifty yards from a lovely old farmhouse.

"Your new home," she announced happily. "I found this for you. The rent is cheap, and you can't buy this view anywhere in town. I've already talked to the landlady. What do you think?"

I was speechless and for the first time in months, which seemed like years, a snowy haze lifted from my mind, the weight of an avalanche lifted off my back and happiness burst back into my life.

I beamed. "I should have given up sooner."

~Dawn Yurkas

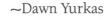

45

My Miracle Baby

Prayer is not overcoming God's reluctance;
it is laying hold of His highest willingness.
~Richard C. Trench

I awoke to April sunlight stretching across the bed in a thin yellow line. Normally I would have reached for the basal thermometer on the nightstand, but not today. Just the night before my husband and I made the decision to stop this crazy pursuit to get pregnant, even if it meant remaining childless.

Pinpointing my most probable days of conceiving was just one of dozens of things we had done in the previous five years, all in our efforts to have a child. There had been endless pills, painful tests, and embarrassing medical procedures. I had endured surgery after surgery, hoping to cure the aggressive endometriosis that plagued my body. My emotions felt like one big roller coaster ride. Up one day. Down the next. Hopes high. Hopes dashed.

In the midst of it all, my daily prayer had been, "Lord, please give me a child."

My family and circle of friends encouraged me, assuring me that God wanted me to have a child. Yet, in all candor, it seemed the heavens were brass. Was God even listening to me?

I threw the bed covers back, more convinced than ever that we'd made the right decision. Perhaps I had been so caught up in the doctors and pills and techniques that I'd never totally trusted God to answer my prayers. No longer would I take matters into my own hands. I would trust in Him to give us a child.

In the weeks following our decision, my spirits lifted. Hope blossomed like the first flowers of spring. I surrounded myself with books about pregnancy, childbirth, and infancy, practically becoming a walking encyclopedia. I knew more about pregnancy than most pregnant women I came in contact with. I studied the latest maternity fashions and stuck out my stomach in front of the bedroom mirror to see how I'd look in them, convinced I would have a baby.

But by summer's end there was no sign of a baby's arrival. Despite all of my prayers, despite all the encouraging words, despite everything, I began to feel as empty as my womb.

One September morning, under a torrential rain, I drove to church, sensing God was preparing me for something. The door to the prayer room was open. The dark and cool interior sent a shiver through me. Filled with a dozen altar benches, the room was designed only for prayer. I found my favorite spot, knelt down and closed my eyes. In silence, I waited. Many had been the times I had knelt before this very altar and begged, "Lord, please give me a child." I had bargained and questioned. But not today.

In the darkness, I opened my hands across the altar. "Lord," I said, "I'm here."

My words curled around the wooden benches and faded away.

"I'm tired and confused, God. The days ahead frighten me, but I know You understand my fears. I cannot carry this load anymore. I'm through trying to understand the reasons. Today — right now — I give up the struggle. If You want me to have a child, I will have a child. If not, I accept Your Divine plan. I trust You with my hopes, my dreams, my future."

At once, an indescribable peace enveloped me like warm oil poured from head to toe. And with it came a release. The emptiness I had carried for five agonizing years suddenly evaporated. In its place was a profound knowledge that all would be well, that I was in God's faithful hands, no matter what happened. I wept tears of relief.

When I left the church the storm had passed, leaving the air hazy and pink. For the first time in a long time I felt at peace. Rooted. Steadied. I remembered the hurricane that had swept through our area a few years back. Some trees were uprooted while others stood firm. The difference was in the roots. Yes, I had been bent and battered, but my faith, rooted in God, was strong.

Autumn blew away and on a blustery January afternoon, I visited my doctor with complaints of pelvic pain. Tests revealed a large cystic mass on my left ovary and a host of problems on the right. A complete hysterectomy was recommended.

Resembling a judge in a white coat, the doctor shut my enormous folder in front of him. Case closed. I took the tissue he offered and cried… for myself, for my husband, and for our unborn children.

Three months later, I underwent surgery. Difficult days of tears and despair followed. But despite my agony, I had an inner peace. Like a barren tree in winter, seemingly stripped of its very life, I knew that underneath it all, God's hand was at work, doing things that, for now, I could not see. Yet, I believed.

On a sunny day in May, just six weeks after my surgery, I sat scribbling out a grocery list at the kitchen table when the phone rang. A woman I'd never met, whose husband worked with my husband, asked, "Would you be interested in adopting a baby?" I stammered through our brief conversation. I hung up the phone, my heart beating a hundred miles an hour.

"Honey!" I yelled to my husband in the other room. "Guess what? That was Doug's wife. She wanted to know if we'd be interested in adopting a baby! She has to know tomorrow! She thinks the baby is due in July!"

Stan and I had considered adoption earlier, but after filling out a dozen forms we saw little light at the end of the tunnel. The cost proved staggering; the wait, agonizing. And there was always the possibility of the birth mother changing her mind—even after giving birth.

I knew somehow we'd come up with the money, but what bothered me most about adoption was whether or not an adopted child would really feel like my own. I didn't know the answer to this question, but I recalled the countless prayers I'd sent up: "Lord, please give me a child." And I trusted His judgment completely.

Stan and I prayed earnestly that night, and in the morning I placed the call. "Yes," I said. "We'd be very interested in this baby." And so began a season of miracles.

Six weeks later, we were called to the hospital to see our new-born baby daughter.

Nothing could have prepared me for the moment when I saw her for the first time. An indescribable emotion surged in me and I could not stop the tears. My baby.

As I gazed at her, stroked her tiny feet, felt her breath on my face, it felt as if she were an extension of myself. I became her mother the minute I touched her tiny toes. We were miraculously bound together by invisible threads. It did not matter at all that another woman had carried her until now; I would gladly carry her from here.

We named her Anna Marie, after my grandmother, and my husband's aunt. Shortly after her arrival, we dedicated her to God. As my father spoke at the dedication service, he summed it up with this scripture from the first Book of Samuel: "For this child I prayed; and the LORD hath given me my petition which I asked of him" (1 Samuel 1:27).

This child. Those words nearly knocked me over. In that moment, I knew beyond a doubt that God had heard my prayers all along. This child was not a mistake. She was not a second thought. She was the answer to my prayers. God had been waiting for me to be still, so He could work in His mysterious way. I had asked for a child, and it would take a miracle. At last, I held them both in my hands.

~Dayle Allen Shockley

46

Dancing with Rachel

The future destiny of a child is always the work of the mother.
~Napoleon Bonaparte

I slammed down the phone and issued terse orders to my five children standing in a half-circle around me, watching like small scared owls to see what would happen.

"Everybody grab some clothes and your toothbrushes. We're going to Grandma's. Hurry!"

My panic must have resonated with them. They scattered, obeying without question. Only one daughter hesitated.

"Is Dad coming back here?" Fear made her eyes as big as cookies.

"Yes, honey. It's best if we leave for a while. We'll be gone before he gets here, but we have to be quick."

She nodded and scuttled away.

Within fifteen minutes, we were all crammed into the van, including dogs, cats and cockatiels, which could not be left to my mentally ill husband's questionable mercies.

"Go fast, Mom!" yelled my little boy.

I didn't feel safe until we pulled into my mother's driveway. He wouldn't follow us there.

My husband's subtle frightening abuse had steadily worsened over the past few weeks until his full-blown paranoia finally turned against me. We'd been through this before; I always knew when it was time to leave. The waiting was the worst. I wanted to be compassionate and support him, but it was only a matter of time before I became the enemy, or worse, he zeroed in on the children.

Living in constant apprehension of the next dreadful occurrence had produced a screaming emotional strain in all of us. I hadn't slept properly for weeks, for keeping close vigil over the kids. My stomach was so tight and twisted with nerves I could barely eat. I'd always been proud of my strength, both physical and mental, but this was too much. For the first time in my life, I thought maybe there was something I couldn't handle.

Safe in my mother's house, the kids and I settled down a bit over the next few days. But still, I jumped at every strange sound, dashing to the kitchen window to make sure it wasn't him crunching into the driveway. My anxious mind churned with what ifs, plans and alternate plans, questions about the future, and especially numbing guilt over my children's suffering.

One day, as my dazed thoughts burned a deeper rut around the same fruitless territory in my mind, I noticed three-year-old Rachel and couldn't help but smile. Chubby arms flung joyfully outward, she spun around and around, making her favorite blue dress float into a blossom. She stumbled about dizzily in a funny dance pattern of her own invention, and then enthusiastically created another spinning dress blossom.

It was one of those sweet and odd moments when you realize that your child can also teach you. Her carefree abandon was a parable—a teaching story. My daughter could play, rest, eat and generally go about her important toddler business without concern for one reason—she trusted me to take care of everything. It struck me then, that as much as I prayed to God and prated about trusting Him, I still spent my days rotating in cycles of senseless worry and fear, proving that I didn't really trust Him at all. If I did, I'd be dancing on the carpet with Rachel.

I felt as though something that had been zipped up tight inside me suddenly unzipped. The tension dumped out of me, and its release warmed me physically. I nearly collapsed with relief. Instead, I scooped up my beautiful trusting daughter. Arms flung joyfully outward, we spun around and around, laughing, making our dresses float into a blossom. And I felt God laughing with us.

~Veronica Farrington

47

Letting Go

No man has ever prayed without learning something.
~Ralph Waldo Emerson

"I can't do this anymore," I told the social worker. "I'd like you to find another placement for the girls by the end of the month. I'm sorry." As I hung up the phone, I questioned if I had done the right thing. How would another move affect them? Would they feel abandoned? Would the next home be a safe place?

It had been one year since my husband and I and our two children, ages eight and ten, decided to become a foster family.

During the training we had high hopes that we would have a positive impact on the lives of the abused hurt children who would come through our home. We figured my background in education would be an asset. We heard the social workers talk about the challenges we might face, but those thoughts were overshadowed by our excitement. Then the call came.

"Kerrie, we are looking for a home for two sisters, five-year-old Paula and two-year-old Katie," said the social worker. "The older girl has some developmental problems as the result of a brain injury from abuse."

The social worker went on to explain that the girls had a new-born sister and older brother who had already been placed in two different homes. Social services would speed up our final paperwork if we agreed to take the girls. We did.

When they arrived, their big brown eyes were filled with anxiety and uncertainty. My children showed our guests their new room where we'd put a stuffed animal, toothbrush, and book on each bed.

The first few days went well, but it wasn't long before our calm household turned upside down. Because of their bad experiences around men, the girls cowered around my husband. Katie began hitting, biting, crying at bedtime, and screaming in the car. Paula's special needs were more severe than we originally thought. She functioned more at a three-year-old level and had problems with her balance and coordination.

Glimpses of hope broke through after a few weeks when I signed Paula up for a special education kindergarten class. We got both girls eye exams and glasses. Katie's outbursts virtually disappeared.

We watched as Katie began talking more, counting to ten and showing more independence. Paula learned to ride a bike, tie her shoes and zip her coat.

I enjoyed the good moments but questioned our good intentions as we watched our own children struggle with this new challenge. The girls followed my daughter around, pestering her with questions and not allowing her a moment of peace. My son, a quiet mellow boy by nature, had a hard time with the constant chatter and listening to the girls fight. Paula antagonized him until he couldn't take being around her and he hid away in his room.

My two kids tried to be good sports, but they were tired of being dragged around in the car for the girls' weekly visits with their mom or therapists.

I knew Paula and Katie needed love, structure, and understanding, but my stress level was on overdrive. Their need for constant supervision made it difficult for me to cook dinner, clean or care for my family. My relationship with my husband started feeling strained. I felt my life falling apart around me.

My heart broke when my son came to me one day in tears. "I want the girls to go. I don't want to do foster care anymore."

I was torn. I wanted things to go back to the way they were, but the intense internal conflict paralyzed me and I couldn't think straight. Good moms do not give up on their kids. Good moms do not abandon their children. Good moms hang in there.

I prayed, "God, please help me. Show me what I am supposed to do." The response that kept popping into my head was "It is time to let go."

I didn't understand what I was supposed to let go of: the exhaustion, the fear, the anxiety?

I finally confided in a friend and told her I felt like a horrible mother. She told me, "Kerrie, it is not your fault the girls are in foster care. You did not put them there. It is okay to let go. It is okay to tell the social worker you can't do this anymore."

Her words echoed in my head for days. I struggled with what to do. Do I continue to subject my kids to this chaos? Do I put my two children at risk in order to help these other two? The idea of having to choose devastated me and all I wanted to do was run away, but I knew something had to be done.

Exhausted, I called Paula and Katie's caseworker. Social services moved faster than I expected, and within a week they had a new placement for the girls in another city. The day we brought them to their new home we put on happy faces for the girls' sake, gave them scrapbooks of their time with us, hugged them and told them how much we enjoyed having them stay with us... and within minutes they were gone.

Time went on and life settled down. Everyone's stress level dropped, the house was quieter and we got back to our family routine. But for me, a small piece of guilt still hung on.

Because of privacy laws regarding children in foster care, we had no more contact with the girls and could not get any information. People would ask, "Where are Katie and Paula?" and I would have to explain to them that we couldn't do it anymore and the guilt clung tighter.

I thought of them often and although I didn't miss the chaos, I did miss Katie's giggle and Paula's singing. I wondered if they were back with their mom or in another foster home. I prayed over and over, "Please God, let me know if they are safe and happy. Let me know I did the right thing."

Four years passed and I was at the local 4H county fair with a friend and my family. We were visiting the area that housed the chickens and I watched a little girl clean out one of the cages. When she turned around I knew in an instant it was Paula. I quickly scanned the room and sure enough, Katie was there too!

My heart raced. I grabbed my friend's arm. "Look there's Paula and Katie!"

"You should go say hello," she said.

"They won't remember me. It's been too long," I said. "I see Mary, the foster mom who used to take care of their baby sister. She is over there." I pointed.

"Let's go talk to her then," my friend insisted.

"I'm not sure. What if..."

My friend grabbed my arm, and led me over to Mary. "Kerrie used to be Paula and Katie's foster mom," she said.

Mary looked at me, "I thought you looked familiar."

"How are they?" I asked.

She explained that the girls were in two more foster homes before finally ending up with her. The courts eventually terminated their biological mom's rights and all four of the kids were put up for adoption. Mary and her husband already had the youngest of the siblings and decided to adopt all four of the kids, so they could grow up together. Each of the kids got new names along with their new family. They loved living on their big property with the animals. Mary home-schooled the kids so they were all getting the attention they needed.

"They are doing really well," Mary beamed.

"Thank you," I said, holding back tears. "I needed to hear that."

I never did talk to Paula and Katie, but I didn't need to. I got the answer I had been praying for; I knew they were safe and happy. The guilt I had carried for so many years was lifted. My purpose in their life was clear. I was to provide them with a nurturing home while God prepared their forever family.

~Kerrie L. Flanagan

48

Trust in the Lord

"He trusted in the LORD, let Him rescue Him."
~Psalm 22:8

When my husband was involved in a motor vehicle accident and hovered near death, I found a babysitter for our three children, borrowed a car and drove to his side. After spending six months in a body cast, he came home from the hospital and several more months ensued before he was able to return to work on a part-time basis.

With a small monetary award from the insurance company, we purchased a building lot and constructed our own home... the largest investment we'd ever made. After the birth of our fourth child, I started working on weekends and, whenever our means allowed, we added to our investment. During the next five years, we sodded the front lawn, planted shrubs, built a patio, bought furniture and did all the things most proud homeowners do. Then, a sump was installed in the woods just down the street from us. Thereafter, every time it rained, our street flooded; the channeled water had no place to go. That winter, the combination of melting snow, frozen ground and pouring rain brought a wall of water through our house. We managed to get out by jumping off the front stoop into the swirling icy water below. Soaking wet and freezing cold, we made our way to the top of the hill to a neighbor, who drove us to relatives, who took us in.

We pumped water out of the house day and night. We cleaned

Trust in the Lord : Let Go, Let God   169

up the mud, removed the rats, ruined furniture, appliances and other damaged belongings and then moved back in. We took out loans to pay off our ruined car, reinforce the basement and try to meet the staggering electric bills caused by the incessant pumping. However, it was not meant to be. That tremendous wall of water hit us over and over again... five times in thirteen months... and we ended up losing everything we owned. Our attorney, claiming it was God who caused our ruin, drew up papers for us to sign to release us from any further financial obligation provided we surrendered all property to the mortgagee. Less than two weeks later, the sheriff arrived at the door with an eviction notice.

Divine Providence intervened. A co-worker who had just inherited an old home in another part of town offered to rent it to us for one year. She planned to sell the home in which she was living, and then move in and remodel the old one. Gratefully we accepted her offer and moved in. The "act of God" had left us with a seemingly insurmountable amount of debt. I began working full-time and we purchased another car. Every weekend we combed any area within a ten-mile radius looking for an available rental. We soon discovered rentals cost much more than our previous mortgage payment. We were so deeply in debt that we wondered if we would ever find a place to live before our one-year lease ran out.

A friend of ours mentioned a house nearby that had stood vacant for four years, ever since the owner passed away. She even managed to track down the name and address of the man, Mr. Carter, who had inherited it. Dutifully, I wrote to him explaining our plight and asking if he'd be willing to rent the house to us. Months passed with no response from him.

The year passed quickly and my co-worker sold her house. We now had two weeks to find another place to live. I did not want to accept the fact that we had reached a dead end, but if there were another place for us to live I had no idea how to find it. I believed in Divine Providence, that we were only to ask and we would receive, yet all my prayers seemed to go unanswered.

Growing weary of sitting in our temporary home feeling sorry for myself, I gathered the children together and we headed for the car. When they asked where we were going, I replied, "To find a place for us to live."

We pulled out onto the main highway leading out of town. I drove aimlessly for about twenty minutes until I spotted a sign, "Our Lady of the Island Shrine." Abruptly, I turned off the highway and wound my way toward it. I pulled into a side parking lot and announced to the children, "We're going to pray."

Stunned into silence, they scrambled out of the car after me and we headed for a beautiful walking path.

An indescribable feeling of peace wafted through me as we walked that path and prayed together. The rhythm... my voice softly leading... the young voices of the children answering... lulled me into believing there was a safe haven all around us. Finding solace in church was not new to me, but this was the first time I'd felt a Divine presence in a cathedral of nature. The tension left my body as I followed after the children, who were racing to a little chapel. There again, I felt we were surrounded by love.

After leaving the chapel, we proceeded on a path up a steep hill. At the very top, overlooking many outstretched miles of Long Island, stood a tremendous statue of Mary holding Jesus. The reality of soon becoming homeless came back to me and I knelt down before the statue. Pouring my heart out, I prayed, "I've tried and failed. I'm beaten. I'm leaving the problem in Your hands." Somehow I knew that was all I needed to do. I gathered up my children and went home.

As we walked in the door I heard the phone ringing in the kitchen.

"Hello, I'm Mr. Carter. I apologize for not having responded to your letter sooner, but I just returned from my winter home in Florida."

He told me he would love to unload that old house of his mother's. He hadn't before because it was sorely in need of repair. He would sell it to us for a ridiculously low amount or we could rent it with an option to buy. And, if our past misfortunes had jeopardized our credit rating, he would gladly hold the mortgage.

"Let's meet there this weekend," offered Mr. Carter. "You can move in right away."

~Margaret Glignor-Schwarz

49

Christmas Wish

A good man's prayers will from the deepest dungeon climb heavens' height,
and bring a blessing down.
~Joanna Baillie

A quiet peace filled the sanctuary as the last notes of "The Little Drummer Boy" softly faded. Then, in total silence, the congregants carefully carried their small lit candles as they filed outside. On the driveway by the main entrance, they regrouped at midnight and sang "Silent Night." My wife Karen, her parents, brother and his girlfriend added their voices to the chorus.

I didn't.

In truth, I had no desire to be there. If the choice had been mine to make we would have attended the much earlier children's Christmas Eve service, but I'd been overruled in favor of the later, more adult one.

My gaze rose upward toward the steeple and beyond. I heard the words of the hymn, "Glories stream from heavens above…." As the faithful sang, my thoughts turned to questions I'd been asking of late: When was God going to recognize that enough was enough? And when would He finally give in and allow us to have children?

Back home, after changing into more comfy attire, we sat in front of the rekindled warmth of our family room fireplace. While savoring holiday wine, we shared memories of Christmases past. For my turn, I recalled how, as a child, I loved attending the Christmas Eve children's services with my family. My memories included the noisy commotion sparked by exciting anticipation of Santa coming. Our minister gathered all the children around him on the floor in the front of the sanctuary where he told the story of the birth of Christ. When he finished, he led us—the children and the rest of the congregation—in singing "Happy Birthday" in honor of the baby Jesus. I ended my recollections without revealing how much I missed those family church services. And I never mentioned how I longed to be attending such a service, surrounded by all of the noisy commotion, while Karen tenderly cradled a sleeping child of our own.

After wishing each other a "Merry Christmas" and saying our goodnights, we all turned in. As I lay in bed it occurred to me that in a home so filled with the love of six adults, for me there remained a profound emptiness. We were childless. Oh, how wonderful it would be if we had a little one to share the magic of the season and our lives.

Unable to sleep, I tiptoed back to our family room and watched the last of the fire's embers slowly surrender. Pouring another glass of wine and slipping into my winter coat and boots, I stepped outside and sat atop the cold brick of the front steps. In spite of the crisp winter temperatures, it was a gorgeous night. Stars twinkled in the holiday skies as the night air carried the fleeting scent of my dying wood fire. In spite of the beauty of this early Christmas morning, my thoughts returned to our problem.

We'd wanted children and had been trying for some time, without success, to conceive. After consultations and examinations, I prayed that should one of us be found medically culpable for our prolonged failure, that it be me. I couldn't accept Karen having to live with the burden of knowing she was the reason parenthood escaped us.

I always believed prayers are answered, just not always in the way we ask. This time, however, the power of one man's appeal sparked divine intervention. When the results were in, I was to blame. Our prospects for conceiving were bleak.

As I sat on the step in the coolness of early morning, looking up toward the heavens, I offered another prayer, perhaps more of a plea. "If it pleases You Lord, grant us a pardon from our non-conception purgatory and allow us the privilege of conceiving a child. This Christmas wish is the only gift I'll ever ask for, not for me, but for Karen. I pray for the day when a child of our making will call her 'Mommy.'"

With my request made, the wine finished and the chill permeating my coat-covered pajamas, I went back inside to bed.

Two years later, we attended the Christmas Eve children's service at our church and it was just as I'd remembered from my childhood… noisy with contagious excitement. Despite the commotion and all the joyous music, our little boy slept through the entire service, contently resting in his mommy's arms.

~Stephen Rusiniak

50

The Miracle by the Sea

Prayer is the principle means of opening oneself to the power and love of God that is already there, in the depths of reality.
~James A. Pike

The umbilical cord was wrapped around my neck so tightly it took twenty-five minutes for me to take my first breath. My brain was deprived of oxygen, and by age two I was diagnosed with cerebral palsy.

CP affects people in many different ways. In my case, brain signals to my nerves and muscles are continually short-circuited. My gait lacks coordination and a regular stride; my left arm jets out to help steady me. My arms make large rolling motions in the basic direction I want them to go. My speech sounds like someone pinching his tongue while trying to talk.

Throughout my life, I have tried not to allow my handicap to define who I am. Though I pressed forward, I found it very difficult to love the person God created me to be.

One New Year's Eve, I heard Josh McDowell speak at a Campus Crusade for Christ conference. Although he addressed 25,000 college students, it felt like his words were specifically challenging me. "If you are wondering where you are going, pray and step out in faith. Don't worry! If you trust the Holy Spirit to guide you, He will lead you to the doors He opens for you."

It seemed I always needed writing on the wall before moving in any direction at all. Josh's words penetrated my being. I now had a desire awakened in me to explore my walk with Christ in a new way, to find the doors He was opening to me. But how?

About seven months later, I was cleaning out my briefcase when I noticed a brochure titled "Josh McDowell's Evidence Tour." It was given to me by a friend months before. I had forgotten all about it, but now I felt drawn to go and see him again. This would be an opportunity to personally meet the man who had such an impact on my life. It was totally uncharacteristic for me to step out this far, but I signed up, not knowing anyone else on the tour.

On Sunday, the sixth day into our trip, we all boarded a boat on the Sea of Galilee and headed to the north shore to Capernaum. I knew this is where Jesus called his disciples and where he performed the majority of his miracles. It was a tranquil day on the water, which made it difficult to relate to the disciples' fear when Jesus calmed the storm and waves.

When our vessel approached the shore, the guide pointed out the very house where the paralytic's friends dismantled the roof to lower him down to be healed by Jesus.

Our guide recounted the various miracles Jesus performed in this place. As the warm sun shone down on the water, an incredible peace and wonderment filled me. I tried to imagine Jesus walking these shores and healing those in need. The closer to shore we came, the more I sensed God wanted to speak to me.

I waited and listened. "Lord," I asked, "are you going to heal me and give me a strong voice? Then I can tell everyone what You did for me in Israel!"

As I got off the boat, I felt the Lord telling me to take time to pray and to seek Him. I was sure He was going to heal me while in Israel. All I had to do was ask.

After the Sunday morning service and Josh's message, he and I joined hands in prayer as we sat at the foot of the cross in an open-air chapel on the shore of the Sea of Galilee. I prayed, "Lord, this is the place where You called some of Your disciples to follow You. I want to follow You too. Heal me of this handicap so that I may serve You better."

Josh added, "Please Jesus, heal your servant Larry."

At that moment, I felt God's presence in and around me and through me like never before. A voice that seemed almost audible filled my being and penetrated my spirit. "Larry, I really love you just the way you are."

"Lord, I'd do more for You if I were healed from CP."

I heard what seemed to be a no, but I wasn't sure.

"Lord," I asked, "can You use my life more effectively for Your kingdom just the way I am?"

The answer came in the still small voice.

That's when the miracle happened, but not the one I expected. The realization struck me that my physical disability was my weakness, and the Lord would use it to His glory. The Lord poured His love into me. I nearly wept. "I get it Lord! For the first time in my life, I love myself despite my disability!"

I thought of the scripture passage 2 Corinthians 12:8-10 where Paul wrote: "Three times I pleaded with the Lord to take it away from me. But he said to me, 'My grace is sufficient for you, for my power is made perfect in weakness.... For when I am weak, then I am strong.'"

I knew then God was using my weaknesses so I could be strong.

The next day, there on the bank of the River Jordan, I put on a long white robe. Two men assisted me down a ramp leading into the river. The waist-deep water was colder than I expected, but the cold was nothing compared to the anticipation waiting for me in there. Josh gently held my shoulders. "I baptize you in the name of the Father, the Son and the Holy Spirit." Then he tipped me back into the River Jordan, the very place where John the Baptist baptized Jesus.

What happened next, I don't quite know how to explain, but my crippled body felt strengthened. It was not my strength, but the strength of my Lord. Through this baptismal water, I gained confidence in Christ.

We spent the last evening in Jerusalem, where Josh gave a talk called "Who Am I?"

"Each person is made in the image of God," Josh began. "Each person is unique. If I act like someone else, who will act like me? God is bigger than our handicaps or weaknesses. He will use our handicaps for His glory."

Then it hit me! God wanted to use me in ministry! I sensed the Lord saying to me, "I want your voice to be a fisher of men for Me." Triumphant, I was ready to begin my journey with the Lord to groom me for His work.

In the last twenty years, God has opened doors for me to speak that I never dreamed possible. He sent me, in this twisted body, to share the gospel, to inspire and bring hope to so many that need encouragement.

I have been sent by the Lord to minister to professional sports teams such as the Detroit Tigers, the Detroit Lions, and the Boston Red Sox. I've spoken at churches, youth rallies, prayer breakfasts, and to youth groups all over the country. I address kids of all ages, from preschool through college. The Fellowship of Christian Athletes makes sure I come back every year. I minister to Youth for Christ, Campus Crusade, and to youth camps both Christian and non-Christian across the nation.

In my speaking ministry, I see the lives of people change. Many reach out in faith to hold Christ and discover what doors God has opened for them... just as He did for me.

~Larry Patton

Chapter 6

Answered Prayers

Ask and You Shall Receive

If any of you lacks wisdom, let him ask of God who gives to all liberally and without reproach, and it will be given to him.

~James 1:5

51

Kisses on the Cheek

*"Whoever is wise will observe these things,
and they will understand the lovingkindness of the LORD."*
~Psalm 107:43

A t 3:30 p.m. the murky sky, draped in soot, shrouded the earth with a premature eerie darkness, blacking out the sun. In the last two days more than 2,500 homes had been decimated by five separate massive wildfires that raged through San Diego County, leveling everything in their flaming paths.

Authorities had finally given us permission to return to our neighborhoods to survey our colossal losses. Sitting in a crowded restaurant, waiting for my good friend Paul, I stared blankly at the food, oblivious to the noise. My world had gone stone cold silent. Salty tears mixed with my tea. I couldn't bring myself to eat. Gut-wrenching shock had robbed my appetite for life. Every inch of me felt numb.

Sliding into the booth beside me, Paul saw my untouched meal. He wrapped a compassionate arm around my shoulder and prayed, "Father please give Sandi kisses on the cheek every day so she will know You still love her."

We left the restaurant and slipped into the long line of cars filing into the charred neighborhood like a funeral procession, headlights piercing the foggy soot, revealing what looked like a war zone.

Massive devastation lay before us: mountains of rubble, twisted steel, chimney bricks, still simmering, flung across sidewalks. Row after row of affluent homes now lay in heaping piles of ashes.

I stumbled numbly out of the car and edged my way toward the wreckage that represented my elegant home and seventeen-year-old prosperous business. While I stood staring, Paul began to dig to see if he could salvage anything from my past.

Staggering blindly through the debris, I opened my dryer. An expensive Egyptian cotton towel, now black, disintegrated in my hands. Ashen powder sifted through my fingers as I opened the files where I had stored the 900 pieces of art I had created over a lifetime. I'd worked so hard to make it to this neighborhood. Now my treasured possessions lay entombed in heaps of ashes.

Just then, Paul cried out. "Sandi, come here!"

Brushing the charcoal off a photo of my father that he had pried from a twisted steel cabinet, Paul handed me my first kiss on the cheek. Neither the frame nor the glass was broken. My dad's photo was not singed—it was completely intact.

Daddy, the man who taught me to believe in God, looked back at me—memories sprang to mind. My parents were missionaries trained by Wycliffe, an organization that made Bibles accessible to all nations. I had watched my father's faith as he survived the loss of our home when African soldiers torched our entire Congolese village and slaughtered those who had not escaped. A few days before, our unsuspecting family had left our compound to vacation with my aunt and uncle who were missionaries in Kenya. We escaped with just our clothes and a few photos. The eighteen-month journey back to the United States took my parents through many difficult trials but their faith never faltered.

As I gazed at my deceased father's picture, it spoke to me of his courage and strength. Daddy had always wanted his four daughters to become women of substance. Seeing my father reminded me of who I was.

I felt God's warm breath and heard His soft whisper as he planted another kiss on my cheek. It was as if I heard my father's voice. "Sandi, you *are* a woman of substance. What you need was planted in you long ago. It is your heritage to survive and thrive like we did when you were a child. Your riches are within."

As I stood reflecting on my father's photo Paul called out again, "Sandi look at this!"

It was my mom's wedding Bible from 1926, the one my father likely used to translate scriptures into African languages.

Paul and I took the few recovered items and headed back to the restaurant. As we waited for our food, he opened my mother's Bible to comfort me with scripture. Out fell a stack of papers that contained writing my mom had penned forty years before, the week after she and my dad lost their home in Africa. She wrote encouraging words about how she coped with the devastation that wiped away all her worldly possessions.

I was blown away! God had seen to it that I had both my mother and father on the day I needed them the most.

That kiss on my cheek etched a new habit in my brain. "In everything give thanks."

From that day on I began to write down at least ten kisses on the cheek each day, even if the only ten things I could write about were my ten toes. Pages and pages of blessings followed. I began to notice that God had always been there. I just hadn't bothered to look for His favor before. I had seldom praised Him or said, "Thank You."

Like us, God loves to be praised. In the Bible, God asks me to have an attitude of gratitude. "Whoever is wise will observe these things, and they will understand the lovingkindness of the Lord." (Psalm 107:43)

Now I focus on the good in my life and it brings me endless joy and contentment. I don't need to wait for the trial to pass to experience happiness. Joy is always available for the taking.

Whereas I used to complain quite a bit, now I find myself breaking out in smiles at the amazing things God does for me. He continually surprises me with things that no one else would even know I needed.

Today I wrote down my 8,342nd kiss on the cheek.

God's loving kindness is new every morning.

Now I notice.

~Sandra McFall Angelo

Reprinted by permission of Dan Reynolds /
Cartoonresource.com © 2010.

52

Snow Angels

It could not happen that any man or woman could pray for a single moment without some good result.

~Alexis Carrel

Record snowfalls had closed the mile-long road to the gravel pit weeks ago. There wasn't much of a call for dirt of any kind in February in Minnesota. During this month of sub-zero temperatures and unpredictable snowfalls, the only business our family's excavation company conducted was snow plowing and preparing bids for spring road projects.

My father's weathered hands unrolled the engineering blueprints across the kitchen table. His favorite and often quoted Bible verse that I cross-stitched for him one Christmas hung on the kitchen wall. *For which of you, desiring to build a tower, does not first sit down and count the cost… (Luke 14:28).*

He placed his coffee cup on one corner and a stapler on the other to hold the plans in place. My brother and he studied them, calculating how much material would be needed and how much Dad could charge to make it profitable and still be the lowest bidder. Every spring he worried whether there would be enough work to keep the company going another year. Every fall he wondered if the weather would hold off long enough for him to complete the projects he'd been awarded.

"We'll need at least 3,000 yards of sand to complete this section of the job," my father said as he calculated each line item of the bid. "Do you think we have that much at the pit?"

"I couldn't say for sure," my brother said, looking up from the blueprints. "I haven't been out there recently. Do you want to check it out now?"

It was 3:00 p.m. and would be dark in an hour. Looking out the window, they saw that the forecasted blizzard had arrived. Roads already in poor driving condition would only get worse.

"It can wait until the storm's over," my father said.

They continued to make calculations for the project, occasionally glancing out the window to watch the storm progress. My father began tapping his pencil on the table. "Let's see if we can get to the pit tonight. The pickup plow should be able to handle it."

My brother eagerly agreed. They suited up in their insulated coveralls, winter work jackets, boots and fur-lined hats and headed for the door, grabbing gloves on their way. Like boys with big toys, they enjoyed the challenge of conquering the snowstorm, which had already dropped four inches on our driveway.

The five-mile stretch of highway between home and the pit road was a white blanket of snow. The center line wouldn't appear until the next swipe of a county plow.

As my father and brother pulled into the mile-long pit road, they saw a faint set of tracks going in and none coming out. "Now who in their right mind would be out on a night like this?" my father asked.

"At the rate the snow's falling, whoever is at the end of this road stands a slim chance of getting out on his own," my brother agreed. "Do you think someone's using the cab windows of the loader for target practice again?"

"So far they've reserved their destruction for Saturday nights," said my father, "but anyone foolish enough to point a gun at a diesel-fueled machine is capable of other crazy behavior."

They drove slowly through the deep snow, my father's face growing beet red with anger. "This seems like an unlikely night for vandalism, but if we catch the hoodlums responsible for any damage, I'll give them a personal escort to the county jail!"

As they descended the hill, their headlights beamed on the loader, crowned with a five-inch cap of snow. Through the flurry of flakes, they saw the windows still intact. When they reached the floor of the pit, a blue VW bus came into view.

My father slammed on the brakes and jumped out of the truck, not bothering to close the door. His weathered work boots hit the ground and he stomped over to the rusted out van in three long strides.

A red-bearded man in his thirties rolled down his window. "I sure am glad you came," he said. "I need a tow." He looked relieved until he saw the storm brewing in my father's eyes.

"What are you doing here in the first place?" my father shouted. "Can't you read the 'Private Property' signs?"

"I came down here to meditate," the stranger said shakily, as flakes congregated on his beard. "When I tried to leave, I got stuck." Then he introduced himself. "I'm Ed Smith, the pastor at St. John's."

Dad calmed down, but he wasn't about to let him off too easily. He said sternly, "It looks to me that instead of meditating, you should have been praying for someone to get you out of here."

"I was. That's when you came."

~Tracy Gulliver

53

Lessons from My Son

Remembrances last longer than present realities.
~Jean Paul Richter

"Stop! Mom! There's a car beside us!" I was about to change lanes on a busy highway when my son called out a warning. I looked over my left shoulder and sure enough, in my blind spot, a vehicle loomed.

Jason had an innate understanding of humans and a sense of timing to deliver the right words at just the right time. His sisters were seven and twelve years old when he arrived on the scene and I thought I was an old hand at child rearing. But Jason came with a guarantee, to teach each of us something new, or at the very least to consider new ways to look at life.

One afternoon he was bouncing his soccer ball off the outside of the house. The neighbor had already mentioned it was irritating her. Despite my earlier request to stop, he was back at it again; maybe he wanted to see how far he could push. Quite irritated with him, I shouted, "Jason, stop with the ball already!"

He grinned at me, which further fueled my anger and I shouted again. Then my skinny, 6' 2" muscular athlete walked over and picked me up! Exasperated, I tried to continue my lecture but the annoyance was soon overridden by a rush of warmth and his winning smile. My frustration evaporated as he teasingly held me. I could feel his love for me. At that moment I saw things through his eyes. I laughed, appreciating his goofy sense of humor.

Another day he went to school in a yellow sweatshirt I'd been given. It bore the emblem of a rival school's football team.

"Surely you didn't wear that to school today, did you?"

"Yes I did."

"Oh my goodness. What happened?"

"Well," he responded calmly, "some kids threw me up against the lockers and called me names."

"Oh Jason, I guess you won't be doing that again!"

"Yes I will," he promised. "Why not, Mom? It builds character!"

The day Jason was to compete in a track and field competition he hugged me just before he left. It was our last hug. Just an hour later, he lost control of his car and within minutes he was dead.

After losing him, trying to find balance, meaning and comfort was a slow, arduous and complex process. Five years passed.

Out of the blue one day, the pain of missing him was suddenly so sharp I broke down sobbing. Between huge gulps I begged, "God give me a dream where I can once more see my beautiful son." I pleaded. "It's so simple for you God. Please, please give me this dream. I miss him so much. All I ask for is just one hug in a dream." I cried and begged as if my life depended upon this one thing.

That night I dreamed of Jason when he was about seven years old. I was chastising him for something he had done. "Don't do that. Do you want to get killed?"

He looked at me, then spoke the most compelling words he ever uttered: "But Mom, death isn't forever."

I awoke, upset. I hadn't received my hug. As I became more fully awake, it dawned on me I'd been given something far better. Jason's words filled me with hope and reassurance for tomorrow. Even after death, this son of mine gave me another lesson, better than a hug—until we embrace again in heaven.

~Ellie Braun-Haley

54

Yes, We Have Room for This Baby

Prayer enlarges the heart until it is capable of containing God's gift of himself.
~Mother Teresa

While I was doing cradle care for a local adoption agency I couldn't predict when the phone would ring and I'd hear the words, "Can I bring you a newborn baby in three hours?"

I was fortunate that a good friend and I shared the duties whenever we had a baby to cuddle and love. Our main job was to hold the baby all the time except when we were in the bathroom, cooking or driving so the baby would not feel abandoned.

One August day, the agency called asking if they could bring me a baby in a few hours. I said, "Yes." Susan replied that I needed to know the baby had Down syndrome. I repeated, "Yes" and started washing the clothes, blankets and toys I kept for infants that found their way into my arms. My friend Monica was at the beginning of her annual two-week vacation to Minnesota, so I would have the baby full-time until she came back.

When Susan pulled into the driveway I went to meet her. I took the baby, Gabriel, out of the car seat and hugged him close. The incredible smell of being so fresh from God still surrounded him and I drank it in. He was so peaceful as he lay sleeping in my arms.

Susan began to put Gabriel's picture and status on local and nationwide adoption websites. She also called abbeys, monasteries, churches, and her friends to pray for this little one to find his family. As time went by, there were inquiries about Gabriel but nothing seemed to work out. Before we knew it Halloween and Thanksgiving had come and gone and the Christmas season was upon us.

Monica and I developed a regular system of splitting our time with Gabriel. One Saturday afternoon as I sat in Monica's kitchen chatting, her phone rang. It was Susan. She asked Monica if Gabriel was going to church the next day. Monica responded, "Yes, we take him everywhere we go and let people know he is looking for his family."

"Good," said Susan, "I just had an incredible vision of Jesus' mother Mary. She said Gabriel's family would find him tomorrow at church."

"Well, should we do a pulpit announcement?" asked Monica.

"No, that's not the way it is going to work. Besides you've already done that a couple of times," said Susan.

"Okay, I'll trust your word and be on the lookout for someone who seems interested in him," said Monica.

Monica hung up and shared the conversation with me. We both looked at each other in wonderment, then at Gabriel who was almost four months old by then. He continued to be a sweet baby, responding with laughter and vocalizations to anyone who played with him.

The first Sunday of Advent, Monica dressed him in a Christmas outfit. The ivory velvet one-piece suit had the words Peace On Earth over a picture of forest animals around a Christmas tree. Monica showed Gabriel off to everyone she met. After church, during faith formation classes for youngsters, there was a speaker for the adults. Monica asked the adult faith formation minister if she could share Gabriel's story prior to the talk.

Somewhere else in town that morning was a young family that had moved from Rochester, New York. Their little boy, Dane, was signed up for classes at our church. They were uncertain about his attendance that day until they noticed it was his turn to provide snacks. Dane and his mother Amy hurried to get ready, stopped by the store for snacks, and made it to church in time for his class. Amy thought about getting coffee and a bagel nearby while he was in class, until she noticed a sign for the topic of the adult session. Art and spirituality, right up Amy's path.

During the session, Amy kept looking back at Gabriel. The speaker announced a hands-on project to make her point—everyone was to create a card. Amy decided to make hers for Gabriel. She designed one with a gold foil star with a comet tail and wrote on it: "There is a place for you, Gabriel, even if you are a little different and don't exactly fit in the same mold as other babies."

Amy noticed that her card didn't fit into the envelope provided. "How appropriate," she thought.

She took the card to Monica, instructing her to give it to whoever ended up adopting Gabriel.

"Do you want to hold him?" Monica asked.

As Amy held Gabriel and talked to Monica and her husband John, she told them her family were newcomers looking for a church and friends. Amy had an instant connection with Monica and John and asked for their phone number.

When she returned home she talked to her husband Ken about Gabriel. The more she talked, the more both of them wanted to see him. They called Monica and asked if they could come over in the afternoon.

Monica called me and told me about the morning's events. She asked me to come over that afternoon too.

During the three-hour visit, Amy and Ken held Gabriel, fed him, changed him, rocked him to sleep and still held him. They kept looking back and forth at each other in apparent surprise.

During the next week, Amy called the adoption agency several times to get more information on Gabriel and the adoption process. She asked me to bring him over to her house one afternoon so her two children and her mother could see him. She was eager to see their reactions. After a pleasant visit their younger child said, "I wish he was my baby brother."

The adoption process began! The adoption agency worked hard

to expedite the paperwork and requirements. The last hurdle was cleared on December 23rd.

The transfer from the cradle care team to his family was to take place on Christmas Eve.

Gabriel wore his Peace On Earth outfit again, with angel wings and a halo that Susan had added. Monica, John, their children and I carried him from our bedroom to the living room where Amy, Ken, their children and grandmother anxiously sat. Gabriel babbled, smiled and slept during the beautiful ceremony Susan conducted. Everyone, happy and excited, shed a few tears.

As Amy cradled him in her arms, I heard earthly and heavenly voices say, "There is room at the inn for Gabriel, and I am well pleased."

~Kerrie Anderson

Granny,
Does God Answer Prayers?

Prayer should be the key of the day and the lock of the night.
~Thomas Fuller

My six-year-old grandson Clem had spent almost every Saturday night with his Pappy and me since before he was a year old. Clem's mommy and daddy split up when he was four and it devastated this little boy.

I taught Clem to pray and we always got on our knees together before we went to bed.

One night, after we had said our prayers and he was tucked in, he asked, "Granny, does God answer prayers?"

"Honey, God hears every prayer you say. Maybe He doesn't answer them as quickly as you would like, and He might not answer them the way you want, but indeed He does answer your prayers."

Clem turned his back to me and in a sweet little voice said, "God, put my mommy and daddy back together, please." Then he turned to me. "Granny, I said please."

"I know you did baby," I soothed.

The very next day Clem's mommy and daddy announced they were getting back together.

Clem exclaimed, "Last night I prayed to God and asked Him to put you back together! God does answer prayers!" He added, "I said please."

They have been together ever since.

~Cledith Lehman

Get Me to the Bridge

It's not that we pray and God answers; our prayer is already God answering.
~Richard Rohr

"I love you, Mom," my husband Tad said, tenderly holding her hand. "What can I do for you?"

"Just get me to the bridge... I can make my way to eternity from there," my mother-in-law whispered. "It's time to call hospice."

The combined effects of Parkinson's and a stroke had caused a significant decline in Bernadine's health, and communication was nearly impossible. It was difficult for her to speak and even harder for us to understand what she was trying to say. Yet Mom was able to communicate a few things very clearly in her final days.

When asked if she wanted to go to the hospital she clearly said, "No." The response was the same when asked if she wanted an IV or a feeding tube. Bernadine had known this time was coming and was ready.

She'd been raised in a family with a strong Catholic faith. They prayed the rosary daily during Lent each year, reciting a Hail Mary on each of the fifty beads. Her mother even crafted a rosary by hand every day for nearly sixty years. No wonder Mary, the mother of Jesus, held a very special place in Bernadine's heart.

Now at age sixty-seven she lay frail, unable to speak. I was struggling to understand what she was trying to tell me when she made the Sign of the Cross and mouthed, "Body of Christ."

"Bernadine," I said as I leaned closer, stroking her cheek, "do you want Holy Communion?"

She nodded and smiled weakly. Tad called our church and a Eucharistic minister brought her Communion.

The next day, Bernadine continued to make the Sign of the Cross over and over again, with a pleading expression in her eyes. At a loss to understand, another family member took her rosary from a drawer and laid it in her hand. Immediately, a peaceful calm blanketed her.

Over the next two days that peacefulness transformed the entire room as hospice chaplains joined the family in prayer.

I brought the rosary Bernadine's mother had made for me many years before and, while reflecting on the suffering and death of Christ, I sat at her side, meditating deeply as caregivers, grandchildren, and others stopped to say their final goodbyes.

Together we surrounded her, whispered in her ear, kissed her forehead and prayed softly as she rested calmly. Then, as we recited the final Hail Mary on the last bead, meditating on the crucifixion of Christ, an indescribable spiritual feeling suddenly permeated the room. We glanced at one another, obviously all experiencing the presence as we continued to pray in unison the last line of the prayer, "… holy Mary, mother of God, pray for us sinners now and at the hour of our death…."

At that moment… that hour… Bernadine simply exhaled and began her journey over the bridge to her eternal home.

~Jona Johnson

Grandpa's Little Man

*"Do You hear what these are saying?" And Jesus said to them,
"Yes. Have you never read,
'Out of the mouths of babes and nursing infants you have perfected praise'?"*
~Matthew 21:16-17

On the day my son Matthew was born, my husband handed him over to my father to meet his first grandchild. Dad looked at his grandson, smiled, kissed his forehead and said, "Hello little man, you're gonna be my hockey player."

When my son turned two, he got his first set of mini hockey sticks and a ball. He forced Grandpa to play hockey for hours. Again, Grandpa would kiss his head, smile and exclaim, "Hey little man, you're gonna be my hockey player."

When my son turned three, he went to his first Ontario Hockey League game with Grandpa and his uncle. Whenever someone talked to Matthew, Grandpa smiled, tussled his hair and said, "This little man, he is my hockey player."

One day Matthew asked, "Grandpa, what do I do when I'm on the ice and don't know which way to go?"

Grandpa smiled. "Don't worry little man, Grandpa will always be in the stands to help you out of a jam."

My son smiled sweetly and said, "Okay Grandpa, thanks."

Sadly, six months before Matthew could play his first real hockey game, Grandpa passed away. During the funeral, my son turned to my husband and asked with tears in his eyes, "Who will help me now when I don't know what to do on the ice?"

My husband hugged him and whispered in his ear, "Don't worry, Grandpa will always be watching from heaven, and you'll know what to do because he will always be there watching you and making sure you are okay."

Matthew looked at his father in amazement. "Really?"

"Really."

As he played his way through his first and second years of hockey, once in a while he'd smile and say, "Grandpa loved the way I scored two goals today," or, "Do you think Grandpa liked my assist today?"

We always smiled and told him, "Grandpa loved it."

When he turned seven, he played at the top level for his age group and even got to travel to his first away tournament. His team slugged it out to the finals.

What a game! Tied at the end of the third period, it went into overtime. They were down to the shoot out. Five players from each team were chosen and Matthew was shooter five for his team.

We watch the first four players from each team take a shot. After four each, it was still tied. It was up to our son now. If he scored, we won.

As my husband and I felt like we were going to throw up from anxiety, our son started to skate to the goalie. Faster, faster he approached the net, went to the right, wound up and at the last second, faked a shot, deked left, and backhanded it into the net. We won the game!

His team poured off the bench to the sound of the screaming parents in the stands. Matthew grabbed the puck, touched it to his heart and raised it up to the heaven. His teammates jumped on him, celebrating, but he didn't let go of the puck.

On the ride back home, trophy sitting beside him in the van, Matthew quietly asked, "Can we go visit Grandpa's grave for a minute? I need to tell him something."

We agreed, understanding that he would want to tell Grandpa about his game-winning goal.

We walked up to the headstone, he bowed his head. "I heard what you said Grandpa and you were right, he would have stopped that shot. I'm glad I heard you tell me go left, little man, go left."

He placed the puck on the grave. "Thanks for the assist, Grandpa."

Years have passed and Grandpa's little man is soon to have his own child. In the nursery, proudly displayed on the future "trophy" shelf is that tournament trophy. Next to it stands a framed picture of Grandpa and his little man. "My hockey player."

~Tracy Cavlovic

58

Keep Your Head High

The feeling remains that God is on the journey, too.
~Teresa of Avila

I stood at the jaws of the ICU ward, watching its huge doors gape open, then close, swallowing blue scrubs draped with stethoscopes. I felt like I'd surrendered to a force that would swallow me too.

After three years battling throat cancer, my husband lay in the ICU attached to a ventilator. The years of radiation eroded anything that resembled throat anatomy. His doctors determined a tracheotomy was Paul's last chance. The hole in his neck and the plastic tube down his "windpipe" were the only path for life-sustaining oxygen to make its way to his lungs. The ventilator kept a constant tempo, retraining his body how to breathe properly.

"God," I finally prayed, "What do I do? How am I going to help Paul through this?"

Dazed, I found my way to the elevator and the familiar ride to the hospital cafeteria. With a slight jerk, the elevator stopped. The doors slid open and one man caught my attention. Around his neck, and barley noticeable, a thin white strap peeked above his ribbed shirt collar. As he faced my direction I recognized, secured just below his Adam's apple, a stoma, the plastic opening to his trachea.

"Excuse me." I hesitated briefly before I walked up to him. Not meaning to be rude, I blurted, "Did you have a tracheotomy?"

"Why, yes, I did!" I expected a hoarse and garbled reply. But his voice was soft, and full, and beautiful!

Tears threatened my self-control. "You, sir, are an angel sent from God."

"No, my name is simply Henry." There among the crowds that came and went, Henry told me his story. Then I told him of my proud husband, upstairs, struggling with this recent setback in his illness.

"What is his name?" Henry asked.

My throat tightened as a sob erupted from my heart. I tried to speak. "Paul," I barely said.

"I will be praying for him," Henry promised. "God bless you both." Then he said the words that I knew God had for me. "Tell Paul to keep his head high!"

Henry lifted his chin, wearing his stoma like a badge, turned, and walked away.

I hurried back to the elevator. Thank you, God! I knew, now, what to do.

My husband and I were on this journey together. We would not look back nor look down. We would move forward, heads high!

~Kennette Kangiser Osborn

59

Living Water

And whatever things you ask in prayer believing, you will receive.
~Matthew 21:22

The summer of 2003, I was a twenty-year-old college student working as a counselor at a camp for the deaf in the blue mountains of Jamaica. Though most people picture the island as a tropical paradise, it's a third world country with one of the highest crime rates in the world. The poverty level is shockingly high, despite the wealth of the tourists and the opulence of their lodging. Disease is a big problem because of pollution.

Though I didn't speak sign language fluently, I had a good enough grasp of the language to hold my own in a conversation. Only a few of the staff could hear and the rest, plus the children, were all deaf.

We spent our days playing games and studying the Bible, laughing and singing songs. Every child, whether deaf or hearing, loved to have fun. Our days were filled with laughter.

On one of our last days there, the camp activity included hiking in the bush. All of us Americans were excited because we loved to hike. So we laced up our boots and set out following thirty deaf children and a Jamaican guide up the mountain.

About fifteen minutes into the hike, we realized our first major communication error. "Hiking in the bush" did not necessarily mean there would be shade. After the initial few steps, we spent the rest of the way under the blistering Caribbean sun. None of us had worn sunscreen and as sweat poured from our bodies, our skin began to blister.

We'd been told to plan on a short forty-five minute hike. For this reason, most of the children carried soft drinks with them and I had a small water bottle half-filled with purified water. Two hours later we reached the top of the mountain.

By this time our drinks were gone. Those of us with lighter skin were already sunburned. One girl, who had given her shoes to a barefoot child, walked without any. This simple act of compassion left her limping on the rocky paths.

The man leading the hike decided to try a different path down the mountain in hopes we'd find a water source. This too was a mistake. We passed several homesteads with bulls tied to stakes. The children, terrified, ran away as the beasts strained against their ropes, scaring the rest of us too.

Finally, we reached a road, relieved, thinking it meant we were close to our destination. But roads presented another danger: vehicles. Jamaicans drive without regard to speed limits or traffic laws. On the twisting mountain roads, we couldn't see cars and trucks approaching and the children couldn't hear them coming. We had many close calls as we herded the children to the side, grabbing them from harm's way.

Out of breath and dazed by the sun, we had reached the stage of dehydration where our skin stopped sweating, as an act of preservation. We wouldn't last long before someone passed out. My hands shook and my heart raced from fear.

I called out loud, "God, please lead us to water."

About ten minutes later, over three hours into our hike, we turned a corner and saw a small village ahead. Relief flooded me. "Thank you, Jesus!" We raced into the only shop open in the entire area. Our hearts sank. It was a bar.

Our leader explained our situation and asked the bartender if he had any water. He shook his head.

"You don't have any water?" our leader tried one more time.

The bartender shrugged. "Just what is from the tap."

Our Jamaican leader and the children would have no problem drinking tap water, but we four Americans would get violently ill. I recalled how the year before a friend had mistakenly swallowed some water and spent the rest of his time on the island in the bathroom, barely able to move.

But at this point, we had no choice. We knew drinking the water would make us very sick, but with at least an hour left to hike, dehydration would be even more life threatening.

My friends and I nodded our consent, and accepted the ice cold unfiltered water. Solemnly, we looked in each other's eyes.

"What are we doing?" one girl asked in desperation.

"We really don't have a choice," I said, and then added, "Let's pray over the water."

We all agreed. So we pleaded, "Lord, please help us not to get sick. We have to drink this water. Please, protect us."

With a final, "Amen," we all began to drink. The ice cold liquid was so refreshing. When it was gone, we knew we'd be able to continue our trek. We thanked the bartender and followed the children down the road.

We never did get sick from that water. That day, I learned that God isn't bound by the laws of this world. He restores us with His purest of living waters.

~Kristen Torres-Toro

Glove Lost, Purpose Found

Success has nothing to do with what you gain in life or accomplish for yourself. It's what you do for others.

~Danny Thomas

The automatic door opened and the wintry weather carried a host of shoppers into the grocery store in its icy blast. Most hesitated a moment at the entrance, removing hats, stashing gloves in pockets, and unzipping coats before grabbing their shopping lists and heading down the aisles. The situation then reversed itself once they passed through the checkout lanes and donned their winter garb and prepared to head out into the cold once more.

The process seemed to take longer than usual for one elderly female shopper who came through my line that winter's day. Her order processed. Then I was surprised to see her lingering in my lane, fumbling in her pockets and looking about with a worried look on her face. Eventually she asked, "Have you seen my missing red glove?"

There was no sign of it at the register, so she reluctantly moved in the direction of the exit door. People leave belongings behind on a regular basis, and this missing item was likewise no big deal—she'd either find it somewhere or get herself another pair.

But instead of leaving, the woman remained, circling the checkout area, obviously concerned. The next time I saw her she told me she had walked the whole store, repeatedly retracing her steps to see if she might have dropped her glove.

Finally realizing there was more to her troubled heart than just a lost item of clothing, I listened as she told me the gloves were a gift from her sister who had since passed on. "They are simply irreplaceable," she said.

Suddenly my heart connected to her problem and I started looking for that glove almost as determinedly as she. I searched through her grocery bags in case she had accidentally dropped it in one. I gently urged her to check her coat pockets one more time. Then I circled my register a couple of times, my eyes scanning all the nooks and crannies on the floor where an item might have been dropped and inadvertently kicked out of sight. No luck. I suggested she leave her name and number at the front desk so the store could contact her if the glove was found and turned in. Despondent, she turned to go and I went back to work, but my mind stayed on that woman and her distress over the missing connection with her departed sister.

A short time later I had a few minutes to spare while nobody was in my line. I realized that, while I could do little else to help her, I could pray. In recent weeks God had been building my faith with many answered prayers, and I firmly believed He would show up in this situation as well. So I lifted a simple request in faith, affirming my belief that He knew where the missing glove was and asking that He direct her to it. I smiled to myself as I realized it was just the sort of situation He specializes in, after all—finding that which is lost and healing broken hearts.

Ten minutes later my white-haired friend was back, a huge grin on her face and her hand madly flapping a red glove in my direction.

"I found it! I found it!" she called. She'd decided to take one more tour around the store and found the glove at last, lying on the edge of the meat counter where someone must have put it. We rejoiced together and I watched as she finally exited the store, her step lighter and her heart happy once more.

I expected God to find her lost glove, but as usual He did more than that. It turned out that more than just a glove was missing. I had clearly lost my focus on why I stood behind that register in the first place. He reminded me that He places me in all my situations each day deliberately, to be a conduit through which His love flows to the people around me. I needed the reminder to be about my Father's business even in my place of business, as well as in my home, my car… and in all the hidden corners of my life where His desires might have been dropped and absently kicked out of sight by the seemingly more pressing problems of the day.

I worked the rest of that shift with a totally different attitude, believing God sent that woman to the store not for groceries, but for me. She may have found her lost glove, but I found my missing purpose.

~Elaine L. Bridge

The Hole in the Sky

The weak can never forgive. Forgiveness is the attribute of the strong.
~Mahatma Gandhi

I pace back and forth, one hand on my stomach, the other nervously fingering the index card with numbers written in red ink. "Just pick up the phone and do it already!" I say to myself. I have never even seen a photo of him. All I know is what my mother told me. "Your father was a heroin addict. He's either dead or in prison."

I pick up the card. There are five phone numbers listed, all belonging to men by the name of Ted Fisher. Amongst thousands of them in the United States, these are the few we whittled it down to. The genealogist marked one of the numbers with an asterisk. "I have a hunch about this one," he said.

My hands shake as I begin to punch in the numbers. 713... the area code for Houston, Texas. I hang up before I hit the last digit. Do I really want to open this Pandora's box? I don't need a father. My stomach tightens. It's been like this all day and I've barely been able to eat.

Okay... be brave. Good or bad, I want to know the truth. I dial the number and quietly close the bedroom door. My husband and son are talking in the kitchen, unaware of what I'm doing. By not telling them, I gave myself the option to chicken out.

The phone rings twice.

"Hello!" Loud and very southern, the woman's voice sounds harried.

I quickly blurt out "Hello, is this the Fisher residence?"

"Yes, it is." Her quick no-nonsense manner lets me know I'd better get to the point.

"Does a Ted Fisher live there?"

"Yes."

Remember what the genealogist said: "don't mention your name. They may not know about you."

"I'm sorry to disturb you. I am doing a family tree research project, and I think we may possibly be related." My husband Troy pokes his head around the bedroom door, eyebrows raised as if to say, "are you doing what I think you're doing?"

I continue, "Umm... did this Ted Fisher ever live in California?"

"Yes, he did. Hold on a minute, I think you found who you're looking for." She says with a certain but matter-of-fact manner.

What? She must have misunderstood me. I turn and look at Troy wide-eyed, my heart starting to race now.

"What? Who is it?" Troy asks. I put my finger up, signaling for him to give me a minute. Breathe...

"Hello?" a man's voice on the phone sends shock waves through me. It's him. Somehow, I know.

"Hello... is this... Ted?" My voice sounds tight and choked.

"Yes... is this... Hollye?" he says with amazement.

My knees buckle, the breath knocked out of me. "Yes," I barely whisper, my eyes brimming with tears. Troy sees my reaction, he laughs joyfully and claps his hands together.

The man's voice becomes emotional: "I can't believe this! We were just talking about you last night! I've been praying to find you!"

"Really?" is all I can squeak out.

"Oh my goodness, my goodness..." he mutters to himself. Then he says loudly as if I weren't aware of it, "Do you know who I am? I'm your dad!" He says it with such exuberance that I laugh and cry at the same time. "You've got a birthday coming up!" he adds.

I manage to squeak out, "Yeah, in Decem..."

He cuts me off, "December 4th! I've got it circled on the calendar. Every year I think of you on December 4th."

I wipe my eyes with my sleeve. "You do?"

"I've never forgotten it. Never," he says.

My heart is pounding. Is this really happening? Troy brings our son into the bedroom, whispering to him in hushed tones. They watch me, wide-eyed, as if witnessing a birth.

"You know," my father says in a shaky voice, "I'm not usually much of a crying man, but this is the happiest day of my life. I prayed to God to bring my children back to the fold... Hey! Did you know... well, of course you don't! You have three brothers!"

"I have three brothers!" I shout to Troy and Taylor, laughing through my tears.

I feel as though my heart will burst. Just listening to him speak in his gentle southern drawl is more than I could have ever dreamed of. This is my father's voice, and I feel safe inside it.

"You can ask me anything, baby," he says, "and it may be hard. But I will tell you the truth."

And he does. He confirms that he was a heroin addict, as my mother had told me, and yes, he was in and out of prison for fifteen years, and it was there, in a prison cell, that he found God.

My father works for the Port of Houston and is a preacher in a Baptist church, ordained eight years ago. Imagine that! A spiritual man, an avid reader, and an oil painter, just like me. We are absolutely stunned by how much we have in common. Chalk one up for the genetics argument.

"What book is on your bedside table right now?" I ask.

"The life story of Mother Teresa," he says. "What's on yours?"

"The life story of Gandhi!" We laugh together. For the first time in my life I am laughing with my father.

He asks me what I do. Am I married? Do I have kids? I tell him he is a grandfather, he has a son-in-law, and I am a singer and an artist. The questions fly back and forth. We laugh and cry in the joy of discovery. With every word, we are changed. There are many difficult questions to be addressed, but not today.

Forty minutes pass but it seems like five. The conversation begins to slowly wind down, and his tone turns serious. "Before we get off the phone, I want to ask you something." He pauses. "How was your childhood, sweetheart? I mean, were you okay?" These words come out heavy, weighted with his regret.

I make it simple for now. "It wasn't easy for me growing up. But I had a strong spirit. I'm okay."

I can hear his relief. "Oh thank God. You know, I always believed your mother would keep you. She was a much stronger person than I was. I was just a punk back then, only seventeen, but I know that's no excuse. I wasn't there for you and I am so sorry."

I exhale and sit down on the edge of my bed. "Thank you," I whisper, just loud enough for God to hear me. Brick by brick, I feel my life burden being lifted.

"One more thing…" he adds in his gentle Texas twang. "Before we hang up, I want you to know… I don't care if you are a one-legged Satan worshipper. You are my child, and… I love you."

In this moment, this one tiny split-second in time, the damaged little girl that I was sees the hole in the sky fill with light and hope.

I belong to someone.

I am loved.

I am whole.

~Hollye Fisher-Dexter

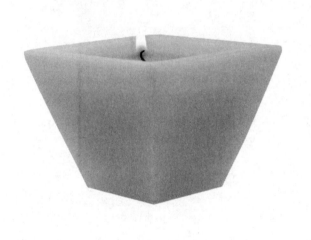

Chapter 7

Answered Prayers

Sign from Above

*And this is a sign to you from the LORD,
that the LORD will do this thing which he has spoken.*

~Isaiah 38:7

62

A Sure Sign

The essence of prayer is the act of God who is working in us and raises our whole being to Himself... Only in terms of wordless sighs can we approach God, and even these sighs are His work in us.

~Paul Tillich

Many mornings I'd sat at my kitchen table, cup of coffee in hand, reveling in the cheery atmosphere. It took me nine years of garage sales to decorate the room with apple curtains, pictures of apples on the walls, a red apple teapot, and even apple knobs on the cabinets. I enjoyed my downstairs bathroom almost as much, since I'd painted the walls a deep pink and hung rose patterned curtains on the window. An antique picture of a rose bouquet graced the wall. Despite a tight budget I'd managed to transform our rented Iowa farmhouse into a comfortable home.

For nearly the first decade of our marriage, my husband David and I worked part-time while attending college, staggering our hours so one of us would always be with our young children. During most of those years we lived in the university's married student housing. By the time we both graduated, we had four children and had decided it would be best if I stayed home with them. We moved a lot, always renting. The one occasion we'd approached a bank loan officer about purchasing a home, she took one look at our application, shook her head, and pushed the papers back across her desk.

"You'll be paying off those college loans the rest of your lives," she said. "No bank is even going to consider you for a loan as long as you're living off one income and have that debt."

Thus, we'd continued renting, finally ending up in a farmhouse seventeen miles from David's workplace. The house was ideal, except for the fact that it could get very cold in winter. By this time, we were the parents of eight children and still living off mostly one income, though I'd done everything from selling used books to freelance writing to help out. The prospect of us ever owning a home seemed remote.

That April, David's family sold some land they'd co-owned since their father's death. For the first time in our twenty-seven years of marriage we had a large sum of money at our disposal. The idea of buying a house resurfaced. We immediately paid off our college loans and credit card debt, setting aside money in savings for a down payment or an emergency.

The emergency was cancer, David's Stage IV oral cancer. Invasive surgery removed the tumor on the base of his tongue and adjacent lymph nodes, followed by a grueling six weeks of radiation and chemotherapy.

For months I cared for David — changing bloody dressings, doling out medications, preparing liquid tube feedings and becoming his companion every Wednesday during chemotherapy.

Even with good medical insurance and accumulated sick days, the huge co-payment on some of the medications and the thirty-mile trips back and forth to the cancer center depleted our savings rapidly.

Six months later, when David had returned to work full-time, the land sale money was gone, along with our dream of owning a house. We easily convinced ourselves it didn't really matter as long as David's good health continued. Cancer had taught us what was really important.

A year after David's cancer treatment ended, Iowa experienced a particularly hard winter. By November our bedroom dropped below fifty degrees and David started sleeping downstairs since he could no longer tolerate the cold. I missed sharing a bed with him and for the first time since living there, I wished we could move.

Shortly before Thanksgiving I read in the newspaper about a program for first-time homebuyers that didn't require a down payment. Excitedly, I filled out the papers and we began praying, asking God to guide us in our search for the perfect house.

"The house will have to be in a quiet neighborhood," I told our daughter Beth on the phone one day.

"Our neighborhood is quiet," she quipped. "Buy the house down the street."

I laughed, although the idea of living near Beth and her husband Ben was appealing. She and I had always been close and we talked on the phone daily. Ben wasn't just our son-in-law; he was also David's co-worker and friend.

"There will have to be an apple kitchen and a rose bathroom," I added, only half in jest. What were the odds of finding a house with either, much less both?

At Christmastime we contacted a realtor who said she had the perfect house within our price range, a small four-bedroom with a nice yard. I quickly jotted down the address and hung up the phone before it dawned on me that it was the house down the street from Beth!

When we stepped into the foyer the next day, I immediately felt at home. I loved the beautiful woodwork and the homey atmosphere. Despite its small size, dark wood kitchen cupboards and drawers covered an entire wall. When I turned from admiring the cabinets, I nearly gasped out loud. A large apple wreath hung on the wall! Then I saw the fruit print wallpaper. My eyes widened as I quickly scanned the rest of the room to see apple canisters on the refrigerator and apples hanging from a shelf. I felt a shiver at the back of my neck as I realized this was, indeed, an apple kitchen.

Before heading upstairs, David and I looked out the kitchen window and spotted a picnic table in the yard.

"I wish the picnic table came along with it," I said wistfully, and David just shook his head. He knew how much I'd always wanted one. We'd never bought outdoor furniture of any kind, since, as renters, the prospect of another move was always in the back or our mind. A picnic table symbolized a sense of permanence we'd never felt in all our years of renting.

Upstairs, I rushed to the open bathroom door, stopping dead in my tracks when I saw the unmistakable pattern of roses on the wallpaper.

A rose bathroom and an apple kitchen? Could God have been any more obvious that this was the house for us?

David tried to talk me out of my certainty that this was "our" house. "We can't buy the first house we look at."

I decided he was right. If God meant this house for us it would still be there after we viewed others.

Over the next week we looked at several more listings, but my heart wasn't really in it. None came close to feeling like home. Still, David resisted the idea that the first house we looked at could be the one for us.

"An apple kitchen and a rose bathroom," I reminded him. "Does God have to hit you over the head with a board?"

He laughed in resignation, my excitement finally contagious.

We were even more pleased with the second showing and called Beth to bring our younger children to look at it. Their eyes shone as they ran from room to room.

"Heating vents in every room?" eleven-year-old Emily marveled. "Let's get it!"

I smiled sadly, not realizing until then how much the cold upstairs bothered the kids, too.

After Beth and our children left, we told the realtor we were ready to make an offer. Our hands shook slightly as we signed the papers in her office, heralding one of the biggest changes in our new life after cancer.

The next morning, on the first day of the new year, the realtor called with the news that our offer had been accepted.

I marveled at the way God had answered our prayers. It was as if He'd had the house in mind for us all along and just pointed the way.

A week after our offer was accepted; the realtor sent an e-mail with a list of things the owner intended to leave if we could use them. I read the tally of items: the curtains, two dressers, and a beautiful vanity I had admired. My breath caught in my chest as I read the last line.

At that moment, David walked into my office. Alarmed, he asked if I was okay. Only then did I realize my cheeks were wet with tears. I couldn't speak past the lump in my throat. I nodded my head and pointed at the computer screen.

Yes, God had provided for our needs. But he also cared about our desires.

He'd given us a picnic table.

~Mary Potter Kenyon

63

God's S.O.S.

Prayer is our humble answer to the inconceivable surprise of living.
It is all we can offer and in return for the mystery by which we live.
~Abraham Joshua Heschel

"I've been thinking about our next trip," my husband Mel announced on a sunny Colorado morning. "Antarctica is the only continent I haven't visited."

I knew this meant he had already surfed the Internet and contacted travel agencies for detailed information. We were going to Antarctica.

During previous travels we had toured cathedrals, mosques, and the Vatican. We cruised the fiords of Norway and New Zealand and roamed through castles and palaces in Europe and Asia. We'd trekked the ruins of Pompeii, the Acropolis and Ephesus, watched the sun rise on the pyramids of Egypt and set on the Taj Mahal in India.

One afternoon, after praying and meditating, I heard an inner voice say, "Don't take that trip." I shrugged it off until I later got the same disturbing message during other prayer times.

I shared my apprehension with Mel, but he was so set on the trip, he shrugged off any negative comments and continued to peruse travel catalogs. As the departure date neared, I went to bed one night weary with concern, and fell asleep. I woke from a vivid dream warning me that I should not travel to Antarctica.

Disturbed, I prayed about it and told Mel. He again dismissed my concerns. "You must have misinterpreted your dream."

My increasing concerns were no match for his increasing

excitement, which continued to accelerate whenever friends who had taken the cruise raved about it.

As he gathered details, he mentioned that there were no public hospitals on Antarctica. Every passenger was required to present a doctor's certification that he or she was in good health. Then he added, "Should there be injuries or illness, the only medical assistance would be aboard the tour ship anchored offshore."

Although we are both octogenarians, we were healthy except for my arthritis. Raised in the Midwest, we had grown up with snow so were not too concerned about freezing temperatures. We would be bundled in heavy coats, hats, gloves and boots as we hiked the frozen tundra, coated with penguin droppings. What if I slipped and fell?

Although Mel agreed it might be too risky for me to go, it did not dampen his enthusiasm, especially when his adult son offered to accompany him instead. They decided to travel on the M.S. Explorer in November 2007.

When Mel called for reservations, however, he was informed that the tour he chose was fully booked. He contacted other Antarctica tours and learned there were no vacancies. Disappointed, he brooded with frustration before deciding to book the cruise earlier next time.

November 2007 arrived and we were watching television on Thanksgiving evening. A breaking news report interrupted the program. "En route to Antarctica, the MS Explorer hit an iceberg that slashed a huge hole in the hull of the ship."

I gasped and glanced at Mel whose face paled as he stared at the television screen.

The news correspondent continued, "All ninety-one passengers, nine guides and the crew of fifty-four were safely evacuated before the ship sank."

Shivering, I said a silent prayer of thanksgiving that everyone survived.

I blotted my eyes and said another prayer of thanks to God for sending me the S.O.S.

~Sally Kelly-Engeman

64

My Worst Nightmare

A mother's arms are made of tenderness and children sleep soundly in them.
~Victor Hugo

For years I was plagued by addiction's vicious grip. Once referred to by my high school English teacher as the girl who would become a successful writer, I had long ago lost my writing ability to a tiny hard rock called crack cocaine. This pebble lowered my standard of living to that of a savage animal. Angrily I gnawed at everything that crossed paths with me. I was no longer following the values my mama and daddy had sternly instilled in me. Rebellion took over and guilt and shame were two of my many negative emotional roommates.

Riddled with disappointment, I hated myself. I couldn't stand to look in the mirror while dressing; I was so frail from weight loss and looked like a zombie. Like a vampire fighting daylight, every night at midnight my built-in human alarm clock intuitively sounded and my body came alive. I'd rise up, stretch my arms high, and creep out of my coffin into the world of addiction.

I would join my using friends who smoked with me. Together we'd search for the dope dealers and once we obtained our fix, we would find a dark abandoned house to take over and go insane. We'd remain there for hours and sometimes even days at a time, only going out when there was no more crack.

Eventually it became harder to get high. The fun and games vanished. To make matters worse, echoes of Mama's voice followed me. Each time the drug stopped working, I talked to anyone who'd listen about my failures and how Mama was to blame for all that was happening to me.

As long as I stayed high, I cared less about what anyone thought about me, and that definitely included Mama. But as soon as I came down from the high, shame and disappointment worked overtime with regret. The only weapon that kept me from going insane was the grace and mercy of Something Bigger and Stronger than me. I didn't know exactly what it was, I just knew it was the only reason I wasn't dead yet.

One night my head hurt so much I decided to go to Mama's house. I prayed she'd allow me to come in for a little while. My eighty-five-year-old mother opened the door wide and shook her head in disgust, yet didn't say the usual demeaning words. I went in, took a hot bath and went to bed. I slept for days and Mama woke me with delicious food. From that day on, Mama and I gelled like never before. There was something bigger, stronger, and different about our relationship. We got along better than ever and argued less. We watched game shows and laughed at sitcoms together.

I knew it was too good to be true. One night came the biggest battle since I'd come home. The craving tiger inside me roared, paced back and forth and yelled, "I need some crack; feed me now!" I was afraid and began to panic, when a soothing voice said, "I've got you, don't move; stay where you are." I tried to argue and didn't know which voice to follow, but again that Something Bigger decided for me. It lifted me off the couch and guided me to my bedroom. I felt light like a feather and I uttered good night to Mama. I lay awake for some time and continued to battle the tiger until eventually I fell asleep.

Sometime during the night I had a dream that I was back in the biblical days. I was with a group of men who resembled Abraham, Joseph, Moses, Paul, and other great leaders. All of us wore pure white long flowing robes with worn dusty sandals on our feet. The men had long white beards and each of us carried flawlessly carved canes to trudge up the mountain. We walked in complete silence and just when we were about to reach the top, I was awakened by a loud pop! It was as if Someone Bigger and Stronger had clapped his hands to bring me out of this hypnotic state. Trembling with fear, I found my pajamas and sheets soaking wet. Sweat dripped down my forehead. I shook violently from side to side trying to make sense of my dream. Then I did something I hadn't done in a very long time. I prayed to the God of my parents. "God, I'm not ready to die and join those great men in my dream!"

At that precise moment I felt a peace come over me and I knew in my heart that everything would be all right. I decided to do something else that I hadn't done in a long time. I got out a pen and paper and tried writing my thoughts. I scribbled for a while and fell asleep again.

The next thing I heard was Mama running her bath water. It was Sunday morning and I knew she was preparing for the Sick Committee from church to come to visit. I'd sit in my room and listen to the hymns, prayers, and discussions when they arrived. I felt good. After a while I went to check on Mama. I took one look at her and knew something wasn't right. She looked dazed and confused. She couldn't move. I knew then that Mama had suffered a stroke. I raced for the telephone and called 911.

At the hospital Mama was unconscious and placed in the Intensive Care Unit. The physician finally came in and told us she wouldn't be the Mama she used to be.

She was hospitalized for about a month and when discharged we took her home. My siblings and I desperately tried to take good care of her, but faced with so many medical issues, it was impossible. Mama needed round-the-clock care. After careful consideration we had to do what we said we would never do… we placed Mama in a local nursing home.

It was on that very day that I made a decision not to use any type of crack, alcohol or mood-altering drugs ever again. I got down on my knees and prayed to that Something Bigger and Stronger than myself.

Today, five years later and still sober, I call Him God. I know

He saved and delivered me from insanity's door. I have reconnected with Him, asked for His forgiveness, and vowed never to leave Him again.

Mama is still here and I oversee her care daily at the nursing home, for I feel that it is my duty as her daughter. It is my way of showing love for all the love she has shown me, especially during my addiction.

Each day when I visit Mama I whisper in her ear that I am still clean and sober and going to church regularly. I tell her I was baptized again and that I started a support group at her nursing home where twenty-five family members meet monthly. I also let her know that the girl whose English teacher predicted great success with writing has written and published a book called *Mending the Hole in My Soul Through Poetry*, a collection of personal poems about my addiction. It's dedicated to Mama.

As for that dream on that strange night, the details are still vivid in my mind. I believe my dream placed me amongst great biblical leaders on that mountain because it is my turn to lead some sick and suffering addicts up the mountain and into the doors of recovery.

What I thought was my worst nightmare turned out to be my greatest blessing.

~Shirley Faye Cobb

Strength in Faith

There is in all this cold and hollow world, no fount of deep,
strong, deathless love; save that within a mother's heart.
~Felicia Hemans

I had only been at the hospital for about twenty minutes. Suddenly I had the crushing realization that Mother's earthly journey was ending. I had left school quickly that morning when my sister called saying the doctor told family to come. Although I prayed all the way that Mother would wait for me, I never really thought she'd die.

"Are your monitors working right? My mother's blood pressure registers zero!" we asked the nurse. She hurried us into the hallway as the emergency team came running. Mother was so strong. She had always rallied. She was a survivor. Surely she would pull through this respiratory crisis. None of us had come to grips with just how weak she was becoming. Just a few days before we were told she was stronger and being weaned off the respirator.

My youngest brother Peter came to us in the hallway from the nurse's station. When we saw his always-cheerful face looking distraught we knew the news was not what we wanted to hear. With deep anguish he said, "They couldn't revive her."

We all rushed to her side again to face the stunning reality that our mother was gone. God had called her home. "She's running now," Peter said.

I gave her one last kiss. "Mother, you have sneaked out on us and gone to heaven."

During that moment I felt as if a thousand light bulbs were going off in my head. I was filled with new insights and awareness of what she had been for all of us. She had shared her life, love, faith and strength with generosity. For each of her children she was a prayer warrior, a fan and cheerleader. Her life had been a testimony to the power of prayer.

One year after her graduation from college she was a beautiful bride in a stunning gown with a handsome groom at her side. A year later her first child was born. Life was all sunshine. The next year, after she delivered her second child, she collapsed getting out of her hospital bed, with a nurse at her side. "My legs feel like rubber," she had exclaimed.

An ambulance transported her to Massachusetts General Hospital where she was diagnosed with polio.

"You will never walk again," the doctor told her.

Mom cried for six months.

She spent nine months at Mass General for rehabilitation, where she learned to use crutches and braces. Visitors brought her religious medals. She pinned so many to her gown that the staff called her "the general." Mom, her family and friends prayed for a cure.

When Mom was discharged, she, Dad, my brother and I moved in with her mother. There she decided to use only the wheelchair because crutches and braces were difficult to manage; she'd lost the use of muscles that helped lift her legs.

Although she was told by a social worker in the hospital not to have any more children, Mom was determined to have the big family she'd always dreamed of. She had two more daughters and four sons over the next fourteen years.

In the mid-1950s she and Dad went up to St. Joseph's Oratory in Montreal to pray for a cure for the paralysis she had from the waist down. After that our family began yearly pilgrimages to the Shrine of Ste-Anne-de-Beaupré in Quebec to beg for a cure. Mother herself went almost every year for forty years; her children helped as aides when she visited the shrine—always praying for a cure. Eventually Mom told us she realized that it was not God's will for her to walk, but she received spiritual strength from prayer and her yearly pilgrimages there.

Mother was strong and healthy as she raised us, working all day at home taking care of the family. We hardly realized she was handicapped—she could do so much. She never complained about not being able to walk. "God is helping me," she said.

Evening prayers were daily rituals. As we grew we helped with the housework and meals. We all had chores. But Mother did all the cooking herself.

In the 1960s when Mom and Dad looked for a new place to live, my grandmother bought them a house, one that could easily be made wheelchair accessible. St. Athanasius, a new church in the neighborhood, had a wheelchair ramp. Mother could finally attend daily Mass without Dad carrying her up the flight of stairs. She was so happy.

When hand controls were put on the station wagon, Mother gained independence after many practice driving lessons with Dad. With one or two of us in tow, she began shopping for her family.

In the mid-1970s she experienced acute thyroiditis, which left her afflicted with chronic fatigue for the rest of her life. Even with severe psoriasis and skin problems for years, her faith was strong and she kept going. She suffered with faith and dignity, united, she said, with the sufferings of Jesus. God was first in her life. The last twenty years she spent several hours every day in prayer and attended daily Mass as long as she could. Her eight children were the center of her life. Her main interest was that we be followers of Jesus Christ, worthy of eternal life with Him. She walked the Way of the Cross—with a smile—and accepted the mysterious sufferings she endured.

At seventy years old, a severe respiratory crisis put her on a ventilator. She was in the hospital for months that late winter to spring and never got completely well again.

We all stood around her in the ICU as her blood pressure plummeted and she received the Last Rites of the Catholic Church.

Now Mother is dancing in heaven. We honor her legacy by

living the faith she exemplified. We learned more about life and faith from our "disabled" mom than if she had been "able." She and God used her immobilization to mobilize our prayers, her weak muscles to strengthen our faith, her paralysis to help us walk closer to God.

Yes, Mother's prayers were answered.

~Sister M. John Baptist Donovan, SCMC

66

It's Raining Dimes

*When thou prayest, rather let thy heart be without words
than thy word be without heart.*
~John Bunyan

In addition to having difficult problems in my marriage, I was also suffering from health issues. I had been meditating, praying for help, and essentially holding on for dear life. My husband and I lived in North Carolina and in order to lighten some of our stress, we took a weekend trip to Myrtle Beach, South Carolina. Although we were in a fantastic place of leisure, I was in a stress-induced daze. I was going through the motions, pushing myself to smile and act happy, yet my overriding feeling was apprehension.

This was my state as I stood in line at an amusement park on a Saturday evening. It was a strange space to be, full of angst, yet surrounded by fun and laughter that I could not feel.

As I stood with my husband, waiting for the line to move, I prayed, "God give me clarity and direction."

Just a few moments later a small object tumbled out of thin air, hit me directly on the top of my head, and dropped onto the ground. I barely caught a flicker of silver as the projectile passed my peripheral vision. The flying object didn't hurt me, but it did take me by surprise.

"What was that?" my husband and I asked in unison.

I examined the ground at my feet and saw a shiny new dime,

the tiny missile that had struck me. As I reached down to retrieve it, I noticed it lay heads up.

I picked up the dime and held it. I knew it was quite literally a message from above. I squeezed it in my fist and I began to feel a bit lighter. I'd always been convinced that signs like these come to us when we seek them. We only need to recognize them as significant, not something to shrug off or consider a coincidence. That day it took a strike on the head for me to get the message that my prayer was heard and I was protected.

I kept that dime for a long time, remembering the magnificence of how it flew into my life to comfort me. Things did work out in my life. That incident was my greatest source of joy, reminding me that I always have a choice, to stay in fear or lighten up, and to know I am never alone.

Since then I have noticed heads-up dimes many times. They have appeared in the washing machine, on the seat of my car, in a public restroom, and many times, simply on the ground just when I needed to know that help was on the way. They have fallen out of my wallet, catching my attention so that I could notice my thinking. Sometimes I find two dimes at the same time.

Just today, I found a heads-up penny buried in my dresser drawer just after I had finished praying. I reverently placed it on my personal altar. It isn't a dime, but it still reminds me of the value of change.

~Karena D. Bailey

67

He Is Able

For He shall give His angels charge over you, to keep you in all your ways.
~Psalm 91:11

Chills ran through me as I gaped at the demolished car. All four tires were flat, the windshield shattered, the roof crushed. While driving her boyfriend Robert's car, my daughter Jaime had taken a downhill curve on a gravel road too fast and lost control. Robert was ejected as the compact car plunged down an embankment, slammed into a huge rock, and landed on its roof—on top of Robert.

An emergency medical helicopter rushed him to the nearest trauma center, where medical personnel suspected he had a crushed chest, two broken legs, and internal injuries. Jaime had been taken to a local hospital's emergency room.

I'll never forget the phone call I got that afternoon.

As I rushed to the hospital fifteen miles away, I was sick at heart and concerned, but not surprised. Two weeks earlier, I'd felt a growing burden for Jaime during Sunday morning worship service at church. I closed my eyes and started to pray. As we sang, "He Is Able," I experienced an overwhelming sense of God's presence. I felt love, light, and warmth, as though God wrapped His arms around me and Jamie, who stood beside me. The words weren't spoken audibly, yet I heard them distinctly in my heart. "She's going to be all right; I have her in My hands."

A week later at a writers' conference across the state, I had the urge to collar everyone I met and ask them to pray for my daughter. "This is silly," I scolded myself. "You're letting your imagination run away with you." But the urge was strong, and I couldn't shake the sense of foreboding.

Back home, I was snuggled on the love seat in the living room enjoying my prayer time when Robert's name popped into my mind.

"You want me to pray for Robert, Lord? Okay."

So I prayed for Robert, as well as my husband and three children, using the words from Psalm 91:11, asking God to give His angels charge over them and guard them in all their ways.

The call came that afternoon. Jaime, who had been thrown around inside the car as it tumbled and overturned down the bank, escaped with bruises and lacerations. After she was discharged, we drove an hour and a half to the hospital where Robert had been admitted. When we got there, he was sitting up in bed, grinning. Eight stitches and a few bumps and bruises were all he suffered. He was discharged from the hospital the next day.

Luck? Coincidence? No, answered prayer.

When the car slammed into the rock, the impact forged an indentation just large enough to protect the small eighteen-year-old boy it landed on.

~Michele T. Huey

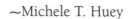

68

Let My Life Change

He shall regard the prayer of the destitute, and shall not despise their prayer.
~Psalm 102:17

"Let my life change, let it never be the same, or let me die!" These thoughts tormented me every day. I was thirty and my life was a mess. My boyfriend had jilted me for someone younger. I had no money, no career, no supportive family, and no self-esteem. But still, I had a thread of hope. "Maybe, just maybe, my life can change." The prayer that whispered in my head again and again indicated that I really believed that possibility.

On March 1, 1978, I was scheduled to fly to Hawaii to emcee the Miss Hawaii Pageant. Being a former Miss Hawaii, I hoped this trip might rekindle my belief that life was worth living.

For seven years I'd struggled to become a Hollywood actress, all the while begging for change. I'd been bulimic for so many years I couldn't remember the last time I'd kept down a meal. Every month I could hardly pay my rent. Year after year, just as I seemed close to success, everything would fall apart. I lived in a fragile turmoil created by a need for approval that drained my spirit. No one knew who I really was; they didn't care. Worse, *I* didn't know who I really was.

I showered and took a taxicab to the L.A. airport. I slipped into my aisle seat on Continental Flight 603, repeating my incessant prayer. "Let my life change, let it never be the same, or let me die."

At 9:25 a.m., the plane moved down the runway. "Let my life cha..." Suddenly—whoosh—life as I knew it was over.

As the DC-10 accelerated for takeoff, three of its tires blew at once and it hurtled into a rocketing death skid. I heard a loud metallic bang and felt the plane quiver as the right wing clipped the tarmac and shattered. Inside the cabin, ceiling panels popped and sounds of wrenching crunching metal and glass cracked through the air. Passengers jerked around like limp cotton dolls. My body snapped forward and the seatbelt nearly cut me in half, stopping my breath. Through the window I saw a part of the aircraft explode into an inferno.

God was answering my prayer. I was going to die.

Outside the windows, flames mushroomed all around. When the flight attendant screamed, "Come to the rear!" I pressed down the aisle with the crowd of passengers, gripping seatbacks to keep from slipping on the tilted floor. Midway down the aisle I approached an emergency exit. The door stood open, but no one was using it because flames were leaping outside. Then death tackled me. I tripped and tumbled onto the angled floor. On my stomach, I slid helplessly toward the exit door and its raging blaze.

My thoughts cried, "Prepare for a slow, painful death!" But suddenly a calming voice in my mind cut through the fear. It asked, "Do you love yourself? Do you have good relationships with your family and friends? Are you living your goals and dreams? If you die today, have you left this planet a better place?"

Lying transfixed by the toxic bonfire, streaming with sweat, I nevertheless found strength to cry a response, "No, no, no, no!" And in the next instant I felt a wave of love. Strange. Here I was, about to burn to death, and I felt pure unconditional love. I was at peace. That's when my thoughts took a U-turn. "I want to live!"

But to do so, I'd have to walk through fire.

Fighting flames and heat, I crawled away from the emergency door. I managed to stand up and creep slowly through the smoky heat with the cramped line of passengers, toward the rear exit where they were sliding on an escape chute to the tarmac. The doorway seemed so far away and small. Would I get out? Would I live? Then came the voice again. "Ask and it will be given to you; seek and you will find; knock and the door will open unto you" (Matthew 7:7).

I asked, begging, "Please let me out!"

A slim opening appeared and I squirmed toward the escape chute, but my left shoe caught on a piece of metal. When I jerked it free, a stroke of pain shot down my left leg. I slid down the ramp and slammed onto the tarmac, into a spray of jet fuel. Another pain explosion in my leg kept me from getting up. "My God I'm going to burn to death!"

With a surge of adrenaline I rose up and limped across the tarmac just as another aircraft section burst into flames. I prayed, "Please let the passengers be safe. Please, God, save them!"

Once again the spellbinding voice spoke. "Your assignment is to help people help themselves. You will speak, you will write, and you will have a daughter later in life who will be a leader." The voice was so strong that I glanced around to see if it came from someone nearby. No one was there.

After being examined by a medical team inside the airport, I returned to my apartment. I closed my eyes and shared my thoughts with God. "You've always been there when I needed You. In the past I asked for this and that; now I want to say how much it means to know You love me and believe in me. I realize now there is a higher purpose to my life, and I want to help do Your work. What am I supposed to do? Will You guide me?"

The answer was revealed to me in fragmented images that echoed the words I heard outside the burning airplane: a stage, a book, and an infant.

A few months later I received a subpoena to testify about the crash at the National Transportation Safety Board's inquiry. At first I was scared. Because of the millions of dollars worth of lawsuits pending, I thought the airlines would attack me. But then I remembered my fellow passengers and the voice that said, "You will speak."

With conviction, I waived my right to sue the airlines and testified on behalf of the passengers who had died or were injured. My testimony helped to change airline safety regulations.

A year after the crash I left Los Angeles and moved to a small California mountain town to pursue a career in speaking and to become a writer. "You will write."

At age forty-seven the third prediction came true. As a single mom, I adopted a little baby girl. "You will have a daughter." Mariah is an expression of pure love, a blessing in my life, a kind soul destined to fulfill her calling.

Thanks to the messages I heard during the horrendous explosion, now every day I tilt my face to the sky and say, "Thank you, God. You changed my life. It's never been the same. I'm glad I'm alive!"

~Donna Hartley

The Innocence of Childhood

In Your presence is the fullness of joy;
at Your right hand are pleasures forever more.
~Psalm 16:11

The rain let up about 1:00 p.m., a good time, I thought, to venture out for a walk in the refreshing cool air. Birds chirped and the smell of the rain-cleansed breeze greeted me. I decided to walk forty-five minutes one way on the trail and then head back.

I took my outer sweatshirt off and wrapped it around my waist. On the trail another woman and I exchanged pleasantries about how nice the day was after the rain. My mood was light and peaceful, my body exhilarated after forty-five minutes. I turned to head home.

Fifteen minutes later, an unexpected drizzle began to fall from a stray cloud. It felt good since I had been walking for an hour. Smiling, I took my sweatshirt from my waist and tied it on my head turban style. I picked up my pace a little. But before I could say, "April showers bring May flowers," the sky opened and a downpour ensued. Drenched, my mood darkened like the clouds.

"Lord, couldn't You have held the rain until I made it back on home?" A scripture verse popped into my head. "Why are you downcast, O my soul? And why are you disquieted within me?" (Psalm 42:11)

Then I realized how fickle I was, one minute singing praises and the very next spewing complaints.

Grimly, I walked on in the torrential rainstorm, soaked to the bone. I lamented, "Well at least it can't get any worse." I recalled the old saying, "When it rains it pours," and sure enough, just ten minutes from home, I encounter a huge deep puddle. There was no way around it. My only choice was to traipse right through, soaking my freezing feet.

But as I stepped into that puddle, I was transformed into a child again as memories came flooding back. The best part of a rainy day was seeing how many puddles I could walk through, run through, and jump into to splash a friend. I'd try to run home before she could catch and splash me, for that was the best fun.

Now as I waded through yet another puddle, I recalled actor Gene Kelly singing and dancing with joy in the rain.

As the chorus of "Singin' in the Rain" resounded in my head, I was reminded that I can choose to allow circumstances to define my emotions and reactions, or I can choose to make the best of them. So I decided to enjoy the rain and rejoice in the opportunity to be childlike once again. Another scripture verse came to mind. "Singing and making melody in your heart to the Lord, giving thanks always for all things unto God the Father." (Ephesians 5:19-20)

With a renewed enthusiasm, I consciously rekindled those childlike qualities of simplicity, faith, trust, and a thankful heart. I would praise Him, my Savior and my God, both in the sunshine and in the rain, for each of them serves their purpose in my life, literally and metaphorically. It is merely my perspective that determines how I'll weather the storm.

Feeling the exhilarating beauty of the pouring rain, I tossed my head back, stuck out my tongue like I did as a kid, and caught raindrops in my mouth. I giggled and stomped my feet, the water squeaking in my squishy shoes.

I was within a few blocks of home when the downpour became a drizzle, and as quickly as it had come, the rain was leaving, as is often the case with the storms in my life. I looked around and truly saw the glory of God. It was as if the whole earth was rejoicing in praises to Him, for the trees and the grass were greener. The bark of the branches, tree stumps, and the mulch around them glistened a dark brown. Flowers bloomed with open petals, as if to say, "Thank you Lord for sending the rain." The sky's bright, crisp, blue freshness echoed the birds chirping once again. Some drank from the puddles as squirrels pranced about.

As I approached my home, a bunny hopped along in front of me and huddled under my favorite tree, whose leaves and branches seemed to stretch out much farther and wider from the nourishment it just received. It made me reflect on how, when I too weather a storm, my faith grows deeper, stronger, as if my roots too, become more firmly planted from the nourishment of His word and my trust in Him.

I looked up to the sky and, along with all creation, gave thanks for the childlike memories that helped me to see His glory, His goodness, and His provision once again. With a final splash up my sidewalk I recited, "The earth, O LORD, is full of Your mercy." (Psalm 119:64).

"Thank you for restoring my childlike fun and faith in You."

~Diana Clarke

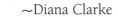

70

Kyle's Rainbow

Prayer is the opening of the soul so that He can speak to us.
~Georgia Harkness

My beloved, blond, blue-eyed adorable grandson never made it to his third birthday. At the age of eighteen months Kyle was diagnosed with a brain mass. Although the operation to remove it was a success, the disease later spread to other parts of his body.

We all know how hard it is to lose a loved one, but when that loved one is a child, it is even more devastating. It is out of the natural order of things. We grandparents should be the first to go.

While parents live out their own private nightmares, we grandparents go through our own torture; not only do we have to sustain the pain of losing a cherished family member, we helplessly grieve the deep hurt of our children.

The September afternoon that Kyle was laid to rest our immediate family had our visit in private. I sat in a corner with my husband John, looking at the precious little one who had just left our lives.

I whispered, "Okay, Kyle, you know what Nana believes in, please show us a sign that you made it to heaven."

My husband heard my barely audible plea and said, "Mary, he is not going to give you a sign yet. It is too early."

John and I were the first to make it back to greet the visitors. The first to arrive introduced himself and said, "I just wanted to let you know there is a beautiful rainbow in the sky!"

That night I was talking to my girlfriend on the phone about the rainbow that Kyle had sent us when we were interrupted by the sound of her doorbell ringing. She excused herself, then came back to the phone. "Mary Ann, there was no one there!" The hairs on my arms stood straight up. A few minutes later the doorbell rang for a second time. She opened the door and looked all around. There was still no one there.

A week later when I returned to work, I got yet a third sign.

After taking my first order to serve a customer lunch, I returned to the place where the menus are stored on the waitress station. In plain view on that counter was the October issue of *Reader's Digest*. In bright bold letters on the front cover the title of the feature article read, "Proof There Is Life After Death."

I knew our little cherub passed through a rainbow on his way to heaven.

~Mary Ann Bennett-Olson

71

Mirror Messages

But even now I know that whatever you ask of God, God will give you.
~John 11:22

I'd always refused to pierce my ears… until I arrived home tired from work one day and noticed something taped to the bathroom mirror. Glistening diamond earrings seized my attention with a message written below in eyebrow pencil by my husband, Mike. "Now you have to get your ears pierced. Am I good, or what?"

A quick painful click in the hairdresser's chair and I made a fashion statement.

Mike's note on the mirror started a joyful new tradition in our family. We communicated through mirror missives. Our son Shawn joined in and soon funny notes, rhymes, and messages adorned our looking glasses, both bathroom and dresser. The game often replaced paper reminders in our household. Shawn left word where he'd be after school. During his teen years he left requests for gas money or field trip permission. He often signed them, "Love, Shawn" or sometimes, "Your son, Shawn."

My Mary Kay saleslady likely scratched her head over frequent orders for lip and eyebrow pencils, but we loved our fun family custom. We thought we'd keep it going forever. We'd be featured in family magazines standing next to mirrors defaced with scrawled prose. We'd tell our future grandchildren about it. The practice would be handed down for generations. Our housekeepers squandered gallons of extra Windex removing the epistles. We didn't care.

When Shawn turned nineteen, senioritis struck and he struggled with grades, anxious to enter the big bright world of jobs, college, and his own living space. We continued our mirror messages and occasionally I'd sneak encouraging cards in his backpack to quell his nervousness about graduation and life on his own.

We'd move at summer's end to begin retirement living in Arkansas. Shawn would remain to start community college and a new job.

Prom night arrived bright and clear. I admired Shawn's tux and his silver vest. "No one else will have one like it, Mom." I hugged him and watched the taillights of the gleaming borrowed Corvette leave the driveway. Our mirror scribe had grown up into a fine young man.

The next morning a drunk driver stole our messenger and stilled the writer's fingers forever.

I grieved for months. A strong faithful person, I struggled for answers. How could I continue without his comedy, his laughter, and his love? No answers came. My husband had a wonderful dream in which Shawn called out to him through an open window and handed him shirts, the same size and type he always wore. When Mike called to him, Shawn turned, smiled and left. I craved such a dream, a whisper, a touch to assure me he was all right.

Eventually, in tiny increments, healing crept into my heart. I gained a measure of peace but still longed for reassurance. I believed in my son's life in a heavenly kingdom, but a mother's heart is never quiet when doubts about her child's welfare are concerned. I looked everywhere and anywhere, praying for a sign from Shawn.

Two years later we opened a fishing resort, furnished the lodge, and our grief journey progressed in our peaceful spot on the White River. We purchased a new dresser for our bedroom and planned to move ours to the guesthouse. I transferred drawer contents, removed dust bunnies, and cleaned the mirror. I looked sideways checking for streaks, and gasped. The words "I love you" appeared in Shawn's handwriting. I wept with relief and gratitude. A new measure of comfort entered my heart.

"All in God's time," a friend of mine often says. The hands of

God's timepiece chose that moment to grace my life. He didn't send a lightning bolt, a burning bush, or a magnificent dream, but the perfect mirror message of love from my child.

~Rita Billbe

Answered
Prayers

Thanksgiving

Offer to God thanksgiving, and pay your vows to the Most High.

~Psalm 50:14

72

O Holy Night!

For me prayer means launching out of the heart toward God; it means lifting up one's eyes quite simply to heaven, a cry of grateful love, from the crest of joy or the trough of despair; it's a vast, super-natural force which opens out my heart and binds me close to Jesus.

~St. Therese of Lisieux

"Where's the baby?" That's how my nightmare always began. As long as I live, I will never forget the terror of being inside a burning building. For days and weeks after we lost our home, the smell of smoke filled my imagination every night, and I lay sleepless with a pounding heart, reliving the whole experience.

I'd awakened to the soft thud of our three-year-old daughter Molly falling from bed to her bedroom floor. When I opened my bedroom door to check on her, I walked into a wall of smoke. In one of those it-only-happens-to-others moments, I ran back into our room to tell my husband that the neighbor's house was on fire. Within seconds, we both knew it was our house that was engulfed in flames.

Below us we heard the blaring smoke detectors and the cracking and popping of little explosions detonating our lives—sounds that didn't wake us because of the carbon monoxide we had already inhaled.

As if we had practiced it many times, Bill dashed one way to Molly's room and I headed for the nursery to scoop up Barry, our ten-week-old baby. I cradled him in one arm like a football and pushed ahead blindly through the smoke toward the window. I tripped over a laundry basket and fell on the floor, curled around my baby. It seemed so easy to stay there and so hard to move. "God help me…"

Feeling as though I were drowning, I managed to crawl to the window. I had to get my baby out. I pushed the screen out and felt the roof over the kitchen. I set Barry down gently and leaned forward onto the roof.

"What if it collapses under us?" I thought. I could see the fire licking upwards from the kitchen; the family room was orange with flames. Bill, after placing Molly on the front porch roof, came barreling back through the thick smoke to make sure we were safely out of the house. He shoved me hard out onto the roof and fell out after me.

"Where is the baby?" he gasped.

I had to feel around to locate him. Barry was alarmingly quiet. I picked him up; he was limp in my arms.

"Help! Help!" I screamed. Where were the neighbors? How could anyone sleep through all of this? We could die on this roof. The heat rose in sheets of acrid smoke that coated our skin, making breathing difficult and speaking almost impossible.

Finally Ben, our neighbor, came running toward the house with a ladder and our trembling bodies descended to the earth. Our little family was soon reunited in an ambulance. One of the attendants worked on Barry to clear his eyes and lungs. Little Molly sat shivering in her Wonder Woman Underoos. We embraced each other, grateful to be alive.

For the first of many times, someone told us, "You are so lucky."

We told ourselves how lucky we were, but I was so sad. We often looked at Barry and sighed, "He is our miracle baby."

Not to be outdone, Molly would pipe up, "And I'm Wonder Woman!"

Yes, we had our miracle baby, wonder girl and each other, but I still didn't feel lucky. Our home was gone. I didn't feel lucky when I had to say our former address over and over to utility companies, the post office, and our creditors.

Why did I feel so attached to that address? "Please, Lord," I prayed. "Help me to feel grateful for our survival and forget about the loss of our things. Didn't You tell us that storing up treasures on earth is storing trash? Help me to accept the truth of those words."

We had no clothes or shoes, but many friends helped us with a generosity that was truly a gift. I'm ashamed to admit that my pride was hurt when I opened boxes of donations. I think God was trying to teach me a lesson about humility, a lesson that didn't really hit home until midnight service on Christmas Eve.

Over several exhausting months, we rebuilt our lives. I was so grateful that our children were healthy, and my husband and I felt closer than ever. Yet I still grieved the loss of our home. The pictures, wedding and baby gifts, our books and records, sentimental objects that marked our ten-year marriage and life together, all our possessions were gone. By the time Christmas rolled around, we were shakily on our feet in a temporary little apartment.

Since the children were awake anyway after the family Christmas Eve party, we decided to attend midnight service in the church where we had been married. St. Leo's was a great old German-looking stout edifice that had marked many signposts in our lives. Bill had practically been the boy next door and we shared a common faith, most of it centered in St. Leo's.

The choir's music rose in the pine-scented church and candles flickered on the altar. I held Barry, a fat pleasant baby who showed no signs of being the limp little bundle of the previous summer. Bill held Molly up to see the crèche. Apple cheeks glowing, she pointed solemnly at the animals, the tiny Baby and His beautiful mother.

I couldn't take my eyes off the little Baby in the manger and His homeless family.

How could I be sad? Everything we needed was in this one oak pew. We had each other, our health, and our faith, which had brought us to this holy night. We possessed all we needed… the love of a family and a generous God who had spared us.

~Rosemary McLaughlin

73

Keys

Prayer also will be made for Him continually, and daily He shall be praised.
~Psalm 72:15

"We'll pray before we get started," said Polly, the enthusiastic director of a local crisis pregnancy center. I thought to myself that we probably should have done that the day before, as we struggled to move donated items and furniture for the yard sale into the center after being soaked by a Texas-sized rainstorm.

Polly, a true Pollyanna, lived by faith. I, on the other hand, firmly believed in specific prayers, giving God advice on not only what I needed but how to accomplish it. He's a busy deity after all and surely doesn't have time to work out all the details.

As a volunteer at the crisis pregnancy center for over ten years, I helped with filing, counseling young girls, teaching computer skills, sorting donated baby clothes, and working on the newsletter. While the volunteers worked hard to help young girls in crisis, which was not always pregnancy related, Polly was a mentor to many and an inspiration to all who crossed her path, volunteers and clients alike.

The storm clouds drifted farther east that Saturday morning and we enthusiastically sold furniture, computers, clothing, and had just negotiated the sale of a workout bench and weights. As I watched the man load the equipment into the trunk of his car, an Asian lady tapped my shoulder. I turned as she opened her hand to reveal a small ornament.

"Twenty-five cents," I said distractedly as I watched exercise equipment being crammed into the car trunk, wondering how on earth he would get all that equipment in there.

Slipping her quarter into a moneybag around my waist, I noticed the lady had not moved. Her smile widened as she held up a key ring. Like blue ornaments on a Christmas tree, the keys were interspersed with hanging baubles catching the sunlight. I nodded politely, smiled and turned back toward the car, which was looking more like a low rider. The man maneuvered a large bench. Just where was all that stuff going?

I felt another tap on my shoulder. The lady held out another quarter. She obviously didn't speak English. Did she think she hadn't paid enough for the ornament? I held up the palm of my hand toward her, and with head and hand gestures, tried to indicate that twenty-five cents was more than enough for the tiny ceramic ornament. I watched the small figure leave, talking animatedly to a younger lady. Maybe her daughter, I thought. The woman's dark head bobbed as she walked to their car, obviously happy with her purchase.

I turned again to the car, overloaded with exercise equipment, and saw the man frantically searching his pockets, while volunteers looked under the tables.

I turned to the volunteer next to me. "Lost his keys," she said shaking her head. "Left them on the table."

"Keys," I whispered, remembering the blue baubles hanging from the key ring. "Oh no."

"I saw that lady holding something up. You didn't sell her his keys, did you?" a volunteer asked, placing her hands on her hips and glaring at me.

I took a step back. Did the Asian woman think she was buying the keys? I remembered her smiling face as she dangled them in front of me.

"Well for heaven's sake, doesn't he have a spare key?" I retorted. "Perhaps someone could drive him home to get it."

I saw the man shake his head. "My house key was on there too."

"We'll pray," said Polly. "God will work this out." With confidence she disappeared into the center.

I knew she would faithfully pray as I tried to think of a way for God to fix this. I shook my head. This was impossible. Parting the Red Sea seemed an easier task than finding a small Asian woman in a large town.

"Who buys keys anyway?" I frowned. "What would someone want with keys?"

"Well, who would sell someone's keys?" a volunteer responded in disgust.

Maybe praying was the solution. I sat on a step and had a heart-to-heart with God, but I was at a loss as to how to advise Him on this one. He'd be on His own sorting out this mess.

I opened my eyes and saw two small dark-haired ladies walking toward me. I blinked. Surely it wasn't the lady with the keys.

I stood and stared. Her daughter held out her hand and dangled the keys in front of me.

"How did you…?"

"We met someone at another yard sale who overheard everyone here talking about keys."

I raised my eyebrow.

"She said someone described my mother."

"But keys?"

"She collects them." The daughter hugged her mother's arm. "She has four hundred sets."

The door from the center opened. "Oh good," said Polly nonchalantly as she watched the man start his car. "God brought the keys back." She nodded as if mentally checking off another prayer request from her list, then scurried back to work.

A single cloud drifted across the now-radiant blue sky. I looked to the heavens, "Maybe You don't need my help after all."

~Ann Summerville

"Instead of an egg hunt this year, the kids will be gathering at the parsonage to look for my lost keys."

74

14k Moment

Prayer is the language of the heart.
~Grace Aguilar

Lighthearted, my husband Lee and I set out for a weekend of fun and business. We drove for an hour, stopped for lunch, and then resumed our journey.

"I hope things go okay at the association's meeting," I said, watching sun-washed South Carolina landscape glide past. "Last year was such a downer, with the organization's power shift and all. Everybody was edgy, and at times, downright snappy. It's all behind us now. Most of those people are friends, and real friends can agree to disagree."

"True. Good attitude, sweetheart."

I smiled at him. "Thanks again for this beautiful gold watch. It's such a special Christmas gift." I rubbed his arm affectionately as he drove. "It was sweet of Pam and Bubba to chip in on it." I would thank our daughter and son-in-law again when we visited them on our return trip home.

I teased, "At least now I won't have to always ask you what time it is." I dramatically hiked up my wrist to demonstrate—then froze. "Lee!" I gasped. "It's gone. My watch... it's not on my arm!"

"I fastened the safety clasp for you," he answered. "How could it happen?"

"It can't be," I repeatedly groaned as I searched every nook and cranny in the van, including all the tote bags we had used along the way. I called the restaurant where we'd earlier dined. They found nothing.

Sprawled on the car floor, I wept and wailed as I hadn't since toddlerhood. "It's not fair!" I threw back my head and bawled harder, figuring I'd earned this uncharacteristic tantrum. "Why, Lord?" I felt so betrayed.

"It'll be okay, honey." Lee comforted me as best he could while driving, encouraging me not to let it spoil the weekend. "After all, watches are replaceable."

"It's not that—it's the love it represents. You three sacrificed to buy it for me. How am I ever going to tell Pam and Bubba?" I burst into fresh tears.

At our destination, we searched the van again. Coming up empty-handed, we concluded the safety clasp had somehow come loose and the watch had fallen off somewhere, perhaps at a rest area or the restaurant parking lot.

"Nobody's going to return a gold watch," I muttered, toting my overnight case into the motel room. Inside, I paused to silently pray but felt as if my words only bounced off the ceiling.

Later, at the business reunion, one dear friend was distinctly cool to me. She'd not forgiven me for what, to her, had been my divided loyalty the previous year during our association's difficult overhaul. My understanding—that we'd agreed to disagree—had apparently been off-target.

On the way home we stopped at Pam and Bubba's. They were sympathetic about the watch's disappearance but I harbored a certainty that I'd disappointed them.

Thereafter, an odd grief seeped into me and refused to leave, compounding fibromyalgia's grip on me. On my best days, brain fog persevered. Depression stalked, smothery and persistent. Inside, exhaustion and pain belied my outward smile.

Romans 8:28 helped keep it from swallowing me whole: "And we know that all things work together for the good to those who love God, to those who are the called according to His purpose."

I truly tried to trust the Lord.

I again recalled the loss of my gold watch. It symbolized the washout I'd become. Finally and deliberately, I repressed the incident from my mind.

In coming days, my mirror reflected a gaunt tragic figure. Hopelessness joined the pitiful parade.

Sunny springtime days began to slowly restore me. And then, a sudden setback toppled me back into bed.

"You're going to be up and about soon." Long-suffering Lee sat on my bed, holding my hand. He prayed for me and I dozed.

I awoke later in the afternoon, feeling worse than ever. I tried to pray. "Lord, help," then sighed with resignation.

Suddenly, a peculiar urge struck to transfer my cosmetics from my old satchel to one I'd recently purchased. I laboriously gathered both bags and returned to my heating pad. Listlessly, I commenced plucking individual, small zipped pouches from the old bag and dropping them into the new one.

Soon, I reached the bottom of the dilapidated satchel I'd carried so long that safety pins held it together. My fingers shuffled remaining debris, searching. "Like my life," I thought dryly as my hand sifted old cotton balls, hairpins, half-used lipsticks. Nothing significant. Ugly.

I sighed, then grabbed the bedside garbage basket to junk it.

"Wait!" screamed a voice in my head.

I stilled. "Turn the tattered bag upside down." The succinct command bypassed reasoning, but I spread a plastic bag over my lap and dumped the contents.

Pure junk.

Then I glimpsed gold peeking through the mess. It shimmered and something inside me shimmered too. I reached out and touched it.

My gold watch.

Wonder washed over me. My heart swelled and pounded with a bliss I'd not felt since childhood. My limbs tingled to dance.

In that sacred golden moment, I gazed up and acknowledged God. "How like you," I thought, unable to speak as tears gathered.

"Gold, the alpha and the omega of this odyssey. At my lowest ebb, in my darkest moment, amid junk and dust, you literally dump this miracle in my lap."

A honey-rich peace poured over me. Energy and clarity enveloped me. In that heartbeat, my healing began.

My little watch sparkles as a daily reminder of that one 14k moment of healing and hope.

~Emily Sue Harvey

A Special Lady

I never went to bed in my life and I never ate a meal in my life without
saying a prayer. I know my prayers have been answered thousands of times,
and I know that I never said a prayer in my life without
something good coming of it.
~Jack Dempsey

I rushed out of the feed store, eager to get home, when I heard
her. I turned to see a darling little filly in a small fenced-in area
in the parking lot. It seemed cruel to keep this beautiful animal
penned up in a four-by-nine stall. Drawn by her beauty, I walked over
to her. Her soft warm nuzzle against my bare arm that hot summer
day almost made me cry.

"Hi! You're a pretty lady!" I rubbed her nose and she immediately
responded with a series of neighs that seemed to say, "Buy me."

I hurried home and tried to go about my business as usual, but
I kept hearing an echo in my thoughts. "Love me."

I had recently begun to seek a closer walk with God. I had a
yearning in my heart to know God in a deeper way. My husband,
Emmitt, did not understand my new commitment and worried I'd go
"overboard with religion."

"Dear Lord," I prayed, "please don't let me turn Emmitt away
from You. Draw him toward You. More than anything in the world, I
want him to love You with all his heart."

I took Emmitt to see the horse, which I already called Lady in my thoughts. Emmitt had a very tender spot for animals, especially horses, and we bought her on the spot!

Since we lived at the edge of town and had an acre of backyard, we thought caring for her at home had more advantages than taking her to our small farm. Emmitt didn't admit how much he loved Lady, but I caught him many times talking to her from the window and he spent all his extra time outside with her. He brushed her mane and tail and led her around the backyard with her halter. When he took her halter off, she followed him anyway. Lady became a privileged character, and she knew it. She ran around inside the yard with the dogs, shaking her beautiful head and prancing like a circus pony.

We kept our animals safely enclosed inside a chain-link fence, but Lady and the dogs ran the length of the fence every time a car went by. One day I found her chasing cars with them. "Oh no! She thinks she's a dog!"

As we loved, enjoyed and laughed at our playful filly, she grew into a very beautiful animal. Summer came, and she ate everything that grew through the chain-link fence and everything she could reach over it. Rose bushes, trees, nothing within her reach was safe. The last straw occurred when she pulled the window screen off the bedroom window. She peeked in.

I finally persuaded Emmitt to take Lady to the farm. Although he couldn't spend as much time with her there, our yard improved considerably.

What a thrill to see her in her newfound freedom. She held her magnificent head and tail high, running like a racehorse.

Then it happened. Emmitt came home from the farm with sorrow written all over his face. "Lady's suddenly gone lame. I can't figure out what happened. She was all right this morning. The vet just left and he can't find anything wrong."

I'll admit that at times I had been a bit jealous of Lady because Emmitt spent so much time with her, but the thought of her hopping around on three legs made my heart ache, too.

Three weeks later, after shots, liniment rubs and many anxious moments, she had not improved at all.

One day a friend just "happened" to loan me a tape about a man who prayed for his horse and it got well. Emmitt and I listened intently to the tape and discovered that God cares about what we care about, even animals.

"Come on," he shouted, jumping up. "We're going to the farm right now and pray for Lady!"

It was a balmy summer night. The moonlight reflected on Lady, and the three of us seemed to sense the awesome beauty and wonder of God. A myriad of stars twinkled overhead, and the distant cooing of doves gave the midnight peace a holy hush. Lady neighed to us in her usual way as we walked up to her. She put her velvety soft nose against Emmitt's shirt and stood motionless on three legs.

"Thank You, Lord," he prayed aloud, "for showing me how real You are. Whether You heal Lady or not, my life will never be the same. And how I praise You for that."

Then Emmitt poured out his heart to God. I cried knowing that no matter how God chose to answer Emmitt's prayer for Lady, He had begun a new work in Emmitt's life.

From that moment on, I had a new husband. He awakened the next morning with a renewed zest for living, grateful for everything in this wonderful world our God has made. We could hardly wait to get to the farm. As we pulled into the gate I saw Lady, still hobbling around on three legs. I hurt most of all for Emmitt's sake.

"I don't care if Lady is crippled the rest of her life, I praise God for everything!" he said.

I silently shot up a prayer of thanksgiving as Emmitt expressed his newfound faith.

It was a gorgeous day at the farm. Lady neighed to us in her loving way. Even the birds seemed to say, "Bless you."

"No use keeping Lady shut up in the lot like this. I'll open the gate. At least maybe she can limp around and eat a little green grass," Emmitt suggested.

The instant he opened the gate, something seemed to quicken in Lady.

She shot out of that gate with her head and tail held high,

running like the wind! A thoroughbred could not compare with her beauty. She galloped the full length of the pasture and back to us on four strong, sturdy legs.

It was then I looked at my husband. Tears streamed down his face and his arms stretched toward Heaven in thanksgiving. My heart leaped; the feelings I felt for this man overwhelmed me and I loved him more than ever.

Not only had God answered Emmitt's prayer for Lady, He answered my prayer for Emmitt.

~Joan Clayton

76

Treasure Stored in Secret Places

I will give you the treasures of darkness, riches stored in secret place.
~Isaiah 45:3

M ight I have thrown those photographs away? I started searching for them several months after my older sister and only sibling, Yvonne, died.

Those photos of her three cats represented much about my sister that I admired and loved, plus memories that comforted me. Yvonne was creative and artistic and photography became her major outlet. But her hobby gave her more than just something to do; it helped her self-image.

Yvonne had been obese, shy around strangers, and lacked self-confidence. When she started taking photography classes at a community college, she met people who shared her interests and instructors who praised her work and encouraged her. She became quite good, in fact, and in an era before digital photography, even purchased equipment and developed her own prints.

Searching for subjects, she would approach a stranger with an interesting face and ask if she could take his or her picture. People often approached her and asked if she'd take a picture of their children, pet or grandmother. These experiences helped her become more outgoing and improved her self-esteem.

Then her husband died suddenly of a heart attack. They were

childless, and I was concerned about how my sister would cope living alone. She had always loved animals, so she adopted three kittens, sibling brothers, almost identical gray-striped tabbies. I was happy she had three little companions, and with her camera she kept a record of her "kitty boys."

Her husband's life insurance was inadequate for her to live on, so she found a part-time job in the small town where she lived. I often visited her comfortable home, enjoying her screened-in porch with white wicker furniture, tropical cushions, and a vase of flowers on a small table. There, in spring, summer and fall, Yvonne sat with coffee or a book. Her cats took a chair and together they watched birds, squirrels, and flowering crabapple trees. For almost eighteen years, the four of them spent many pleasant hours together on the porch.

When Yvonne died, I promised myself not to go overboard keeping stuff. I retrieved only things I could use or that had special meaning to me. From the hundreds of photographs, I threw many away. Among them was an album full of cat photos, some taken on Yvonne's porch, capturing the characteristics, postures, and behaviors that cat lovers appreciate. Those I removed from the album, still in their plastic sheets, and brought home. I put them, along with some letters and cards from my sister's house, in a cardboard box and placed it in a storage room.

Several months later, I wanted to show those cat photos to a friend. But they weren't in the box. I searched through all our photos, thinking I'd moved them. Over the next two months, I searched through that storage room two more times, opening every cupboard, searching all the shelves. No photos.

One night I was in bed thinking of Yvonne and missing her. I'm a believer in prayer, and I pray every day. That night I talked to God, saying, "It really bothers me, Father, that I can't find those pictures of the cats. I can't imagine I threw them away. Please help me find them."

While praying, I got an image in my mind of a particular plastic storage box. Could I have put those photos in there? Maybe I buried them under other stuff in that container.

I got out of bed and searched the container, taking everything out. No pictures. I turned around and stared at the cupboards where we store our own photo alums, the cupboards I'd searched through at least three times before. I flipped through a couple of albums, sighed, and replaced them on the shelf.

Then I stretched, barely reaching the knob on a top cupboard. When I opened the door, a white business-size envelope fell out and landed on the floor. I picked it up and I turned it over. On the front, in my own handwriting, were the words "Y's cats." Sure enough, inside were the cat photos. I sorted through them over and over, breathing, "Thank you, Father."

I still have no recollection of moving those photographs, but no doubt I did in my haze after Yvonne's funeral. I wondered, though, why I'd visualized a plastic storage container as I'd prayed. In Isaiah 45:3, God spoke to a king, promising him victories and the spoils of battle. "I will give you the treasures of darkness, and hidden riches of secret places…." God told him. But they would come through miraculous means, not by anything that the king could picture in his mind. Why? "So that you may know that I am the Lord."

That's a secret I will share.

~Paulette Zubel

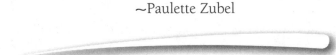

77

God, Hear the Cry of My Heart

I will not leave you as orphans; I will come to you.
~John 14:18

Rain pouring steadily outside chilled me until I wondered if I would ever feel cozy and cheerful again. The loneliness was unbearable on this bleak, dreary January day.

I felt desolate and listless. In trying to pray, I couldn't find peace because of my despair.

I lived in the country and was somewhat homebound due to my blindness and lack of transportation. At these times, I kept occupied listening to audio books and CDs while cooking and cleaning house. Today not even praise music helped my mood.

Others understandably were involved in their own busy lives yet it seemed as if the world was passing me by.

I continued to cry out to God, hoping he would somehow console me.

Soon after I got up from my knees, the phone rang.

"Hi Pam!" Mary's smile came through the phone line.

"Oh, hi Mary, it's good to hear from you. How are you doing?"

"I slipped and fell on the ice and broke my leg."

"Oh Mary, I'm sorry."

"Pam, there's another reason I'm calling besides to get your sympathy." Mary paused. "Now that I'm laid up, I realize how you must feel with your limitations yet I complain more than you ever do."

I chuckled. "Wow! Someone's worse off than I am. I feel better already."

"See why I called? You always give me a boost."

"Seriously, Mary, thank you for thinking of me while you're having your own challenge."

"That's because you are an example to me, Pam. You never give up and your disabilities are not stumbling blocks. I need to see my life as more of an adventure like you do."

"I've been down today too," I admitted to Mary. "It's nice to hear someone remind me that life isn't so bad."

"We all have our problems. I lie here bored with reading and restless, wanting to be active. If I have to look at these four walls one more minute I'll go crazy."

I laughed. "At least you can see the four walls."

"Hey! You've got me there. I take for granted being able to drive. As soon as I'm mobile, let's go out to lunch, okay?"

"You've got a date."

"One blessing: this accident gives me time to meditate and to value my friends."

"There's always a bright side. I'm not glad you broke your leg but I'm happy you called."

I hung up the phone, feeling all aglow inside, like a renewed person. Mary understood. She couldn't walk yet she had run a mile in my shoes. I experienced gratitude that someone cared.

The sun had broken through the clouds. It streamed through my window and felt warm on my face.

"I'm not alone," I whispered.

God had answered my prayer. The Lord's words filled my mind, "I will not leave you comfortless."

~Pam Johnson Bostwick

From Princesses to Pirates

Behold, children are a heritage from the LORD.
~Psalm 127:3

T he day we became foster parents to two-and-a-half-year-old twins Damian and Darian our "ship" changed course and all we could do was hold on for the ride.

For ten years our home had been filled with princesses, ponytails and politeness. As the parents of four girls ranging in age from three to ten, my husband Eddie and I felt we had everything under control.

We had a good understanding of what girls were all about. As the one male in this world of princesses, Eddie was great at fitting in and was the knight in shining armor in this pink fairytale world. He attended more tea parties than I'm sure he'd ever admit to his friends, and he could put the girls' hair in ponytails faster than you could say "Barbie."

Manners were important and instilled in the girls early on. Pleases and thank yous filled our home. Hair ties, barrettes and frilly hats covered the bathroom counter. When we took the family out to dinner, we often received compliments regarding the girls' good behavior.

Around age three, each of the girls went through a princess stage. They dressed up in the pinkest, shiniest, laciest clothes they could find and slipped into some over-sized heels. The linoleum kitchen floor became their runway.

"Mommy, look at my fabulous dress," they would say while sauntering across the room. This phase in their lives was all about looking good and being sure to accessorize properly.

Playtime was organized with rules and lots of discussion. It didn't matter if the girls were playing ball outside or playing a game inside, whatever they did, there always seemed to be some level of control.

Don't get me wrong, it wasn't always tea parties and rainbows. The girls had their share of arguments, screaming matches and even the occasional tantrums. Just the fact there were four of them meant activity always filled the house. But when it came time to relax, the girls had no problem sitting and reading a book, coloring or watching a movie.

Eddie and I always felt for the sibling groups in foster care. We knew that many brothers and sisters were split up because the system simply didn't have the resources to keep them together. We prayed for years that God would open our hearts and home to a sibling group. We waited patiently for several years until we heard God clearly say, "Permission to climb aboard Captain!"

That was when our two little pirates, Damian and Darian, clamored onboard. Adorable, with sweet smiles, they were filled with the true essence of two-year-olds and boyhood—energetic, curious, fearless and constantly on the move.

Our calm princess ship was rocked to the core. We had to batten down the hatches, revise our course of action and prepare for the journey ahead. Any sense of direction and predictability was immediately thrown overboard.

As foster children, the boys had more than your typical two-year-old issues. Their lives had been filled with uncertainty, inconsistency, many changes, and limited boundaries. To them everything was fair game to touch, taste and ultimately destroy.

The noise level in our house went from chatty to thunderous. Gone were the days of all the kids sitting down reading a book. The boys would have no part of it; they had a whole world to conquer.

And conquer they did. Sticks became swords; spoons became

guns; stairs became slides. They were oblivious to the potential consequences of their actions. It seemed their motto was "smile and go for it!"

I spent my days trying to keep them safe and alive. While one of the boys slid down the banister, the other bolted for the front door. I'd have to make a mad dash for the banister boy and yell to one of the older girls to nab the other one. After rounding them up and bringing them to what I thought was a safe location, I would try to take a moment to recover.

Then one of the girls would run up to me. "Mommy, look at my sparkly purple dress."

"Oh, that is beautiful honey. Turn around let me…"

Another daughter declared, "Mommy, Darian is eating something from the trash and I don't know what it is."

I would stop him just in time to see Damian taking off the plastic safety cover from the outlet, ready to stick something into it. By the time Eddie came home from work, I'm sure I looked liked I had been fed to the sharks.

Every day it felt like our ship traveled through a big storm with waves crashing against us, winds howling, sailing in no direction, and all we could do was hang on. By the evening the storm would subside and our crew would sleep. Eddie and I often prayed, "God, is this really what you wanted for our family? If this is Your will, shouldn't it be much easier?" Then it would be morning again: "All hands on deck!"

This went on for several long months. Just as Eddie and I were at the end of our rope, something amazing started to happen. The storms became rain showers, then just overcast, then the sun started to appear more often and our ship became more steady.

Our pirates began learning from the princesses. There were more pleases and thank yous, they sat for a few minutes to hear a story and occasionally I spotted a pirate running around in a pink sparkly skirt.

Our princesses began learning that not everything had to begin with a plan and discussion. Sometimes it was just fun to let loose, jump in and try something new. Plus, pirates have some great toys to play with.

Since the boys first arrived, our lives have changed dramatically, but it is clear now that God had an amazing plan for the boys and our family all along. Damian and Darian did not come into our lives the same ways the girls did, but that doesn't matter.

The boys' adoption was finalized a few years ago. Our permanent crew is now complete. With God at the helm, we don't always know the direction we're sailing, but with all our princesses and pirates onboard, we are grateful and excited about the adventure that lies ahead.

~Heather Stephen

Reprinted by permission of Off the Mark
and Mark Parisi © 2010.

79

To Susie with Love

You pray in your distress and in your need;
would you might pray also in the fullness of your joy
and in your days of abundance.
~Kahlil Gibran

When Dad was killed in an auto accident, the tragedy jerked the earth from beneath my feet, robbing me of my father's rock-steady presence. During my time of bereavement, I felt compelled to write a book of family memoirs from my storyteller Dad's perspective. The idea excited my married children.

"Go for it, Mom," encouraged Pam, my oldest daughter. "Papa and his stories were certainly colorful enough. And you two were so alike. You talked a lot, so you should be able to remember lots of them."

"Oh, we talked." I had to laugh. "Did we ever talk! But I wish I'd probed deeper and listened, really listened, instead of wishing he'd not tell me the same things again and again."

I wanted to weep now, wondering just how many golden nuggets I'd passed up by being too busy with life to listen.

I paused, letting memory fragments surface. They were sporadic and scattered, my recall of Dad's adventures in a sharecropper's family of fourteen kids. He'd managed, against all odds, to survive and go on to rise above the ordinary.

"Such intelligence," I murmured, "... and his preoccupation with armchair writing."

The next morning I went into my office and began. By noon, the Dad-factos list stretched long: WWII veteran who refused a medal for bravery... finished high school/business college under the GI Bill... though never attaining affluence, he was an excellent provider who exemplified character and integrity... handsome, regal bearing... musical. I decided to call it a day.

That night in bed, I prayed, "Father God, I'm sorry for the times I've not listened to your voice, just as I ignored Daddy's. I've missed so many vital messages and truths. Please help it not hurt so much. Thanks for loving me and allowing me to lean on you more. Amen."

When I arose the next morning, a mild lethargy weighted my limbs and dulled my brain. I now faced giving the story life, vitality and substance. But as I sat before the computer, my mind blanked. I'd exhausted my Dad-data reservoir. I swiveled my chair away from the half-finished sentence.

At lunchtime, Lee, my husband, took one look at me. "What's wrong?"

It all came pouring out. "There are so many gaps. Why didn't I listen more to his endless rambling about bygone days?" I spread wide my hands. "Such wit and wisdom. Why didn't I really listen? Now I hunger for all those tiresome details. I grieve not only for him but for all the unfinished talks. I long to know the aunts, uncles, cousins, grandparents..."

Back at my desk, the melancholy refused to lift. I said a listless half-hearted prayer.

"Music," I muttered, "that's what I need." I rummaged in my filing cabinet for tapes to spring me from my depression. When I couldn't find them, I dashed upstairs to search.

Grief still hovered as I descended the stairs. "Lord, please help me."

Compelled, I returned to the filing cabinet and opened the same drawer I'd earlier searched. Where were those tapes?

Something new drew my attention. Protruding from a folder in the back jutted the corner of a composition book. Where did that come from? I hadn't seen it earlier. Across the unfamiliar cover I saw a familiar scrawl. Dad's handwriting filled the entire back cover. A chill rippled up my spine.

The front cover read: "A History of James H. Miller and his ancestors. This is not a complete history, mind you, only recollections I've committed to memory, a faulty memory at that."

Like a slow-motion tidal wave, the enormity of it crashed in on me, leaving me awash with wonder.

"Thank you, Lord," I whispered again and again, sensing keenly the sacredness of the moment. Reverently, I turned the notebook over again. That's when I saw the words: "To Susie With Love."

I hugged the book to my heart, then sat and read for hours, wiping away tears. Gaps filled in. A three-dimensional James emerged. His voice rang full and nurturing. I met my great-great-grandfather, a wealthy landowner who emigrated from England in the early 1800s and sired three sons. I met caricature cousins and visited a kind-hearted Aunt Sis.

I could hardly contain the joy, the sheer wonder of it all.

I recalled a hectic family dinner at my house a few weeks before Dad's death. He'd sat in my office as I dashed about hosting. Was that when? His busy daughter could not be harnessed for a ceremonial presentation of his handwritten journal, so had he merely slipped it into my filing cabinet, knowing one day I would find and appreciate it?

God knew the perfect timing. I threw my head back and laughed from sheer bliss. Imagine, Father God and Daddy in cahoots!

My melancholy vanished. I spent the afternoon with my father. Dad did all the talking, and I finally listened.

~Emily Sue Harvey

80

Say Thanks

I not only begin praying when I kneel down, but I do not leave off praying when I rise up.
~Thomas Adams

I wrapped my arm around the pillow and pushed it under my head. Though I was absolutely exhausted, sleep would not come. I tried to lie still so I wouldn't disturb David. My pastor husband would be up by 4:00 a.m. on Sunday as usual.

Tears spilled as I cried out to God. For over a year a growing weakness had crept over my body. For the past five months I couldn't walk from my recliner in the family room to our bedroom without stopping in the hallway to lean against the wall and rest. First a hacking cough caused me to leave my job as a radio program host. I tried to hang on to my work, but pre-recording everything so I could edit out my coughing squashed spontaneity and made interaction with listeners difficult. My full-time job went down to a three-hour day, and even then twice I was too weak to get out of my chair at the end of my shift. The receptionist called David to come carry me to the car. Finally I had no choice but to leave my job.

I relinquished my Bible study group to another leader because I couldn't talk above a whisper without breaking into fits of coughing. We cancelled my weekly sermon for children and found another person to teach the junior high Sunday school class. Instead of leading every activity, I could only sit and watch.

I had been to three specialists and had every test in the book.

Every lab test, procedure and doctor reported the same findings... there was no explanation for my symptoms.

"God," I ranted, "what do You want from me? Why are You doing this? I can't go on without hope that my strength will return."

Although the coughing had stopped, the weakness deepened its grip and squeezed out every ounce of energy. It was so unfair to David—he hadn't signed up as caregiver for a wife who sat in a chair while he cooked and cleaned. He didn't complain, but I could see that caring for me was tearing him away from his work at the church.

I finally slept for a few hours, and when I awoke, David had already left. I moved to his side of the bed and snuggled into his pillow, comforted by his lingering scent. Again I pleaded with God to heal me, not for my sake, but for David's. He needed his life back.

This time as I begged God, I clearly heard Him say, "Julia, you haven't told Me thank you."

Tell Him thank you? "What do I have to be thankful for? My life has been ripped from me. I've done every good thing I know to do. I've followed You all my life. I've served You by serving Your people. My reward had been sickness. It isn't fair!"

God ignored my ranting and continued. "I've cleared your schedule, you have no responsibilities and no one expects anything of you. I've given you a chance to start over with your time and you've not told Me thank you."

My anger and resentment melted. God was right. There was not one thing I had to do. "Thank you," I murmured. "Thank you for letting me start over."

After church later that morning we drove from our home in southern Oregon to Seattle to see friends heading back to their mission in Mongolia. After the seven-hour drive, I was exhausted when we got to our hotel. I may have told God thank you, but nothing had changed for me. David still had to carry me into our room.

Before I fell asleep I thought about my conversation with God the night before. What good was a fresh start if I still didn't have enough energy to do anything?

In the early morning hours God spoke to me again. "I will heal you," He said, "but it will be a long obedience in the same direction." What did "long obedience in the same direction" mean? When would He heal me? What exactly did He want me to do? I was more confused than ever.

After breakfast with our friends, they decided to visit Seattle's aquarium. As we entered, David pointed out some benches where I could sit and rest. I shook my head.

"So far I'm feeling all right," I said. As we moved slowly through the facility David hovered over me, urging me to take it easy. "I'll sit at the next resting place," I told him.

When our friends, who knew little about my illness, suggested we walk five blocks to a restaurant for lunch, I cringed. "I need a head start," I warned. "I'll have to stop to rest along the way."

Surprisingly, I walked straight to the restaurant.

After lunch we meandered all through Pike Place Market. My husband and I stared at each other in disbelief, amazed at my ability to keep walking.

As the day went along, my astonishment grew. I wasn't overflowing with energy, but neither did I have to stop to rest.

Finally we stood before an art booth at Pike Place. David hugged me and shared my joy when I exclaimed, "God stepped into my life and worked a miracle!"

Together we gazed at a print there, by artist Beth Hendrickson Logan, of children waiting for a school bus under an umbrella in the rain. One boy is standing off to the side, joyfully looking up to the sky, with rain splashing his upturned face. The caption reads, "Smile at the rain."

Every time I see the picture hanging in my home I'm reminded that no matter what I go through, I can smile. God always has a plan with a loving purpose in mind. He is in charge of my time, He controls my agenda. I must simply commit to long obedience in the same direction… and lift my head to the rain and say, "Thank You."

~Julia A. Ewert

81

A Snowy Hospital Holiday

And the child grew and became strong in spirit, filled with wisdom;
and the grace of God was on Him.
~Luke 2:40

Christmas Eve 1955, I sat on the wide marble windowsill of my third floor hospital room in the Essex County Isolation Hospital. I looked longingly at the circular driveway leading up to the front entrance and let my tears flow freely. Not because the predicted snowfall turned into a major blizzard, but for me, a twelve-year-old girl diagnosed with tuberculosis, confined to six months of isolation and forced to swallow handfuls of pills.

And because it was Christmastime and I wasn't home.

A white blanket of snow covered the hospital's grounds and shiny ice coated the trees… a scene any photographer would describe as a perfect postcard picture. Who wouldn't appreciate this wonderful winter Christmas gift from God? Me, that's who.

"God," I prayed, "I'm really mad at You and not sure I like You much." That was true. I wanted to be with my family, not in a hospital. I also had a slew of questions, which I didn't hesitate to ask: "Why did you let my daddy die? Why did I have to get sick? Why am I stuck in this room? Nobody can come in but the nurses, and then they have to put on those ugly green gowns and gloves before they even touch me. Why does a glass wall separate me and the rest of the world?" In between my angry tears I told Him, "It's not fair that I can't celebrate Christmas with my mom and brother."

I soon realized that nothing I said made a difference and I had to accept what was. Besides, He was probably not even listening.

I'd have to spend the day alone in my room, on my ugly brown metal bed, reading another chapter of my favorite Nancy Drew mystery. Alone.

There'd be no going to church to celebrate Jesus's birthday, no caroling, no presents, no gathering of the relatives around the table, no sharing the stuffed turkey with all the trimmings, no playing games, no listening to family stories late into the night. This would all have to wait until next year when I returned home... if I got better.

I said "if" because my father died of TB just three months after he found out he had it. And I believed I would die too. I knew about God and heaven and eternal happiness but I was young and wanted to go to college, get married, have kids, and live to be a grandma. I prayed about that too, but got no sign that He even heard me.

I sat alone on the hospital room windowsill on Christmas morning. The nurses on duty bubbled with holiday spirit as they carried out their morning routines. They brought in the breakfast tray with a candy cane stuck in my bowl of oatmeal. They gave me my medication in a small red cup. "A splash of Christmas spirit," said one.

Later in the day they strolled up and down the hallway, sang Christmas carols and took requests for favorites. They passed out gifts, wrapped with jolly-faced Santa Claus paper.

Regular visiting hours weren't until two o'clock in the afternoon. I knew not to expect any visitors, especially after Father Francis, a priest from the nearby church, didn't show up with Holy Communion. His absence only proved how bad the blizzard was, because if he could have come, he would have. Just like my mother and brother. If they could have come, they would have.

Just after lunch, a loud "Ho! Ho! Ho! Merry Christmas!" and the jingling of sleigh bells echoed down the hallway. From my isolation room I observed through the glass wall. Most kids stood at their doors smiling with delight. A few of the younger patients made a speedy dash to the nurses' station shouting, "It's Santa!"

Yes, Santa Claus, dressed in his best red Christmas outfit and shiny black boots, had found his way to the hospital. Over his shoulder he toted an oversized black bag, bulging at the seams. He made his way to every room with gifts. For me, he handed gifts to a nurse who dressed in a green isolation gown to bring them into my room. I ripped open a Paint-by-Numbers kit, a new Nancy Drew mystery and a jar of multicolored hard candies. This surprise brought joy to my dreary room and heart.

The day went on and I still felt sad without my family there to enjoy the festivities with me. I looked out the window and noticed the driveway had been cleared and cars were inching their way toward the front door. A few people walked up the sidewalk after getting off a public bus. Traffic along the main road showed signs of things getting back to normal in the world outside.

Then out of nowhere, people bundled in winter clothing; carrying Christmas wrapped bags and boxes, filled our hallway. Families arrived, one by one in small groups. I heard squeals of happiness and hoped against hope that my mother and brother would show up too. But they didn't even have a car; there was no way they could come.

I wanted to pray, again, but so far, God had ignored every prayer I whispered. There was no use. I decided to take a bubble bath to pass the time.

From the bathroom, I heard a knock on the glass wall and I peeked out. There they stood, my mom and brother with rosy cheeks, wrapped presents and great big smiles. "Merry Christmas!" they shouted.

I rushed to the window and cried with happiness. "I didn't think I'd see you today!" They must have ridden the bus two hours to get there.

I wanted to burst out into the hallway, hug them and never let go. But instead, we put our open hands on the glass wall, palm to palm, pretending we were touching. I could feel their love through the glass.

That night my prayer included an apology. "I'm sorry God for doubting that You were listening. I really knew better. Thank you for getting my family to the hospital. This was the best Christmas ever. I'll never forget it as long as I live."

And I haven't.

~Helen Colella

82

Selfless Love

We will give ourselves continuously to prayer and to the ministry of the word.
~Acts 6:4

I watched our son envelop her in his arms as she sobbed. "It's okay, it's okay," he soothed.

She stepped back, looked up at him and, half laughing and crying, whispered, "These are tears of joy and answered prayers."

They both chuckled, lightening the moment. The ten of us surrounding the two of them mopped our tears too.

Drying her eyes, the woman held my son's hands and gave him a head to toe once over, as she had done eighteen years earlier, when she gave birth to him. This time he looked back at her with the heart of a wise, mature young man. As if the two were alone in the room, he said tenderly, "I hope you have no regrets, I have not a one. I am proud of you for choosing life for me."

Eighteen years earlier, my husband Tom and I were in the process of adopting overseas when a local adoption agency called. We anxiously submitted our profile to the seventeen-year-old mother. After combing through numerous prospective parent profiles, she wanted to meet us right away.

We walked into the agency, shook hands with our adoption counselor, and out of the corner of my eye, I saw her sitting in a chair swinging her legs nervously. Her hands folded over her five-month pregnant tummy, protruding from her petite frame. Before our counselor could introduce us, I moved toward her. As if we had known each other a lifetime, I put my arms around her. We pulled away and her deep brown eyes met mine and we embraced again. Then she hugged Tom. The moment I feared would be awkward was comforting. There was an instant bond. We would be her son's parents.

A few months later I woke to the sound of the phone ringing at 12:42 a.m. Groggily, I mustered, "Hello?" Within three seconds and hearing the words, "She's in labor," I scrambled into my clothes, grabbed the two bags by the door that had been packed for three weeks, and quickly jumped into my car to drive the 100 miles. Luckily, Tom was working in the same city where I was heading. I ran back into the house and called him. Awakened from his sound sleep, he exclaimed, "I'll meet you there... Mom."

That word sounded foreign, yet right. The day we'd prayed for had arrived. Smiling, I hung up the phone, ran outside and began my travels into motherhood.

Fog hung low as I drove too fast that early March morning. "God, you have walked our journey and know what we have been through trying to start a family. Please get me there safely to witness the birth of my son." Then I prayed for the young girl in labor. "Please make this delivery as painless as possible for our young Tawnya. May she come to know our appreciation of her selfless love, letting us raise her son to be our own."

Driving along I was thankful for North Dakota's flat and straight roads. My head spun with excitement and fear. My pounding heart propelled me to the parking ramp of the hospital. I nearly leapt out of the vehicle and ran to the maternity floor. I found Tom sitting next to Tawnya as they talked and smiled. I gave our dear girl a squeeze and she returned the heartfelt hug.

The nurse came in, checked Tawnya, and told us she had a way to go. Tom left to get coffee and roam the halls and perhaps wrap his head around what was soon to come. I took his chair next to the bed, held Tawnya's hand and stroked it as she fell asleep. I felt concern, sadness and joy all at the same time.

I dozed off and woke to the nurse drawing the curtain around the bed. Soon she said, "It's time to push!"

The doctor swept in with a smile, took Tawnya's hand and spoke softly to her, then turned to us and declared, "Let's have a baby!"

Two hours later, a red, curly-haired, big baby boy was born and placed on Tawnya's chest. Tom cut the cord, then we stood back and watched as Tawnya stroked the baby and talked to him. Tom and I and the nurses all cried.

Then Tawnya placed our son into my arms.

Now I watched him, a strapping eighteen-year-old man, hug her again and say, "You gave me life and chose two incredible people to be my parents."

He stepped to Tom and me. The more he talked, the tighter we held him and each other. He continued, "I've had a life rooted in faith, family, and many friends. I have been blessed a hundred times over. My life has been an answer to all of our prayers."

~Reneé Wall Rongen

Chapter 9

Answered Prayers

Trust in Him

Trust in the LORD, and do good;
dwell in the land and feed on His faithfulness.

~Psalm 37:3

83

Jesus Be My Eyes

When my spirit was overwhelmed within me, then You knew my path.
~Psalm 142:3

That January morning began beautifully. Even at 4:30 a.m., my husband was wide awake and in a silly mood. Getting ready for work, Steve teased me and told jokes, leaving me breathless from laughter.

After handing him his lunchbox and the cell phone, I kissed him goodbye and watched him drive away, offering my usual prayer for his safety.

Ten minutes later, as I sorted the laundry, the ringing phone startled me. No one ever called at 5:00 in the morning, so I instinctively knew it was Steve and that something was wrong.

When I answered, all I heard was my husband's voice weakly repeating my name.

"What's wrong?" I blurted out in a panic.

"I don't know," he gasped. "Help me, please help me!"

I fought back tears, my heart pounding in my chest. "Where are you?"

His voice faded. "I... I... don't know."

I screamed, "Hold on! I'm coming to find you!"

Slamming down the phone, I stumbled up the stairs, frantically pulling jeans on over my pajamas, and sliding into my slippers. I grabbed my purse, fumbling for the truck keys and my glasses. It was only then that I realized I was in trouble.

I had just undergone a series of six eye surgeries, and my vision was severely clouded, making me unable to drive and causing night blindness. Now, here I was in the middle of winter preparing to drive in the dark to look for my husband.

Fear socked me in the gut. By the time I found Steve, he could be dead or I might be killed, driving blind.

Then, like the Psalmist, in my moment of despair I cried out to God, "Jesus, be my eyes!"

I didn't take time to defrost the windshield. Screeching out of the driveway, I started down the road Steve traveled on his commute to work. Hanging my head out the window, I couldn't see the lines on the road.

Twice I narrowly missed sliding into the ditch, but I never stopped praying, "Jesus, be my eyes! Help me to find him in time!"

Somehow the normally heavy traffic during that time of morning stayed a safe distance from my weaving truck. I could barely make out enough landmarks to know which way to turn.

I didn't know if Steve had stopped in the street, pulled off to the side, or even into a parking lot. It would be so easy to go right past him.

"Jesus, be my eyes!"

So many lights glared. So many colors moved in every direction. How would I ever be able to see him?

Then, just ahead on the right, taillights glowed from a vehicle parked awkwardly between the edge of the road and a cornfield.

I pulled behind the car and jumped out, leaving the truck engine running and ignoring the vehicles speeding past me just inches away. Inside, I found Steve slumped over on his side, one arm outstretched, the cell phone still in his hand.

"Steve! Steve!" I shouted.

He roused enough to moan and mumble.

I dialed 911, then did my best to stroke and calm him until the paramedics arrived.

Many hours later, sitting by his hospital bed in the cardiac ward,

I finally broke down. As Steve rested, I told him what had happened, and about how I literally could not see to find him.

Together we agreed. God granted us a miracle in our moment of need, when I cried out, "Jesus, be my eyes!"

I recalled my favorite scripture passage, Psalm 142:3: "When my spirit was overwhelmed within me, then You knew my path."

That day, I truly understood what that verse meant.

When we are unable, God is able. When we are lost, He knows the path. When we cannot see, He will be our eyes.

All we need do is ask, and trust.

~L. Joy Douglas

84

Rain, Rain, Go Away

*Trust in the Lord with all your heart
and lean not on your own understanding.*

~Proverbs 3:5

R ain, rain, rain! I didn't know it totaled 4.5 inches when I set
out for church after dark that January night, like I'd done
for many years.

Seeing no signs or reflectors, I rounded a corner and drove right
into bumper-high water across the road. The car engine died immediately. There I sat with water up to my waist and rising. I knew I
couldn't get out of the car and risk being swept away, so I just sat
there getting very cold. The water rose inside the car. I needed to get
up higher. I pulled the console down between the two front seats,
climbed on it, put my feet on the dashboard and waited for help. And
waited. And waited, freezing.

I saw car lights, but when the driver saw the high water, the car
turned around and went back.

"Please God," I prayed, shivering. "Send help. Save me!"

Two hours later, a car came again and blinked the lights. A
woman called out, "I came back! I called for help!"

A while later, help came and rescued me by boat. An ambulance
took me to the hospital where I stayed for the night and next day. I
had frozen legs and was in shock, but no permanent damage, not
even a cold.

With faith, prayer and calm, I came through this in very good shape.

I'm a thankful eighty-nine-year-old!

~Alberta Wimsett as told to Sharon Orndorff

85

When Your Ship Goes Down

Prayer is not eloquence, but earnestness; not the definition of helplessness,
but the feeling of it; not figures of speech, but earnestness of soul.
~Hannah More

R oss was a sweet five-year-old child in the early 1900s when he admonished his much older brother Clarence for speaking crossly to their mother. In a wise but peculiar statement that far exceeded his youth, Ross said, "Clarence, someday you are going to remember how you spoke to your mother when you are far across the blue waters."

These words came back to haunt Clarence when, a decade later and half a world away, he was in Guadalcanal on a World War I fighter ship.

At the same time, on a Sunday evening, the last rays of a late summer sun shone through the pines surrounding the stately Nordeck United Evangelical Church near my grandparents' farm. As the last strains of "How Great Thou Art" reverberated under the high ceiling, the small congregation nestled in the homemade wooden pews. After Benediction, Clarence's mother, my grandma, gathered her long skirt about her and started down the aisle. Suddenly her face creased with the most grievous look. She laid her Bible and shawl on a pew, threw her arms heavenward, and prayed aloud fervently.

One old-timer exclaimed, "'Taint never heard such a prayer. Makes the hair stand up on the back of my neck."

After an ardent petition, Grandma breathed a holy, "Amen." She raised her head, opened her eyes, fell weakly onto one of the slatted wooden seats and gasped, "It was Clarence. He was in mortal danger, but is safe now."

Months later a letter from Clarence arrived, telling how his ship had been torpedoed. At the very moment of Grandma's intercessory prayer, Clarence was clinging to a piece of drifting debris until a rescue ship finally arrived. Clarence wrote that he knew at the moment the twisted tree trunk floated into his arms that his mother was praying for him. That's when he recalled the words of his little brother years earlier and felt a little sorrow and great relief.

Most of all he felt the love of a saintly mother who was in accord with God.

~Shirley Nordeck Short

Reprinted by permission of
Steve Barr © 2011.

86

When Touch Is a Whispered Prayer

Jesus came and touched them. "Get up," he said. "Don't be afraid."
~Matthew 17:7

I t was dawn, two days before Christmas, and my roommate had left earlier on a long road trip to spend the holidays with her family. It was also trash pick-up day. I had already dragged one bag out through the rear garage door and backyard to the alley. Since I have a physical handicap and walk with crutches, I'm slow at this chore. I left the alley gate and garage door propped open, then went back into the house for the other trash bag. As I approached the kitchen door into the garage, I heard a noise.

"What's going on out there?" I said with a laugh, wondering what trouble my cat had gotten into in the garage.

I flung open the door. A man stood there, all but his eyes covered with a blue bandana. In his hand was a small dark gun. He motioned me back into the kitchen. I'm surprised that I didn't have a heart attack right there; it pounded so hard I could hear it. I dropped the trash bag, stumbled backward as well as I could on my crutches, and whimpered over and over again, "Please don't hurt me."

"I ain't gonna hurt you, lady," he said. "I just got outta jail and I need cash."

My purse was in my bedroom. "Please Lord, don't let him touch me!" I prayed all the way down the hall. He followed me and stood in the doorway as I fumbled so badly with my wallet that the eighteen dollars in cash fell to the floor. I sat on the end of the bed and picked up the bills with trembling hands. He stepped forward, took them, and jammed them in his pocket. Suddenly, an unimaginable feeling of calm touched me like a gentle breeze. The gunman turned and headed down the hall before hesitating a moment.

"You shouldn't leave your garage door open, lady," he said. Then he was gone.

"He never touched me," I repeated in awe to the kindly policeman who came to take my report.

"I think this was a crime of opportunity," he said. "He was probably walking down the alley, saw the back door open, and went in the garage to see if there was anything to steal. And you know what else? I think he had a degree of compassion—and regret—when he saw your crutches."

Perhaps so. My burglar was never caught, but I have prayed for him. Mostly, though, my prayers have been thanksgiving that instead of the burglar or his gun touching me, God's touch calmed me in my moment of distress.

~Kathleen M. Muldoon

87

Lost and Found

I know of no blessing so small as to be reasonably expected without prayer,
nor any so great but may be attained by it.
~Robert South

I t wasn't the dollar amount of the jewelry that mattered. It wasn't losing not one but three pieces that was so important, even though on a scale of one to ten I am definitely a "ten" jewelry lover. The three missing pieces were sentimental treasures. First, there was the antique cameo pin, a gift from a former student who went on to become a close friend. The second piece was a small gold ring with value that far outshined its miniscule chip diamond, given to my younger son for his eighth birthday. The third item was the irreplaceable heart grabber—my mother's platinum filigree diamond ring. It was one of the very few things left to me when she died at the young age of forty-four. Dad held onto the ring over eighteen years before giving it to me. It was especially precious since he passed away shortly after gifting it to me.

We seldom misplace anything at our house as I am one of those mothers who insist that things be put back exactly where they belong, much to the dismay of my less particular teenage sons.

I first realized the box containing the treasures was missing the morning I decided to wear the antique cameo pin on a favorite blouse. I was only mildly disturbed, thinking I must have taken it to the safety deposit box the last time we went out of town. I would merely stop at the bank for a look during lunch. The mildness of my earlier response suddenly turned frantic when I found the safety deposit box devoid of my lost jewelry. I tried to pinpoint the last time I had seen or worn one of the missing pieces.

When the boys got home from school, we began the most thorough search ever undertaken at the Patterson household. By this time I was offering extra allowance to the first one to find the jewelry. No place was off limits: not even my son's sacred note box he had since first grade. We looked for over two hours until my husband got home from work. He joined in until leaving for his Tuesday night men's meeting at church.

"I'll pray," he promised as he left.

My eyes filled with tears while I prayed and cleaned the house as completely as the poor woman in the Bible who scoured her house for one lost coin. I could barely stand to think that Mother's ring would not be among the heirlooms to be lovingly passed on to my boys. Finally, after another three hours of searching, with no other place to look, I sat down in the recliner in the den and decided it was time to release my struggle to the Lord.

The boys were no doubt glad for their frantic mother to stop and calm down. I prayed and sang quietly until my tears dried. When I finished, the atmosphere in our home was more peaceful and so was my heart. I walked upstairs to my bedroom. My younger son came in. "I'm so sorry we didn't find your jewelry, Mom."

After thanking him for his help and sweet concern, I was prompted to look once more in my closet. I groped the pocket of a sweat suit I had looked through earlier. I felt a bulge. The neighbors ten doors down heard my, "Thank you, Jesus!" exclaimed over and over. My younger son frowned in disbelief. "But Mom, you found it... not the Lord. You must have missed it the first time you looked."

Just when I was going to try to wipe away his doubts, I heard the front door open. Knowing it was my husband returning from church, I yelled downstairs, "Honey, guess what?"

Before I could go on he yelled back without a pause, "I know, you found the jewelry!"

Astonished at the certainty in his voice, I asked, "How do you know that?"

"I asked the men if they would pray. While we were asking the Lord to help you find your lost jewelry, one of the men said he felt the Lord was showing him a pocket."

My son stood speechless.

The former skeptic told the story of the "lost and found jewelry" the following night at his youth meeting at church.

God answered two lost and found prayers for our family that Tuesday evening: recovery of my treasures and turning a young man's doubt to a deeper faith.

~Sharon L. Patterson

Show Me Lord

Never was faithful prayer lost. Some prayers have a longer voyage
than others, but then they return with their richer lading at last,
so that the praying soul is a gainer by waiting for an answer.
~William Gurnall

I was desperately lonely. After my job relocation to San Diego, I felt deep pangs of homesickness. I missed my family and friends back in the small Midwestern town where I was born, grew up, and raised my two sons. I tried unsuccessfully to connect with fellow workers and customers at my new workplace in the downtown area, but they were commuters who had already established lives in the suburbs. As soon as work finished each day, they disappeared from the downtown scene.

Being an outgoing person, I grew up enjoying the friendships of many. But those friends were now a long distance away. Was it going to be possible to develop new relationships? I decided to explore what I vowed I would never do—resort to something as impersonal and scary as a blind date, a computer dating service or a singles' group. I had to switch gears if I were going to survive this pothole of self-pity.

"Show me Lord," I prayed. "Lead me where I need to be."

Plan A emerged: Check out a local singles' group. If that didn't work out, I'd implement Plan B—whatever that would be. The catchy name of a local church group, SinglePhile (single file), aroused my curiosity. Would it offer a painfully lonely person a social life?

In spite of apprehension about being the new kid on the block, I attended. The size of the group was surprisingly large. Between 150-200 singles gathered weekly at the friendly meetings. About half of the attendees had never been married. All were between the ages of twenty and forty-something.

The same format was followed each week: announcements, special programs, fellowship with refreshments, and group sharing time. Everyone formed a circle around the spacious room to ask for prayers about their concerns, joys or victories. After we lifted up those requests in prayer, attendees announced upcoming events such as movies, athletic events, activities, or dining opportunities.

One Tuesday, one of the long-time well-liked members who I hadn't met yet, Doug, announced that on Friday a local restaurant was hosting a Happy Hour with free food from 4:00-6:00 p.m.

"Anyone interested in joining me?" he inquired.

Offering free food to SinglePhilers always got overwhelming responses. At least 150 people raised their hands with genuine enthusiasm. I was one of them.

Taking extra time preparing for my group date on Friday, I chose a new outfit and refreshed my tired looking make-up after work. I was ready to party but I wasn't ready for the unexpected.

My heart raced a little faster as I drove to my first social function since joining SinglePhile. Would I be able to find a place in this group to end my loneliness?

As I pulled into the parking lot of the restaurant, I glanced around for familiar cars that had been at the Tuesday meeting. I didn't see any. Nevertheless, with a spring in my step, I bounded into the "Happy Hour" smiling with anticipation. I looked for the SinglePhilers group, but didn't recognize any faces.

"Oh no. I have the wrong day, the wrong time, or the wrong location." Deflated that none of my potential new friends were there, I sat down with my free chips and dip ... alone... again.

Just as I was finishing, Doug walked in. He approached my table. "Where is everyone?"

Shrugging my shoulders, I confessed, "Looks like I'm the only one from SinglePhile that made it."

"Mind if I join you then?" he inquired undaunted as he held his plate of guacamole and warm tacos. "Wouldn't want any free food to go to waste."

"Have a seat," I offered. But I was privately wondering where the other 150 hungry SinglePhilers were.

For the next three hours, Doug and I shared a delightful and revealing conversation about life, love and loss. He had just returned to San Diego after exploring a seminary near Los Angeles. Doug confided that he had never been married and prayed very specifically for ten years for the perfect wife for him. He knew exactly what he wanted in a life mate… someone who was a few years younger than he; tall and thin with long, straight blond hair; and no children or previous marriage. He admitted he felt restless since he had searched unsuccessfully for so long, so he was exploring the possibility of a new career instead.

I shared that I was definitely *not* looking for a husband after being the product of a failed marriage. I also admitted my loneliness after moving so far away from home. I assured Doug that most job changes and new beginnings were not as easy as anticipated.

We agreed that God was working in our lives in ways that hadn't yet been revealed, and that sometimes He answers prayers in totally different ways than we ever dreamed. We also agreed it best to wait patiently on God's timing and amazing plan for each of our lives.

As we parted, we both admitted we wouldn't have gotten to know each other so personally had a group of 150 fun-loving friends entertained us with trivial banter. We said goodbye, grateful for our new friendship, with aspirations for nothing more. After all, I was a few years older than Doug. I was relatively short at 5' 5", sturdily built, and sported short, red, curly hair. I had been single for twelve years since my divorce and had two grown sons attending local universities. I was the opposite of Doug's perfect wife.

Our relationship held no pressure, no aspirations or expectations of one another, so we simply became best friends. Then that friendship grew closer and closer—deeper and deeper—to engagement—marriage—and a twenty-fifth wedding anniversary.

Today Doug and I counsel couples all over the world about answered prayers and heavenly arrangements, teaching them that God gives us not what we think we want but exactly what we need.

~B.J. Jensen

A Birthday Miracle

Our prayer and God's mercy are like two buckets in a well;
while the one ascends, the other descends.
~Mark Hopkins

My husband was recovering in the hospital from cancer surgery, so he hadn't been able to work for some time. With seven children to provide for, there wasn't any money left in my budget to buy a birthday gift for my son's ninth birthday.

The night before, I lay in bed trying to decide how I should spend my last five dollars. My public assistance check wouldn't arrive in time. "God," I prayed, "I can either buy ice cream and ingredients for a birthday cake, or put gas in the car to visit my husband in the hospital. Help me know what to do."

I wanted so much for our little boy to have a nice birthday, but in my heart I knew the money needed to be spent on gas. I closed my eyes and placed my trust in God. A feeling of peace settled over me and I drifted off to sleep.

Early the next morning the ringing phone woke me. Fearing it might be the hospital calling, I rushed to answer it.

An unfamiliar woman's voice asked, "Can you use any ice cream at your house? I know you have a large family and my husband just brought home gallons of ice cream a local store was about to discard and we can't possibly use it all." The caller, a casual acquaintance who lived several blocks away, knew nothing about my husband's illness or that it was my son's birthday.

I burst into tears and told her my dilemma. After assuring me that my son would have ice cream for his birthday, she added, "I just finished a class in cake decorating and would love to try out my new skill. You go to the hospital and visit your husband. I'll drop by later with the ice cream and cake."

I spent the five dollars on gas and drove to the hospital where I was surprised to see my husband at the door.

"The doctor discharged me!" he exclaimed. "I'm going home!"

When we walked into the house the children squealed with delight and ran to their dad.

The excited birthday boy rushed to us. "Look! I have a Snoopy birthday cake!" Then he opened the freezer, took out a gallon of ice cream and the celebration began.

~Priscilla Miller

The Pumpkin Man

"The King will answer and say to them, 'Assuredly I say to you,
inasmuch as you did it to one of the least of these, my brethren,
you did it to me.'"
~Matthew 25:40

As a young man, I set out on a path to become a farmer. It started in our first garden, but worked its way to owning sheep, cows and a pig or two.

Each winter I perused an endless supply of seed catalogs. In one I saw a photo of a child standing beside a giant pumpkin. The ad announced a challenge to grow the first 1,000-pound pumpkin. This quest would carry us for the next fifteen years.

Our first challenge was the Michigan State Fair where we received our first ribbon. Later our family set a new state record for the heaviest pumpkin, at 545 pounds.

I set a goal of becoming the best pumpkin grower in the world and coined the name, "The Pumpkin Man."

In the spring of 2001, I decided to retire from growing pumpkins after one more season. As the summer ended, our biggest pumpkin, 700 pounds, cracked open. That disappointment confirmed my decision.

Then came September 11, 2001. We all held our breath. America was asked to give our best to heal our nation. One morning I woke and knew exactly what to do. I would take one of our best remaining 500-pound pumpkins to New York to help them smile.

On October 10, I started to carve. The Red Cross returned my call saying they would love to have our pumpkin. I told them I wanted to deliver it the next day, on the one-month anniversary of 9-11. I explained that I would carve it, then leave my home in Michigan at 3:00 a.m. and arrive in New York City 3:00 in the afternoon. They loved the idea.

My wife Lorraine and I started carving at 4:00 p.m. and finished at 10:00 p.m. We carved only one-half inch deep into the skin, in hopes it might last until Halloween. The finished pumpkin face had, for the left eye, a little boy praying and for the right eye, a little girl in prayer. A heart encircled them both. The nose was the firefighters putting up the flag at Ground Zero and the mouth was the word AMERICA shaped to make a smile. We wanted to show everyone who had lost so much that they were in our hearts and prayers.

I left for New York on the morning of October 11, 2001 at 3:00 a.m. The trip passed quickly and I made it to the mountains in Pennsylvania. In the night, the mountains stood so dark and powerful, with shades of gray gently cascading into blackness. As the sun began to rise, my field of view broadened. My senses started to wake up and I felt a renewed energy. On the horizon, the sun rose, cresting the mountain ridge ahead, it lit up the mountains with depth of color that stretched as far as I could see. The orange, red and yellow colors flowed from the top of the mountains to the valley, a beauty only God could give.

I felt a presence that overwhelmed me. With tears in my eyes I thanked God for this beauty and asked for blessings on my journey.

As I neared New York City I saw the remains of the World Trade Center across the Hudson River. A broken wall was all that stood, like a stairway straight to heaven. Tearfully I asked God, "Help me touch the hearts of those who lost someone."

I made it to the Red Cross Family Assistance Center on the West Side of Manhattan. It looked like a converted warehouse. There were policemen everywhere. They went through an extensive search of my truck. One policeman chuckled saying, "You should have a license plate that says 'The Pumpkin Man.'"

I smiled. "Thanks, I once was that man and I guess I am again today."

While I waited to unload the pumpkin, a New York City police officer walked up. "How long did it take to carve the pumpkin?"

"About six hours."

He shook his head. "God Bless you man." He ran his fingers over each of the carvings, asking about the water beads around the little girl and boy. I told him it was normal for a carved pumpkin to seep water in an area of the carving. I shared with him that my daughter said, "The little girl and boy are crying for all who lost their mommies and daddies."

The policeman asked how long it took me to drive to New York.

"About eleven hours."

He again said "God Bless you man. You can't imagine how many kids you'll make smile."

He took a deep breath. "My brother was in one of the towers that went down."

I grabbed his shoulder. "Dear God, I am so sorry."

"You came so far; I can't believe you care so much."

"Everyone I know in Michigan and all over the United States cares as much as I do."

He then pointed. "All these police officers from all over the United States, they all really care."

"I've had a knot in my stomach and tears in my eyes since this all began. People like you are why I came."

On the long drive home I had a smile on my face and tears in my eyes. I had achieved my goal to help the people who had lost so much feel a little better. And I became "The Pumpkin Man" for one more day.

Then I prayed for everyone who lost someone. "God bless you man."

~William Garvey

Adoption Miracle

If one draw near to God with praise and prayer even half a cubit,
God will go twenty leagues to meet him.
~Sir Edwin Arnold

Only the death of my mother was as painful—and this pain would never fade. A two-year journey to give a beautiful young boy a safe, nurturing foster home had ended in failure for my wife and me. It began on the day that fate took a seven-year-old boy from us.

Teams of therapists, hours of prayer, and months of perseverance weren't enough to overcome the nightmare of abusive and violent behavior of a troubled little boy. Facing my wife's deteriorating emotional and physical health from the situation, I made the heartbreaking decision to have him placed back into a therapeutic home nearly a thousand miles away in the state charged with his custody. From that day forward, I never gave up hope that he would come back to us, though at times that hope faded almost completely.

The story actually began more than twenty years earlier, when my younger sister was born. The last of seven children in a dysfunctional American family, she was cherished by all her older siblings. But with my mother's valuable love already divided six ways, and the corresponding financial and logistical burdens of a huge family in the trailer park, she didn't get the attention the rest of us did. She struggled through school and her brothers and sister were often her primary caretakers. When my adored sister was nine years old, our mother passed away after an eighteen-month battle with cancer that included months away from home for a liver transplant.

Troubled relationships with family led my little sister to spend her later teen years with my other sister. But her difficult childhood had taken its toll, and emotional troubles continued. At age nineteen, she met "someone special," became pregnant and got married. Justin was born into a troubled environment and four years later, he was in the custody of the state. Justin was placed in our care because we were his closest relatives. The decision to have him join our household was one we labored over as a couple. We had spent years working to improve our marriage by overcoming our own personal challenges, and we enjoyed a comfortable carefree lifestyle. Brenda's full-time job as a travel agent meant frequent and fun vacations. I was fulfilling my dream to race cars. We had a nice lakefront townhouse that we shared with Brenda's mother. By the time Justin reached us at five years old, his behavior was quite explosive and he had great difficulty following rules in daycare and school. In addition to his challenges with boundaries, we had to teach him virtually all his life skills. He needed help with toilet hygiene, tooth brushing, dressing, and even fundamental English. He didn't have enough strength to support his own weight and was on powerful prescription medication that kept him lethargic. We loved him dearly, though, and sought out therapists and behavior specialists to help us.

We replaced our idyllic lakefront townhouse with a single-family home better suited to raise a young boy. I gave up racing and Brenda retired from her travel career to dedicate all her efforts to Justin's well-being.

Despite our efforts to catch him up academically, emotionally and physically, his behavior became increasingly difficult. Weeks of vacation were replaced with weeks of behavior camps and intensive therapy sessions. Instead of racing, I spent my weekends giving my wife a break from the overwhelming stress of caring for a special needs child. Trips to the Caribbean gave way to trips to therapists a hundred miles away. Even spending several months away during the week at group home to work on his behavior had no effect.

Justin became increasingly violent, began attacking us daily and verbally threatened us with bodily harm and even death. We dreaded giving up on him and hated the thought of losing him even more, but we had to let him go back into the foster care system to preserve our sanity and our marriage.

During the two years that followed we ached with the pain of the loss. The experience was worse than having someone die, because we felt we had given up. The emotional abuse he subjected my wife to left substantial doubt that she would ever heal from the scars. As much as I begged, she couldn't bear the thought of having him back in our house. "What will he be like when he's twelve years old and is bigger than me?" she asked.

Without even a glimmer of hope for his return, we continued to be a consistent factor in his life. Every week we painfully peeled the scab off our emotional wounds to call him on the phone—we never missed one call. We sent gifts and even visited him on holidays. When the rights of his parents were terminated and he became eligible for adoption, Brenda still couldn't bear the thought of enduring his abuse again. We had to accept the painful fact that he might end up with strangers, out of our lives.

When the next Thanksgiving approached, Justin still hadn't been adopted. We scheduled a visit, anticipating the pain we'd feel knowing it was likely our last chance to see him. With heartfelt sincerity, Justin told Brenda that he knew he used to hit her and he spoke of his regret.

Then he said, "I wish I could come back to live with you as my forever home and have you for my mom."

Whether it was his genuine sincerity, the look on his beautiful face, or the influence of a higher power, we'll never know. But Brenda's heart softened and the emotional pain melted enough for a glimmer of hope that perhaps he could come back into our lives. We said our tearful goodbyes at the end of the weekend, and on the long drive home, she tearfully admitted she still wasn't ready to have him back.

Yet the desire never left us, so we soon called his social worker to see what it would entail to adopt him. We were told a placement decision was about to be made. With an insanely short timeline, we completed our adoptive home study and paperwork.

When the big day came, we waited on pins and needles for the call about the committee's choice for Justin's permanent home. We were crushed to hear we weren't chosen. None of the prospective families was selected.

However, we were told we still had a chance. We invested nearly a hundred hours attending every parenting class we could find to prove that we were committed to being Justin's family, and that we were in it for the long haul. We studied books about his new autism diagnosis and sought out every support group and disability resource we could find to ensure that if he came back, we would be as equipped as possible to have a successful placement—and more importantly, give Justin the permanent home he deserved. We did everything in our power, then waited—and prayed for a miracle.

For a lifetime I'd believed in dreams and miracles. And though I'd been blessed enough to see many dreams to fruition, I had never been party to a miracle—at least one that I was aware of—until the call. After twenty-seven months of emotional torment, Justin would be our son. For life.

The following months were filled with anticipation as we pre-pared to pick him up on his last day of school to bring him home. Six months later, only days before Christmas, we three stood beaming before the judge and committed to be Justin's forever family.

~S.L. Delorey

A Match Made in Heaven

And the people kept shouting, "The voice of a god, not of a man."
~Acts 12:22

"There's a young woman in this congregation who is in desperate need of a kidney transplant. If she doesn't receive one soon, she isn't going to make it. Please pray for her this week."

The pastor's words chilled me. I thought about the young woman all the way home. I'd found out that her name was Ruth and she wasn't much older than my own beautiful daughter.

Later that afternoon I walked beneath our pine trees enjoying the gentle breeze when I suddenly felt goose bumps up and down my spine.

"Give Ruth one of your kidneys, Debbie."

Stunned, I wrapped my arms tightly across my chest, feeling chilled to the bone.

"Lord, donating a kidney doesn't exactly sound like a picnic to me. Are you sure about this?"

My heartbeat raced along with my quickening steps. Was I trying to run away from this overwhelming sense of duty that was growing more and more intense by the second?

That evening, as I read my Bible, I came to a decision. "Lord, I'll tell you what. I'll take the test to determine whether I'm a match for Ruth. If by some miracle I am, I'll give her my kidney. I'm doing this because I love You so much, Lord. You've done so much for me."

I'd heard other members of the congregation had tested to see if they could be donors; no one came close. I had the tests. I was a perfect match. Ruth was informed that a donor had been found.

We were scheduled to have surgery the end of January but Ruth came down with an infection. The surgery was rescheduled for a week later. That too was cancelled. Suddenly I began feeling apprehensive about it all. "Lord, are You sure this is what You want from me?"

For some time I'd been planning a trip to visit our daughter in San Diego. The surgeons suggested I go as surgery wouldn't be possible for several weeks. Two days before we were to leave, I received a call from the hospital. Ruth was not doing well. There was a short window of time in which the surgery would be lifesaving. They told me the decision was mine; we could wait to do the surgery until we returned from our trip.

As I hung up the phone, I glanced into my husband's compassionate eyes. He smiled sympathetically. "We're not going to California, are we?"

"If anything happened to Ruth while we were away, I'd never be able to live with myself."

Arrangements moved along faster than any of us could have imagined. The doctor visited us both before the operation. He confided that if Ruth had contracted another infection before this surgery she wouldn't have survived. I knew I had made the right decision.

The kidney transplant operation was performed without a hitch.

At church we were nicknamed, "Ruth Recipient and Debbie Donor." Ruth named the kidney as well. She christened it, "Faith."

Now, when I sit staring at the back of Ruthie's head on Sunday mornings, I can't help grinning from ear to ear.

God had plans for her and me all along... a match truly made in heaven.

~Debbie Moran as told to Mary Z. Smith

My Three Amigos

When He comes, in that day, to be glorified in His Saints and to be admired among all those who believe, because our testimony among You was believed.
~2 Thessalonians 1:10

Birdsong and butterflies filled the air and threads of sunlight pierced through the canopy of trees as I walked along the lane outside the ancient city of Pompeii. It was lovely and serene. I, however, was far from peaceful; I was a very damp basket case.

In just a few moments, I was due at the Villa de Misteri office to interview the chief archaeologist for the Vesuvius area. My interview questions were prepared, but I was not only nervous, I was as hot as a grilled sausage in the only business outfit I'd brought. A winter suit. Who knew that in late October in Italy, the temperatures could be unseasonably hot?

Some women "glow" when hot, others might perspire. Me, I flat out sweat. Torrents of water poured off my head, down my face and spouted off the end of my nose. Hardly the way to conduct a dignified interview.

I'd already had a few bad moments in Italy. In Rome I somehow managed to break security at the Vatican and ended up in the Papal courtyard. As the Swiss Guard grabbed my arm and two others ran over, I quickly prayed to Saint Peter to put a good word in for God to help me. This was his house; surely he knew I meant no harm. After a mere two minutes of questioning, the guards determined that this grandma in tennis shoes was no terrorist and released me with the admonition to, "Go and trespass no more."

Another harrowing incident occurred in Herculaneum. I was so busy photographing all the glorious sights, I somehow allowed my bag to slip off my shoulder. Not only was my credit card in there, so was a considerable sum of money and, most importantly, my memory card with about five hundred photos of Rome. After running wildly up and down the ruins without result, I reported my loss and gave my cell phone number to the guard office, then left for Naples.

"Gee, Lynne, you're handling this well," my companions commented.

"We gotta have faith; there are still good people in this world."

But, in my secret heart, I was worried. I sat on a bench and lifted my head in prayer. Noticing the church of Saint Anthony across the piazza, I petitioned him to intercede. Twenty minutes later, I received a call... my bag had been found! A messenger delivered it to me that afternoon with all the items intact.

The third incident took place in Sorrento. I have the language skills of a pigeon, so an Italian friend was to confirm my appointment with the archaeologist. It was essential that I meet with him the next day, as my window of opportunity was very tight. I stood on the Corso Tasso waiting for my translator so we could place the call. The archaeologist's office would be closing soon; time was running out. I toe-tapped, strutted and muttered and still my friend didn't show up.

Across the street I saw a church dedicated to Saint Francis. Since prayer had already worked so nicely for me, again I prayed. Before I even got to the Amen, my friend came stomping across the cobblestones on her stilettos.

So, now I was in Pompeii about to meet the professor. A little bit shaky and quite damp, I prayed one simple prayer, "Oh, God, please help me."

Immediately, an indescribable peace wafted over me like a clean linen sheet. I felt cool, both in body and spirit. As I continued to stroll toward the Villa di Misteri, I had a physical sense of Saint Anthony behind me, Saint Peter in front and Saint Francis beside me.

The interview went splendidly. Today my three amigos still walk with me wherever I go, putting in a good word to God whenever I need them.

~Lynne Zielinski

Answered Prayers

Angels Among Us

*But the angel said to them, "Do not be afraid;
I bring you good news of great joy that will be for all the people."*

~Luke 2:10

The Gift Shop Angel

Do not forget to entertain strangers,
for by doing so some have unwittingly entertained angels.
~Hebrews 13:2

A middle-aged woman with a bandaged arm waved down my sister-in-law, Barbara Jean, as if she were a New York City taxi cab driver. "Can you give me a ride home?" the woman asked.

Barbara Jean was leaving the hospital parking lot after her shift at the hospital auxiliary gift shop where she'd volunteered weekly for over twenty years.

"Where do you live?"

The woman replied with a street address that Barbara Jean recognized as being in the poorest part of town, an area she avoided as a rule because of the vagrants that roamed the streets, the graffiti-covered walls, and the overall reputation of the neighborhood as being "rough." These thoughts were quickly dismissed. "I'll be glad to take you home," she told the lady.

The woman opened the front passenger door and took a seat. Barbara Jean asked, "How did you get to the hospital?"

"My grandson brought me because I had hurt my arm this morning and it needed attention. I had a long wait though, and he had to go to work. That boy can't afford to risk losing his job. I just sent him on along without a worry. I told him, 'The Lord will provide a way,' and He did. He sent you." There was a note of conviction in the woman's voice, but not a trace of concern.

"Well, I'm glad I was leaving the hospital at just that moment. Sometimes things have a way of working out," Barbara Jean said.

"I prayed to the Lord for help, and He sent you to help me," insisted the woman. "By the way, dear, what is your name?"

"Barbara Jean."

"Well, isn't that something!" the woman chuckled. "My name is Barbara Jean, too!"

The two traveled along for a few moments, making small talk. Then the woman said, "Oh, dear. I almost forgot something. The doctor gave me a prescription to drop off at White's Pharmacy. Would you mind taking me there?"

My sister-in-law's eyes widened. "Well, it just so happens I was heading there when I left the hospital. I have some papers I need to leave there for a charity event."

The coincidences did not startle her guest whatsoever. When they reached the drugstore, my sister-in-law offered to take the prescription in. The name at the top was clearly legible — Barbara Jean.

She took her flyers to the manager and the prescription to the pharmacy counter. When she returned to the car, she asked, "How will you get your medicine when it is ready?"

"Someone will pick it up for me tonight."

"I have no doubt about that," my sister-in-law replied. They drove to a rundown apartment complex. She helped the other Barbara Jean out of the car.

"Thank you for the ride," she said, "but I knew you were coming. I asked the Lord to provide me a ride and He did."

"I am glad to be able to help." She pulled away from the curb and turned toward home. A church on that route always had a clever or insightful proverb on its marquee. Barbara Jean glanced to read today's message. "TODAY, YOU COULD BE SOMEONE'S ANGEL."

"Amen," thought Barbara Jean. "Amen."

~Kimberly Seeley

Grow Old with Me

In vocal prayer we speak to God;
in mental prayer He speaks to us.
It is then that God pours Himself unto us.
~Mother Teresa

When Dad passed away, Mom never thought she'd fall in love again. Pushing seventy, she'd lived a full life. Then one morning as she was posting a letter at the mailbox, a handsome man appeared. The two fell in love.

Eventually, Bob asked us all for Mom's hand in marriage. Looking into her eyes, he declared, "I can promise you this, if you'll grow old along with me, the best is yet to be!" This became their special promise to each another.

Having so many grown children and grandchildren between them, they decided on a quiet wedding back in Pennsylvania with just the minister and two witnesses attending.

The morning of the wedding dawned sunny and filled with promise where I lived in Virginia. I couldn't help feeling anxious however. Had Mom and Bob really not wanted their kids present at their ceremony or were they simply being considerate about all the traveling expenses and arrangements involved? All morning I stewed. Maybe keeping busy was the answer. Reaching for the car keys, I headed for the church to set up the first grade Sunday school room.

I thought about Mom and Bob all the way down the highway. Finally, I turned to the source of my strength, whispering a simple prayer. "Lord, send me a sign that all is well with our folks, that this is really the way they want their wedding day to be."

Releasing a sigh, I turned the radio on. The car filled with the beautiful voice of Mary Chapin Carpenter. "Grow old along with me the best is yet to be…"

Unable to believe my ears, I slowly pulled off the highway, finding a safe place to park. Reaching for the cell phone I dialed my sister's number in Florida.

"Sis, you aren't going to believe this!" I explained my feelings of anxiety and how I'd prayed for a sign.

My sister gasped, dropping whatever she'd been holding with a clang.

"Are you okay?"

"Oh, sorry. I dropped the spoon I was holding. I was feeling the same way so I decided to keep busy by baking chocolate chip cookies. I switched on the radio. "Grow Old With Me" filled the kitchen!"

"It can mean only one thing…"

"What's that?"

"The angels are already on the case. After all, they're playing their song."

~Mary Z. Smith

96

Heaven's Music

Prayer, to the thinking person, is almost inescapable.
~Marjorie Holmes

M y grandson would be entering the world today. "We still haven't decided on a name, Dad. Any ideas?" my laboring daughter-in-law asked between contractions.

"I'm going to go pay a visit to the chapel downstairs," I said. "Be back shortly."

Pushing the button for the elevator, I whispered a prayer. "Send your angels with the perfect name for my grandson, Lord."

Sunshine streamed through the chapel window sending beams of hope to my soul. "Be with Deb as she labors, Lord. About that name..."

A short while later, I ended my prayer and slowly made my way out the door, with no name for my grandson in my heart.

At the elevator I suddenly froze in place. The song "Oh Danny Boy" filled the air from the hospital intercom.

"Thank you!" I whispered, whistling all the way back to the delivery room.

"I think we should name my grandson Daniel!" I announced, hearing the excitement in my own voice.

Deb's mouth dropped open.

"What's wrong?" I asked.

"Chuck," she cried as my son entered the room. "Tell your dad what name we just decided on."

"Daniel. The name came on a breeze as I walked across the parking lot. I called Deb on the cell phone to tell her," my son chuckled.

It seems the angels had been whispering my grandson's name all over the place. I couldn't wait to set eyes upon our bundle from heaven.

Welcome to the world, Danny Boy.

~Wayne Terry as told to Mary Z. Smith

97

A Glance at Heaven

Likewise I say to you, there is joy in the presence of the angels of God...
~Luke 15:10

Sean Robert, born addicted to cocaine, alcohol and nicotine, was abandoned in the hospital by his birth mother and father. He spent much of the next two years in and out of hospitals and foster care. The diagnosis of fetal alcohol syndrome presented in a myriad of ways, from the loss of his leg to a hole in his heart. Many people would have easily written him off as another damaged, unwanted child.

But maybe there is no such thing as an unwanted child.

My daughter met this little boy while working in his daycare center. Shannon, always a loving and nurturing person, adored children, but circumstances and health reasons kept her from being able to conceive. She was a single woman in her thirties looking at a future without motherhood.

When she first met Sean Robert she watched him smile and play with other children and said, "I could take that kid home."

"Actually you could," the director said.

Shannon discovered the precious toddler was in foster care and available for adoption. The next two years found her in a whirlwind love affair. After a great deal of prayer and paperwork, he was placed in Shannon's home as a foster child with the intent to adopt. Slowly, and with a lot of support, Shannon was taught to care for a little one with extensive medical needs… but she didn't have to be taught how to love him.

When I first met my new grandson he was two years old, small for his age, did not talk, had chronic illnesses and only one leg. Within weeks he began to smile, laugh, and even use some sign language. Within months he was scooting around the floor and walking with a prosthetic leg. He rarely took his eyes off his mother and the interaction between them was beautiful to watch. Shannon's world had blossomed and Sean Robert suddenly came to life.

Tragically, over the next two years his health deteriorated. His life included many doctor's visits, hospital stays, medical tests and surgeries. He was no longer able to eat. Tubes and IV's were placed again and again. Shannon and I sometimes wondered if he would survive. But he surprised us with a smile on his face and the will to live. He lit up when his mother took him in her arms.

There were good days that turned into weeks, but then Sean would be sick again. I learned from him to enjoy life as you receive it. He taught us to focus on today. Today he was smiling and playing and going to the circus. Today he was watching Elmo, coloring with his cousin and riding his rocking horse. Today he was dancing with his mom, celebrating his birthday and going to see Santa. Today he was loved, and teaching the rest of us to love unconditionally.

When local hospitals and doctors ran out of ways to help Sean Robert, he was taken a long distance to Boston where renowned surgeons and specialists did their best. Shannon didn't leave his bedside. For weeks at a time she and her son faced the world and all its pain together. His aunts, uncles, cousins, grandparents and friends cried together, laughed at his silly antics and prayed for a miracle.

One day he was playing with pretzel sticks and dropped one on the floor. It broke into a dozen pieces and he laughed hysterically. We spent the next half hour tossing pretzels on the floor of the hospital room and cheering as his face lit up with joy.

One night in bed Sean suddenly began to babble, making sounds he had never made before. Smiling and waving at the ceiling he said, "Hi, hi." He appeared to be having a conversation with unseen guests.

We laughed and watched in awe. We'd heard these kinds of stories and felt blessed to watch as Sean was being prepared for his journey.

That's when Shannon decided it was time to let her son go back home to God.

Sad and afraid, we knew it was our job to make his last days as joyful as possible. We took him to my home filled with friends and relatives. Hospice workers, nurses, and doctors came to offer support. His teachers and therapists stopped to see him. We received spiritual support through cards, phone calls and prayers. Our lives centered on giving this little boy a goodbye party. Sean didn't seem a bit disturbed that the doorbell rang constantly, that his many relatives came and went or that eighty-nine balloons filled our living room.

But each hour he grew weaker.

On his last day he became less and less responsive, sleeping a lot, and then waking for short periods. Shannon and I took turns walking him in his stroller. On one walk, Shannon pushed and I walked beside him.

He suddenly woke up and said, "Mama?"

"Yes, Sean Robert, I'm right here," Shannon responded.

He said in a soft voice, "Love ya."

Soon afterward he fell asleep.

Later that night, Shannon needed a well-deserved break. As she rested I sat in the darkened living room cuddling him. His breathing got very shallow. His pain was ending but I knew our family's pain was just beginning. I prayed that his transition to heaven would be soon. He began to struggle with each breath; I knew his journey was almost complete.

Then I saw a glorious light so bright I could not look directly into it. I said, "Sean Robert, the light is waiting for you."

I told him not to be afraid, that I would take him as far as I could go. As I carried him closer I felt a warmth and saw the light separate into four beings. I knew these were angels welcoming him home. I saw myself hand him to the first light. He was held close and the lights encompassed him, passing him from one angel to another. Tears poured from me. I knew he was gone but left with the gifts of protection, love, peace, and lasting joy. I held his body close and said a prayer of thanksgiving for him and this moment.

I never imagined that a little boy, who the world saw as imperfect and unwanted would give me the gift of a glance of heaven.

~Maggie Whelan

98

Angel in Uniform

The angel of the LORD encamps around those who fear Him,
and he delivers them.
~Psalm 34:7

My travel alarm buzzed at 4:30 a.m. I smacked it and let my feet drop from the couch to the floor. It was never easy leaving Mom's efficiency apartment in Cleveland, Tennessee on those Monday mornings and driving the eighty miles to my job in Knoxville by 7:30 a.m. I wished I could stay with her. She was in the beginning stages of Alzheimer's disease; but I had a job to go to, and a husband at home.

Another sister, Jan, lived in the same apartment building, but as a dialysis patient Jan couldn't help as much as she wanted. My three sisters and a brother drove long distances to take turns staying with Mom.

As I dressed, I sipped my cup of creamy instant coffee. Balancing the cup of coffee in one hand, I grabbed my overnight bag and tiptoed from the apartment. I slid behind the wheel of my Buick, assuring myself that Mom would be okay until Jan checked on her.

It was quite foggy as I drove through the back streets of Cleveland toward the Interstate Highway. I felt uneasy about driving that morning. "Lord," I tossed up a prayer out loud as usual. "Please put your angels around this car. I ask for protection as I drive this distance once again, in Jesus's name. Amen."

The fog grew thicker. I could barely see street signs and houses.

Angel in Uniform : Angels Among Us   339

Four years earlier on a densely foggy morning there had been a ninety-nine vehicle pile-up twenty miles north of here. At about 9:00 a.m. that fateful day, vehicles smashed into each other like the layers of an onion, one wrapped around another. Twelve lives were lost and another fifty injured.

I should have turned around and gone back to Mom's. But my family's strong work ethic prevailed.

Approaching Interstate 75, my heart lurched. A patrol car appeared just ahead of me. I watched it pull slowly across the north entrance to the Interstate and stop. The officer got out of her car and stood with her hands on her hips. Pulling my car alongside, I rolled down my car window and asked her the unnecessary question, "Is something wrong, officer?"

"The Interstate is closed. Fog is worse further ahead," she stated matter-of-factly.

I sighed, knowing I'd have to call my supervisor to say I'd be late for work on a Monday. "Thank you," I said, without feeling thankful at all.

I turned my car around and headed back to Mom's apartment to wait for the fog to dissipate and the Interstate to open again. The delay meant I'd have to work late to make up my time at the doctor's office, but that couldn't be helped.

As I headed back to Mom's, I thought again about the officer, and how I hadn't noticed the police car in front of me until it pulled over to block the Interstate entrance. I also thought about how good God is at taking care of us when we forget to take care of ourselves. Truthfully, I was relieved that I didn't have to make that trip in the fog.

Mom and I had breakfast and visited for a while. About 10:00 a.m. the fog was lifting so I called the State Highway Patrol, and asked, "When will I-75 be opened again?"

Silence. Then the officer answered, "You must be mistaken, the Interstate has not been closed."

I told him about the police officer who blocked the highway, but he continued to insist, "The Interstate was not closed."

After hanging up, I sat thinking, "Who was that officer? Did God see my own lack of wisdom and send her to keep me from danger? Did He indeed put angels around my car?"

No longer do I take my routine prayer for granted. When I ask God to protect me I pray with the expectation that He will send help.

~Phyllis Qualls Freeman

Reprinted by permission of
Steve Barr © 2011.

99

From a Canvas Tent

You can't defeat a praying man. He finds his answers everywhere he looks.
~Margaret Lee Runbeck

R ain pelted against the windows. I worried about Roy alone in his canvas tent. It was five miles from his makeshift shelter to the drop-in center where I worked, but he made the trip twice a week and was overdue.

When I last visited Roy's campsite, I saw the squalor. A green tarp hung between two trees to create a wind barrier for his patched canvas home. Cooking utensils were scattered on the ground with a few pieces of firewood.

The tap tap tapping of a pencil on the counter interrupted my thoughts. There stood Roy in his droopy cowboy hat, a thin coat, overalls, no socks, and tennis shoes. Drenched from head to toe, he placed his shivering arms on the counter.

"I'm here to get my dog back," he blurted.

Expecting Roy to ask for food or clothing, I was shocked.

"I bought an old truck a few weeks ago," he said. "Spent every dollar I had and drove to Florida to see my son. My dog, Shadow, went along. My truck engine blew up and we hitchhiked. Once we arrived, I realized my son was living the life of a drug addict. We couldn't stay. I begged a Greyhound bus driver to let Shadow ride back to Seattle. His answer was, 'No dogs on the bus!' So I called a pastor friend and he said he'd keep Shadow until I returned home.

'I'll fly him back to you Roy,' he said. Well, it's been a few weeks now. Please, can you help me?"

"Yes," I assured him, "we will help you."

The center contacted the pastor and made arrangements to fly Shadow home. We knew of Roy's living conditions, so we all began to pray for a miracle.

A miracle arrived with a telephone call from a local resident.

"I own a trailer lot," he said. "I have a camping trailer and a piece of land to donate to your center."

"I have the perfect person in mind," I replied. "Thank you God," I whispered.

On the day of Shadow's return not only did the employees from the drop-in center go to the airport with Roy, but television news crews also joined our team.

I hugged Roy as we walked through the crowded airport. He was dressed in clean clothes, wore a new shirt from the mission barrel, and was clean-shaven, compliments of the drop-in center. Roy stared at the conveyor belt as we waited for Shadow. Soon, the animal crate made its way down. Local news cameras were poised.

When Shadow saw Roy, he whined and barked.

"Hey Shadow boy," Roy called, clapping his hands.

Shadow shook with excitement as Roy lifted the terrier out of the crate. The dog's ears perked up, and he wiggled from the top of his head to the tip of his tail, then sprang into Roy's arms and licked his face.

"Oh Shadow," Roy said with tears running down his face. "I didn't think I'd ever see you again."

"That's what God does. He brings miracles," I said.

My supervisor wrapped his arm around Roy. "We have one more place to go with you and Shadow."

When the van stopped in front of a sixteen-foot trailer on a rural plot close to town, Roy sat speechless.

"The trailer is stocked with food and blankets for you, Roy," I said. "Here are the keys to your new home."

Roy and Shadow stepped in and the man cried. When we left, he waved to us from the window, smiling his toothless grin.

The center didn't hear from Roy or Shadow for a while, but during a lunchtime stroll I saw them sitting on a park bench. I was thrilled to see them and I unraveled the story about the trailer.

"It was a miracle, Roy. It was what I call a God thing."

"Maybe it was. That's what God does. He brings miracles. Isn't that what someone said?" he chuckled, nudging me.

Through the winter months, Roy and Shadow didn't frequent the center so I assumed they were doing well. Then, I was asked to work the midnight shift and declined because of my family situation.

Worried that I would not see Roy and Shadow, I wrote a letter and left it with the midnight shift supervisor who promised to deliver it to Roy.

Dear Roy,

I had to leave my duties here at the center because I cannot work the midnight shift. I was afraid I would not see you and Shadow again. When I first saw you and Shadow, I could not stop watching the love you had for your friend. What a team! I want you to know that Jesus loves you just that much and more. He has walked with you, kept you safe, and brought you to a new home. He has surrounded you with love from the people here. You can make it Roy! Remember to pray. Know too, that I will always pray for you. God bless you Roy!

Your friend, Shirley

My last workday arrived. With no hope of ever seeing Roy again, I walked out to my car. As I turned the key in the car door, I heard a dog panting and a familiar voice.

"Hey, Shirley, I got the letter." Shadow rubbed against my leg.

"Oh Roy, I'm so happy to see you. I wanted to talk to you."

He smiled. "What you said in your letter is true. I know God has something better for me. I've been praying and going to a little church. I want you to know that I'm a believer now. How can I not be? God created a miracle — for me."

~Shirley A. Reynolds

100

God, Do You Exist?

Last night an angel of the God to whom I belong whom I serve stood beside me.

~Acts 27:23

"God, if you are really there, I need your help. What am I going to do with my life now?" I was not brought up religious, nor did I have any real understanding of God. But there was a part of me that wanted to believe that someone looked out for us. At the same time I couldn't help wondering, if God did exist, why would He make things so difficult for my family? After all, I had "done the right thing" by walking away from my job. Didn't I deserve a break or some guidance? Anything?

No answers came.

It had been a few months since I left my job, a job that not only fully supported my family, but one I had considered my baby before I ever had children. I had helped to start the company five years earlier and was proud of what I had built and accomplished as a young woman. And yet the day came when I could not stomach the unethical practices of the owners. To leave was definitely a financial risk for my family, especially since we had just moved cross-country back to my small hometown to start again.

It didn't take long to realize that job opportunities were scarce. We were struggling to get by, my husband stringing together several part-time jobs while I took on any project I could get my hands on. I was becoming desperate. "Please God, please help me find direction," I moaned.

I lay in bed wide awake. It was another sleepless night. I glanced over at my husband, peacefully asleep, wishing I could do the same. Every now and then, I checked the clock next to his side of the bed, hoping morning would soon save me from this restless night. On my last check it was only 3:00 a.m. Hours to go.

After what seemed like an eternity, I rolled over to check the clock one more time. I gasped in shock to see a boy about thirteen years of age standing there, with long brown hair and dressed in a robe resembling a young monk. I stared at him in total disbelief. He appeared to be lit up from the inside. I could actually see through him! Lights danced inside him like swirling colors on the surface of a bubble, beautiful hues of deep blue, purple and fuchsia.

He looked at me with no particular expression, then slowly turned and walked away, fading gradually with every step.

He faded more. I sat straight up in bed to get a better look. I squinted to make out the last of him before he completely vanished. Then I just sat there motionless until morning, wondering if he would return, knowing that if I let myself sleep, I'd awaken convinced it must have all been a dream.

The experience ignited a fire within me, a yearning to understand what it meant. I searched the Internet for similar stories, perhaps even of the dancing lights, but I found nothing.

Next, I went through old family photos, carefully studying the faces of those who passed long ago, in search of any slight resemblance to this spirit boy. I visited the library every week, borrowing as many books as I could on ghosts, spirit guides, or anything similar. Nothing I researched resonated.

Then one day at the library I came across a book on angels. My first thought was, "But he didn't have wings." Nonetheless, my selection of books was becoming limited, since I had read nearly everything they had on spiritual encounters. So I brought home several angel books and began reading.

Unbelievably some of the stories reminded me of my experience, and there were several accounts of angels without wings. One even spoke of colored lights. Shivers ran up and down my body. I finally had my answer.

There was one last piece to this puzzle though. The books claimed angels were messengers. But I hadn't received a message. I had a once in a lifetime visitation from an angel and I missed my message! Had I been too shocked to receive it? How would I ever get my message now?

Some weeks later, I started to feel ill. I developed a persistent nausea and my energy was so low I couldn't work out anymore. Soon more strange symptoms developed, some that vaguely reminded me of when I was first pregnant with the twins. But this was not morning sickness—it was all-the-time sickness. Besides, it was impossible that I could be pregnant. I'd been unable to conceive without the help of a specialist.

Another month went by, and when I didn't menstruate, I knew something was wrong with me. To rule out the impossible, I bought a pregnancy test. It was positive! I was pregnant! I wondered how this was even possible through my tears.

Then it crossed my mind… could the visit from the angel have something to do with it? I quickly did the math. No, the timing didn't add up. It had been over three months since my angel experience. I couldn't be that far along.

My doctor immediately scheduled an ultrasound. The technician determined that the baby was fourteen weeks and two days old. I was much further along than I thought. Perplexed, I grabbed a calendar, counted back fourteen weeks and two days… the exact day I saw the angel in my room!

So, as it turns out, I did get my message… a beautiful baby girl, brought lovingly into this world by her guardian angel.

God answered my plea and proved He does exist.

~Candace McLean

God's Answer

More tears are shed over answered prayers than unanswered ones.
~Mother Teresa

Teenagers made up the majority of volunteers on our mission trip to West Virginia's Appalachian region. They had decided to forgo part of their summer vacation plans to join with other members of our congregation in making homes warmer, safer and drier.

One seventeen-year-old girl, a third year volunteer, said, "As soon as my pastor gave that sermon, I knew I wanted to volunteer. Instead of sitting around and saying things like, 'I wish there was something I could do,' I can actually do something!"

Her brother, a veteran of five previous trips, added, "I worry about the people who have no roofs over their heads, and the families who have to watch where they step so they don't fall through their own floors."

The ride to the school that would serve as our weeklong home-away-from-home was almost twelve hours long, but by the next day, rested and ready, we went to work.

We were assigned the task of refurbishing a water-damaged roof for a family living in a hollow on the other side of the mountain. The family had tried to fix the problem themselves, but lack of money and materials to make lasting repairs made previous attempts fail. Rain and melting snow seeped through the roof of this forty-plus-year-old trailer home, and ultimately, into the lives of the family below.

And so we volunteers went to work, and soon found ourselves laboring under the heat of a hot summer's sun, trying to remove the damaged roof—in reality, five roofs, one atop the other. With hammers and crowbars, sturdy work gloves and sheer determination the teens began to peel back layer upon layer of deteriorated shingles and old decaying tar paper. When the roof was finally stripped and the damaged sections of decking replaced with new wood, the new felt and shingles were finally installed. Despite the litany of problems that seemed to crop up almost daily, when Friday afternoon came around, two truly amazing things happened: the job was completed, and moments later, as if to test the volunteer's efforts, it began to rain. The family within remained dry!

Later that night, the last before returning home, all the volunteers staying at the school gathered to share their Appalachian experiences.

One roof-crew member said that just as we were about to leave the jobsite for the last time, the family for whom they'd labored all week became emotional.

So did he as he shared, "Charles, the father, was crying, and so was his wife and all of their kids. And yet, they were smiling, and giving us lots of hugs and saying 'thanks.' Charles said he'd been praying for help for a long time for someone who could fix his roof. He said that finally, this week, God had answered his prayers."

The young volunteer looked at his calloused hands. "I thought about that for a minute, and then all of a sudden I realized: I was a part of God's answer! I guess I started crying too."

And so did most of us listening to his story.

~Stephen Rusiniak

Meet Our Contributors

Kerrie G. Anderson is a writer currently working on a novel, poetry, prayers and children's books. She is a mother and grandmother. Kerrie lives in Colorado where she enjoys life. E-mail her at lightspirit49@gmail.com.

Art Coach for absolute beginners, **Sandra Angelo** has authored numerous home study art courses including Draw101.com, which takes people from "Wimpy to Wow" in just sixty days. Her daily thirty-minute lessons help absolutely anyone master art in days instead of decades. Read more at www.LearnToDrawFAST.com or e-mail her at Sandra@SandraAngelo.com.

Karena D. Bailey is a speaker, trainer and writer, with twenty-five years experience teaching high tech systems. She holds a Bachelor of Science degree in Mass Communications and is producing media to remind us of the true human state: beautiful, loving, and magical even as we experience our own imperfections. E-mail her at Karenadbailey@gmail.com.

Janice Banther received her diploma in Christian Education from Trinity College of Florida. She is a certified birth doula, childbirth educator, and on the faculty of CAPPA. She is the founder and Executive Director of Birth Behind Bars (birthbehindbars.com). Janice enjoys collecting old quilts and spending time with her family. E-mail her at janice@janicebanther.com.

Shinan Barclay's stories appear in *A Second Chicken Soup for the Woman's Soul* and *Chicken Soup for the Soul: Think Positive*. Shinan is the author/editor of *Align with Global Harmony*, and the co-author of *The Sedona Vortex Experience* and *Moontime for Kory, A Rite-of-Passage Adventure*. Contact her at www.facebook.com/shinan.barclay.

Steve Barr is the author and illustrator of the popular *1-2-3 Draw* series of art instruction books. He's also a co-creator of the new "1-2-3 Draw" app for iPads. In his spare time, he likes to draw.

Dot Beams resides in California. She has published short stories in *Chicken Soup for the Soul: Twins and More* and *An Oasis Moment*. She recently published her first cookbook, *Treasures* (family favorite recipes). She is a Christian women's speaker and loves speaking to single parent groups.

Mary Ann Bennett-Olson resides in the little Canadian town of Tillsonburg, Ontario. She is a certified reflexologist practicing her craft in her home-based business called The Oasis and spends her free time writing children's stories. She was blessed with two sons, Murray and Bill, is happily married to her Johnny Angel and has five grandchildren.

Rita Billbe is a retired Oklahoma City high school principal who now owns a resort, Angels Retreat, on the White River in Arkansas. Her passions are her church choir and fly fishing. Visit her blog at www.flyfishing4faith.com.

Pam Johnson Bostwick's many articles appear in Christian magazines, newspapers and in several books in the *Chicken Soup for the Soul* series. Although she is visually and hearing impaired, she enjoys her new condo and its peaceful, sunny surroundings. She plays guitar and loves being with her seven children and thirteen grandchildren. She happily remarried on 7/7/07.

Ellie Braun-Haley frequently contributes to the *Chicken Soup for the Soul* series. She is the author of a number of books and her inspirational stories have been published in numerous books. She enjoys traveling, writing, making handcrafted cards and spending time with her family. E-mail her at ellie@evrcanada.com.

Elaine L. Bridge worked in the woods on the West Coast as a forester before becoming a stay-at-home mom to her three boys. Now living in

Ohio she stays busy working in a grocery store, caring for her family, and writing inspirational material. E-mail her at lanie0b@brecnet.com.

Connie Sturm Cameron is a speaker and the author of the book, *God's Gentle Nudges*. She's been published dozens of times, including several in the *Chicken Soup for the Soul* series. Married thirty-two years to Chuck, they have three children and four grandchildren. Contact her at www.conniecameron.com or via e-mail at connie_cameron@sbcglobal.net.

Danielle Cattanach lives in western New York trying her best to be mindful of magnifying the too often overlooked beauties that are all around to be seen. She is a mother of six—four at home and two stepchildren. She lives a life full of love with her husband Patrick, celebrating each smile. E-mail her at daniellecattanach@ymail.com.

Tracy Cavlovic lives in Ontario, Canada with her husband and three boys. She hopes to be a magazine writer some day soon.

Diana Clarke is an avid outdoor cyclist; she started riding again in her 40s and completed three centuries, and a biathlon in her 50s. She lives in Maryland with her husband Carlisle and daughters. She enjoys reading inspirational stories best, which was her motivation to write this first publication in hopes to inspire others.

Joan Clayton is a retired elementary school teacher. She is currently the religion columnist of her local newspaper. She and her husband have three sons and six grandsons. Her passion is writing. She has written nine books of her own and has published stories in various anthologies.

Angela Closner was born and raised in Norfolk, England. She has been happily married to a USAF pilot for forty-four years, raised two happily married children who have given her six wonderful grandchildren, and has traveled all over the world.

Shirley Faye Cobb is a native of Memphis, TN, and a former radiology technologist. She is very compassionate to the sick, elderly, homeless, and addicted. Her book, *Mending the Hole in My Soul Through Poetry: A Collection of Poems*, is available at www.publishamerica.net. Learn more at shirleyfayecobb.com or e-mail her at shirleyfayecobb@publishedauthors.net.

Helen Colella is a writer of educational books/materials, magazine articles/stories for adults/children. Her stories have appeared in several *Chicken Soup for the Soul* books and parenting magazines. She works for Blue13Creative, a professional writing, editing, and creative services company in Denver, CO. Learn more at www.underthecuckooclock.org.

Karen Danca-Smith teaches ESL to adults from around the world and Spanish to children. She is the co-host on *Good News with Father Jim*, a television program that highlights inspirational people around the country. Karen enjoys running and triathlons. She lives on Long Island with her husband and two children. E-mail her at kdanca1000@aol.com.

Beth Davies' life is built on her faith in GOD and listening to her grandmother read the Bible. Beth attended school in Colorado but was unable to graduate due to a horrible automobile accident. Beth loves to write, craft, crochet, and spend time with her family and friends. E-mail her at bethidavies@yahoo.com.

Diana DeAndrea-Kohn is the owner of a small business. She is married to her husband, Scott. She has three boys Kenny, Alex, and Brodie. She spends her free time reading and writing.

Martha Deeringer writes for children and adults from her home on a central Texas cattle ranch where she is surrounded by a large loving family, two geriatric horses, cattle, dogs and cats, and three naughty orphan raccoons. Visit her website at www.marthadeeringer.com.

S.L. Delorey is an author and freelance writer who resides in Florida, and is building a career as a motivational speaker. He also works with special needs and at-risk children as a behavior assistant and tutor.

Sister M. John Baptist Donovan, SCMC is a member of the Sisters of Charity of Our Lady, Mother of the Church and works in the Academy of the Holy Family in Baltic, CT, as a guidance counselor, boarding school staff member, and teacher of psychology. E-mail her at guidance@ahfbaltic.org.

L. Joy Douglas resides in Indiana with her husband and their two dogs. She currently writes a monthly column for an online magazine, and her first book of inspirational articles was released in September 2010. Her other interests include reading, photography and music. Contact her via e-mail at joy4rain@aol.com.

Melissa Dykman is a happily married twenty-seven-year-old mother of one. She has been blessed with a wonderful family. God has been good to her.

Julia A. Ewert writes a weekly column for a local newspaper and has hosted a talk show on a local radio station. She is a pastor wife and writes the curriculum for their church children's programming. Julia enjoys speaking at retreats and seminars, traveling, home decorating, and visiting her three grandsons.

Veronica Farrington and Rachel live happily in the country, surrounded by many oddball pets, including two spoiled and hilarious sheep. Veronica plans to start an informational website to help abused women in the near future.

Hollye Fisher-Dexter is the author of the memoir *Only Good Things* and co-editor of the anthology *The Shame Prom*. She received the Agape Spirit award from Dr. Michael Beckwith for her work with at-risk youth. Hollye lives in Los Angeles with her husband and three children. Contact her at www.hollyedexter.blogspot.com.

Kerrie Flanagan is a freelance writer and the Director of Northern Colorado Writers. She loves being outside in her garden or hiking in the mountains; she bakes to relieve stress and she hopes to someday see the Northern Lights in person. Learn more at www.KerrieFlanagan.com.

Karen Freeman lives in Colorado where she enjoys anything involving family, friends and laughter. "The Swing" is her first published story. Karen will continue to write, as she desires to share her story of grief, loss and hope with others. E-mail her at donf80104@aol.com.

Phyllis Qualls Freeman is the author of more than 350 published stories. She teaches Sunday school and offers conferences on Emotional Healing. Learn more at www.sanctuaryofhope.us or e-mail her at pqfreeman40@yahoo.com.

Dan G. was raised in Colorado and studied philosophy at the University of Denver. He is a sales and marketing contractor and also plays electric guitar in several musical groups. His home is in Loveland, CO, where he lives with his wife Paula. E-mail him at gambat13@yahoo.com.

Writing, music, poetry and ministry all have been a part of **Sue Stover Gaither** and her life for years. She enjoys Gospel music in concerts and recording, volunteering as a law enforcement chaplain, and in most recent years writing devotions. Learn more at www.Thegaithers. org and www.spiritears.blogspot.com.

William Garvey, his wife Lorraine, and family live in Michigan. He enjoys writing, photography, and gardening. He believes life is truly about the moment—make it one that takes your breath away. Learn more at HeartOfOurHeroes.com.

Lynn Gilkey received her certification in drug and alcohol counseling from Butler Community College. Lynn is the founder of Caring Ladies Assisting Students to Succeed (CLASS), a program that mentors adolescent girls (www.sisterhoodofclass.com). Lynn enjoys reading the word of God, traveling and spending time with her family. E-mail her at goodheart316@hotmail.com.

Margaret Glignor-Schwarz worked with the late, renowned author, Budd Schulberg, for seven years before becoming immersed in several ghostwriting projects. She enjoys spending her spare time with her family and plans to write several biographies in the near future.

Martha Pope Gorris received her B.A. in Creative Writing from George Mason University. She is the author of *Parenting 20-Something Kids: Recognizing Your Role as They Find Their Way*. She loves to travel, watercolor paint, and write fiction. She resides in Southern California. Contact her at www.marthapopegorris.com.

Tracy Gulliver has had essays published in magazines and anthologies including several *Chicken Soup for the Soul* books. She is founder and director of RiverVoices Writers Group. She has received grants from the Lilly Endowment and the McKnight Foundation. E-mail her at tracygulliver@gmail.com or visit tracygulliver.blogspot.com.

Donna Hartley is an inspirational speaker, owner of Hartley International, former Miss Hawaii and author of *Fire Up Your Life!*, *Fire Up Your Intuition!* and *Fire Up Your Healing!* Donna survived a DC-10 plane crash, melanoma and open-heart surgery. She adopted a daughter late in life who brings her Firepower! Learn more at www.donnahartley.com.

Emily Sue Harvey, author and speaker, has six novels being released in 2011. See Amazon.com. She also has stories in *Chocolate for Women* and numerous other anthologies. An expert on renewal, Emily Sue has dozens of articles on websites such as Dr. Laura and Shine. For speaking engagements contact her at emilysue1@aol.com.

Jonny Hawkins draws cartoons full-time from Sherwood, MI. His work has been in over 600 publications since 1986 and in hundreds of books. He has five Cartoon-a-Day calendars available as well as his latest books; *The Hilarious Book of Heavenly Humor* and *The Awesome Book of Hilarious and Heavenly Cartoons*.

Jan Henrikson writes, edits, and coaches other writers around the country. She is the lucky editor of *Eat by Choice, Not by Habit*, by Sylvia Haskvitz. She gets her best inspirations riding a Harley and hiking in the mountains of Tucson, AZ. Learn more at www.eatbychoice.net.

Miriam Hill is a frequent contributor to the *Chicken Soup for the Soul* series and has been published in *Writer's Digest, The Christian Science Monitor, Grit, St. Petersburg Times, The Sacramento Bee* and Poynter Online. Miriam's manuscript received Honorable Mention for Inspirational Writing in a Writer's Digest Writing Competition.

Deborah Howard is an avid student of the Bible. Her willingness to obey, one step at a time, has opened doors of ministry around the world. Her life's mission is to live and teach the unsearchable riches of Christ. She currently resides in Wilmore, KY. E-mail her at LetTheWordSpeak@aol.com.

Michele Huey writes an award-winning newspaper column and produces a daily radio program, "God, Me & a Cup of Tea." A writing mentor for the Jerry B. Jenkins Christian Writers Guild, she is a teacher at heart, teaching at writing conferences and a Christian high school. Learn more at www.michelehuey.com.

Penny Hunt is the wife of a retired naval officer/attaché and mother of five. She is the author of the Amazon.com bestselling children's book, *Little White Squirrel's Secret*, a motivational/humorous speaker, faith columnist for *The Citizen News* of Edgefield County and popular contributor to Christiandevotions.us. E-mail her at penny@thechangespeaker.com.

B.J. Jensen is a song-signing artist, author, speaker, dramatist, and director of the international traveling Love In Motion Signing Choir since 1990. She is happily married to Dr. Doug Jensen, her favorite cheerleader and encourager. They enjoy living in sunny San Diego, CA, near three wonderful granddaughters. Learn more at www.signingchoir.com or e-mail her at Jensen2@san.rr.com.

Jona Johnson grew up on a farm in Colorado, and later studied agriculture at Colorado State University. She home-schools her son and has volunteered in music ministry for over twenty years. Jona enjoys gardening, cooking, fishing, and hiking. E-mail her at jonafury@hotmail.com.

Amber Paul Keeton is a stay-at-home mom and wife to her high school sweetheart. She is a former volunteer firefighter and EMT. Amber loves the beach, camping and reading. She enjoys writing non-fiction stories that will encourage and inspire others through her real life experiences. E-mail her at mommy2manymiracles@yahoo.com.

Sally Kelly-Engeman is a freelance writer who has had numerous short stories and articles published. In addition to writing, she enjoys reading and researching. She also enjoys ballroom dancing and traveling the world with her husband. E-mail her at sallyfk@juno.com.

Mary Potter Kenyon graduated from the University of Northern Iowa in 1985. Mary's writing has appeared in magazines and anthologies and she blogs about writing, saving money and parenting at http://marypotterkenyon.wordpress.com. She lives in Manchester, IA, with her husband and four of their eight children.

Terry Kirkendoll-Esquinance received a Bachelor's degree in Education from Lee University. She is a wife and mom of four children. She enjoys writing, teaching, and sharing in Children's Ministry at the church she attends in Cleveland, TN. Contact her at www.livingalive.org.

Mimi Greenwood Knight is a mother of four and freelance writer with over four hundred articles and essays in print. She lives in South Louisiana with her husband, David, and enjoys Bible study, butterfly gardening, artisan bread making and the lost art of letter writing. Visit her blog at blog.nola.com/faith/mimi_greenwood_knight.

Carrie M. Leach is a missionary wife and mom-of-many in Eastern Europe. When she's not home-schooling, folding laundry, cooking, or working among the Gypsy children of her area, she is writing. Her goal is to write a book about her experiences. E-mail her at cmleach5@gmail.com.

Cledith Lehman is a grandmother of five and great-grandmother of five. She was raised on a sharecroppers farm in Texas and graduated from a country school at seventeen, married at eighteen and had her first of three sons at nineteen. Her hobbies include family, cooking, computer and the casino. She is still going strong at seventy-one.

Sandra McGarrity lives and writes in Chesapeake, VA. She is the author of three novels. Her writing has appeared in many publications and she maintains a regular column at TidewaterCrossSection. com. More information about her writing may be seen on Facebook under Sandra V. McGarrity.

Rosemary McLaughlin loves the written word and has since childhood. Becoming an English teacher was the perfect fit, combining literature with her love of young people. Teaching creative writing, she always wrote with her students to share the pain and joy of writing. E-mail her at rosemarymclaugh@gmail.com.

Candace McLean is a clinical hypnotherapist, speaker, writer and host of the inspirational talk radio show "Everyday Miracles with Candace McLean: Opening Your Mind to Unlimited Possibilities!" Candace is an avid cruiser and kayaker, and loves spending time in nature with her family. Connect with her at www.candacemclean.com.

Rosemarie Miele, retired, spends her free time reading, traveling, enjoying her grandchildren and writing children's stories. She was previously published in *Chicken Soup for the Dog Lover's Soul* and *The School Magazine* in Australia. She plans to send in her children's stories until they are accepted for publication, After all, she believes in miracles!

Priscilla Miller retired to northern Michigan, and at the age of sixty-one, despite being diagnosed with macular degeneration, began her career as a writer and author. Two previous *Chicken Soup for the Soul* books have featured her stories. Although visually impaired, she continues to write for local newspapers and has published a book.

David S. Milotta is a retired pastor living in Hawaii with an interest in the miraculous and paranormal. He enjoys windsurfing, stand up paddle surfing, and Great Danes. He was previously published in *Chicken Soup for the Soul: A Book of Miracles* and *Angels on Earth*. E-mail him at milottad001@hawaii.rr.com.

Martha Moore, a retired Texas English teacher, spends her time tutoring at a community college and writing. She is the author of three novels, including *Under the Mermaid Angel* which won the Delacorte Press Prize for a First Young Adult Novel. She enjoys inspiring others to tell their own stories.

Debbie Moran is fifty-six years old and lives in Powhatan, VA, with her husband Bill and Golden Retriever named Tucker. She has worked as a Customer Service Representative with a local community bank for the past seven years. Debbie enjoys reading, gardening, and traveling with her husband.

Kathleen Muldoon is the author of *Sowing Seeds: Writing for the Christian Children's Market*, as well as several other children's books. When not writing, she enjoys playing with her parakeet Abraham and literary feline Walter.

Kennette Kangiser Osborn received a Teaching degree and a Masters in Educational Technology. She taught elementary and middle school in the Puget Sound area of Washington State for fifteen years. Kennette plans to continue writing inspirational pieces for women and is working on several educational children's books. E-mail her at kennetteosborn@aol.com.

Mark Parisi's "off the mark" cartoons appear in newspapers worldwide. You can also find his cartoons on calendars, cards, books, T-shirts and more. Visit www.offthemark.com to view 7,000 cartoons.

Mark resides in Massachusetts with his wife and business partner Lynn, along with their daughter Jen, two cats and a dog.

Sharon Patterson, retired educator, career military wife, and leader in women's ministry has written works of inspirational encouragement for thirty years. She was a contributor to *Chicken Soup for the Soul: A Book of Miracles* and has two published books: *A Soldier's Strength from the Psalms* and *Healing for the Holes in Our Souls*.

Larry Patton was born with cerebral palsy. Rather than allow this handicap to control him, Larry faces life with a lot of courage and motivation. He began his career at IBM. In 1985, he founded Hurdling Handicaps Speaking Ministries. Larry travels the country sharing his story. This story was adapted from *If He Can Do It, I Can Do It* by Diane Wyss. Learn more at www.hurdlinghandicaps.org.

Saralee Perel is a national award-winning columnist. She is a multiple contributor to the *Chicken Soup for the Soul* series. Her book, *The Dog Who Walked Me*, is about her dog who became her caregiver after her spinal cord injury, the initial devastation of her marriage, and her cat who kept her sane. E-mail her at sperel@saraleeperel.com or www.saraleeperel.com.

Justina Claire Rausch is a twenty-one-year-old from Kansas, currently living in Nashville, pursuing a career in music as a singer/songwriter. She hopes to use her talent to praise God and please others. Visit her website, www.reverbnation.com/justinaclaire or e-mail her at justinaclaire@hotmail.com.

Dan Reynolds' work has been seen by millions in every city in the United States via greeting cards for American Greetings, Papyrus, NobleWorks, and other companies. He is the most frequent cartoon contributor to *Reader's Digest*, and also regularly appears in *Esquire*, *Christianity Today*, *Saturday Evening Post*, *Catholic Digest*, and many others.

Shirley Reynolds is a freelance writer living in the mountains of

Southern Idaho. Since her retirement several years ago, she has found the freedom and time to write. She is working on two books and has published many short stories and articles. She loves to go four-wheeling on mountain back roads, hike, and take multiple pictures.

Lucille Rowan Robbins is now with the Lord. When she and her friend, Elsi Dodge, wrote this story, Lucille said, "If you have lost loved ones, know this: as long as God is there, leading and guiding you, you don't need to fear." Elsi blogs at www.RVTourist.com/blog.

Reneé Wall Rongen is a wise and witty mom, an international humorous and inspirational speaker, and an award-winning entrepreneur and author. She is the international spokesperson for the Pay It Forward Foundation. Renee enjoys horseback riding, kayaking, gardening and spending time with her family. E-mail her at renee@reneerongen.com.

Stephen Rusiniak's stories have appeared in various publications, including three previous *Chicken Soup for the Soul* anthologies. He's a husband and father of two from Wayne, NJ. To read some of his other stories, please visit him on Facebook or e-mail him at stephenrusiniak@yahoo.com.

Betty Scheetz received her B.A. in Communications, with honors, from Regis University in Denver, CO, and is a graduate of the Catholic Biblical School of the Archdiocese of Denver. Betty primarily writes with a religious intent and has been published in *New Theology Review*.

Elizabeth Schmeidler is a happily married mother of three wonderful sons. In addition to being an inspirational public speaker, she is a singer/songwriter and author of poetry, children's stories, novels, and short stories. She is currently working on her upcoming fourth CD entitled *Believe*. She can be reached at www.willyoubemyvoice.com.

Kim Seeley is a former English teacher and librarian who resides in Wakefield, VA, with her husband, Wayne. She teaches handicapped adults part-time and loves to travel and read. She is a frequent contributor to *Sasee* magazine and this is her second contribution to the *Chicken Soup for the Soul* series.

Jeanette Sharp is a graduate of Jerry B. Jenkins Christian Writers Guild, The Apprentice Program. She is a freelance writer in Houston, TX. Jeanette enjoys traveling, speaking and writing. She writes Christian non-fiction inspirational stories and her first book, *Hurray God! Hope, Pray, Believe*, will be released in late 2011. E-mail her at Jeanette-sharp@sbcglobal.net.

Dayle Shockley is an award-winning writer, the author of three books and a contributor to many other works, including the *Chicken Soup for the Soul* series. She and her retired fire captain can often be found traveling around the country, enjoying God's handiwork. Visit Dayle's website for more information at www.dayleshockley.com.

Shirley Nordeck Short has been writing since the 1950s when she started pounding out stories on a 1908 Oliver typewriter. Retired now at age sixty-five, she has traded in the manual typewriter for a computer but her enthusiasm for writing remains. She's been published in *Reader's Digest* and *Guideposts*.

Marsha Brickhouse Smith attended the College of The Albemarle. She worked with a national television network for over twenty years before retiring to coastal North Carolina. She has been published by Blue Mountain Arts, *Christian Life Magazine*, and in three previous *Chicken Soup for the Soul* books.

Mary Z. Smith is a regular contributor to the *Chicken Soup for the Soul* series as well as *Guideposts* and *Angels on Earth* magazines. When she isn't penning her praises to God, she can be found gardening, visiting with her children and grandchildren or spending time with her retired husband, Barry.

Heather Stephen is a dedicated wife and mother of six terrific children. She works and plays in her native state of Colorado. She enjoys traveling, camping, hiking and just about anything involving the Rocky Mountains. Heather also loves to attend the various activities her family participates in.

Two of **Carol Strazer's** essays have appeared in the *Chicken Soup for the Soul* series. Her essay was a winner in *Woman's Day* and American Library Association's contest. Her poem was a second place winner, appearing in *Sunflowers and Seashells: Nature's Miles*. Carol and her husband are active in their mountain community church.

Ann Summerville, author of *Storms & Secrets*, was born in England and in search of a warmer climate moved to California before settling in Texas. Ann is a member of Trinity Writers' Workshop and resides in Fort Worth with her son, two boisterous dogs and a somewhat elusive cat. Learn more at www.AnnSummerville.com.

Jean Tennant has been writing for more than thirty-five years. Her books have been published by Kensington, Silhouette, and Warner Books, and she has an essay in the recently published anthology, *Amber Waves of Grain*, by Shapato Publishing. Learn more at www.JeanTennant.com.

Wayne Terry recently authored *Ezekiel's Wheel Vision: Strength for Patients with Dementia* (Publish America). Wayne considers success to be a little nose pushed up against an inside window where he views lips saying, "I love you Grandpa." Learn more at hopeforalzheimerscentral.com.

This is **Kristen Torres-Toro's** second contribution to the *Chicken Soup for the Soul* series. Her first story, "Sarafina," appeared in *Chicken Soup for the Soul: A Book of Miracles*. Kristen is a missionary with Adventures in Missions and lives in Georgia.

Ashley Townswick received her Bachelor of Arts degree in Social Work. She just started writing in the last few years. She's written a few

Christian fiction novels she is hoping to get published someday. In the meantime, she enjoys reading and music. She's also in a singing group that travels around and performs at churches in the Midwest. E-mail her at atownswick@gmail.com.

Maggie Whelan is the mother of eleven and grandmother of fifteen. She is a retired special education teacher from Albany, NY, whose passion is writing and storytelling. She enjoys singing in a choir and visiting with hospice patients. Maggie is currently taking classes and writing her memoirs. E-mail het at mags9119@yahoo.com.

Alberta Wimsett and Sharon Orndorff have both lived in a rural community in the same houses for many years. While living there their addresses have changed four times, their zip codes are from another county, and the telephone numbers are from another town. It is very confusing for the UPS man. They both enjoy spending time with their families.

Jamie White Wyatt loves to laugh and share "Joy on the Journey." She is a writer, editor, speaker, Bible teacher, event/retreat planner, and ballroom dancer. Jamie, her husband, and two children live in Georgia, where Jamie has owned several businesses, including a bridal shop. E-mail her at rockhavenw@mc.com; or visit www.dancingonthejourney.blogspot.com.

Dawn Yurkas is a retired navy wife, mother of three sons and a full-time realtor in Hampton Roads, VA.

Mother of seven, Nana of nineteen grands and six great-grands, **Lynne Zielinski** lives, laughs and loves in Huntsville, AL. She believes life is a gift from God—what we do with it is our gift TO God.

Ruthie Zimberg is a teacher, writer, editor, composer and singer. She specializes in producing stories, workbooks and songs for teaching English. Born and raised in Toronto, Canada, she now lives in Safed, Israel, with her podiatrist husband, Avraham. E-mail her at zimberg.r@gmail.com.

Paulette Zubel is the author of *Canine Parables: Portraits of God and Life*. She and her certified therapy dog, Forester, visit seniors and hospital and hospice patients. They also participate in a children's literacy program in which children with reading difficulties read to dogs. E-mail her at pkzubel@iserv.net.

Meet Our Authors

Jack Canfield is the co-creator of the *Chicken Soup for the Soul* series, which *Time* magazine has called "the publishing phenomenon of the decade." Jack is also the co-author of many other bestselling books.

Jack is the CEO of the Canfield Training Group in Santa Barbara, California, and founder of the Foundation for Self-Esteem in Culver City, California. He has conducted intensive personal and professional development seminars on the principles of success for more than a million people in twenty-three countries, has spoken to hundreds of thousands of people at more than 1,000 corporations, universities, professional conferences and conventions, and has been seen by millions more on national television shows.

Jack has received many awards and honors, including three honorary doctorates and a Guinness World Records Certificate for having seven books from the *Chicken Soup for the Soul* series appearing on the New York Times bestseller list on May 24, 1998.

You can reach Jack at www.jackcanfield.com.

Mark Victor Hansen is the co-founder of Chicken Soup for the Soul, along with Jack Canfield. He is a sought-after keynote speaker, bestselling author, and marketing maven. Mark's powerful messages of possibility, opportunity, and action have created powerful change in thousands of organizations and millions of individuals worldwide.

Mark is a prolific writer with many bestselling books in addition to the *Chicken Soup for the Soul* series. Mark has had a profound influence in the field of human potential through his library of audios, videos, and articles in the areas of big thinking, sales achievement, wealth building, publishing success, and personal and professional development. He is also the founder of the MEGA Seminar Series.

Mark has received numerous awards that honor his entrepreneurial spirit, philanthropic heart, and business acumen. He is a lifetime member of the Horatio Alger Association of Distinguished Americans.

You can reach Mark at www.markvictorhansen.com.

LeAnn Thieman is a nationally acclaimed professional speaker, author, and nurse who was "accidentally" caught up in the Vietnam Orphan Airlift in 1975. Her book, *This Must Be My Brother*, details her daring adventure of helping to rescue 300 babies as Saigon was falling to the Communists. LeAnn has been featured in *Newsweek Magazine's Voices of the Century* issue, FOX News, CNN, PBS, BBC, PAX-TV's *It's A Miracle*, and countless radio and TV programs.

Today, as a renowned motivational speaker, LeAnn inspires audiences to balance their lives, truly live their priorities and make a difference in the world.

After her story was featured in *Chicken Soup for the Mother's Soul*, LeAnn became one of Chicken Soup for the Soul's most prolific writers. That, and her devotion to thirty years of nursing, made her the ideal co-author of *Chicken Soup for the Nurse's Soul*. She went on to co-author *Chicken Soup for the Caregiver's Soul, Chicken Soup for the Father and Daughter Soul, Chicken Soup for the Grandma's Soul, Chicken Soup for the Christian Woman's Soul, Chicken Soup for the Christian Soul 2, Chicken Soup for the Nurse's Soul: Second Dose, Chicken Soup for the Adopted Soul, Chicken Soup for the Soul: Living Catholic Faith*, and *Chicken Soup for the Soul: A Book of Miracles*.

LeAnn is one of ten percent of speakers worldwide to earn the Certified Speaking Professional designation award and in 2008 she was inducted into the Speakers Hall of Fame.

She and Mark, her husband of forty-one years, reside in Colorado.

For more information about LeAnn's books and products or to schedule her for a presentation, please contact her at:

LeAnn Thieman, CSP, CPAE
6600 Thompson Drive
Fort Collins, CO 80526
1-970-223-1574
www.LeAnnThieman.com
e-mail LeAnn@LeAnnThieman.com

Thank You

Our first thanks are to our contributors. Your stories of answered prayers will truly bless so many people—countless letters prove how our books change their lives.

We can only publish a small percentage of the stories submitted, but we read every one, and even those that do not appear in the book influence us and the final manuscript.

We thank D'ette Corona, our Assistant Publisher, who seamlessly manages a dozen projects at a time while keeping all of us positive, focused and on schedule. Our gratitude also goes to Barbara LoMonaco, Chicken Soup for the Soul's Webmaster and Editor, and Chicken Soup for the Soul Editor Kristiana Glavin, for her assistance with the final manuscript and proofreading.

We owe a very special thanks to our Creative Director and book producer, Brian Taylor at Pneuma Books, for his brilliance on our covers and interiors.

The ultimate thank you goes to Amy Newmark, Publisher of Chicken Soup for the Soul whose vision, expertise and diligence create each book and make it excellent.

Finally, none of this would be possible without the business and creative leadership of our CEO, Bill Rouhana, and our president, Bob Jacobs.

Thanks to Dan Gamble, LeAnn's Director of Marketing, who manages her speaking business while she writes… and writes.

A special thanks to LeAnn's husband Mark for his forever love and support and to her mother Berniece Duello whose role modeling provided the foundation for LeAnn's faith and abilities.

And to God for His divine guidance and abundant blessings.

~LeAnn Thieman

Improving Your Life Every Day

Real people sharing real stories—for seventeen years. Now, Chicken Soup for the Soul has gone beyond the bookstore to become a world leader in life improvement. Through books, movies, DVDs, online resources and other partnerships, we bring hope, courage, inspiration and love to hundreds of millions of people around the world. Chicken Soup for the Soul's writers and readers belong to a one-of-a-kind global community, sharing advice, support, guidance, comfort, and knowledge.

Chicken Soup for the Soul stories have been translated into more than forty languages and can be found in more than one hundred countries. Every day, millions of people experience a Chicken Soup for the Soul story in a book, magazine, newspaper or online. As we share our life experiences through these stories, we offer hope, comfort and inspiration to one another. The stories travel from person to person, and from country to country, helping to improve lives everywhere.

Share with Us

We all have had Chicken Soup for the Soul moments in our lives. If you would like to share your story or poem with millions of people around the world, go to chickensoup.com and click on "Submit Your Story." You may be able to help another reader, and become a published author at the same time. Some of our past contributors have launched writing and speaking careers from the publication of their stories in our books!

Our submission volume has been increasing steadily—the quality and quantity of your submissions has been fabulous. We only accept story submissions via our website. They are no longer accepted via mail or fax.

To contact us regarding other matters, please send us an e-mail through webmaster@chickensoupforthesoul.com, or fax or write us at:

Chicken Soup for the Soul
P.O. Box 700
Cos Cob, CT 06807-0700
Fax: 203-861-7194

One more note from your friends at Chicken Soup for the Soul: Occasionally, we receive an unsolicited book manuscript from one of our readers, and we would like to respectfully inform you that we do not accept unsolicited manuscripts and we must discard the ones that appear.

Chicken Soup for the Soul

www.ChickenSoup.com